I Still Miss Someone

I Still Miss Someone

FRIENDS AND FAMILY
REMEMBER JOHNNY CASH

COMPILED BY

HUGH WADDELL

CUMBERLAND HOUSE
NASHVILLE, TENNESSEE

Copyright © 2005 by Hugh Waddell
PUBLISHED BY
CUMBERLAND HOUSE PUBLISHING, INC.
431 Harding Industrial Drive
Nashville, TN 37211-3160

Cover design: James Duncan Creative
Text design: John Mitchell and Mary Sanford

Library of Congress Cataloging-in-Publication Data
I still miss someone : friends and family remember Johnny Cash / compiled by Hugh Waddell.
    p. cm.
  ISBN-13: 978-1-58182-398-1 (hardcover : alk. paper)
  ISBN-10: 1-58182-398-3 (hardcover : alk. paper)
  ISBN-13: 978-1-58182-528-2 (paperback : alk. paper)
  ISBN-10: 1-58182-528-5 (paperback : alk. paper)
  1. Cash, Johnny. 2. Country musicians—United States—Biography. I. Waddell, Hugh, 1958–
ML420.C265.I67 2004
782.421642'092—dc22

2004010735

Printed in Canada

1 2 3 4 5 6 7—12 11 10 09 08 07 06

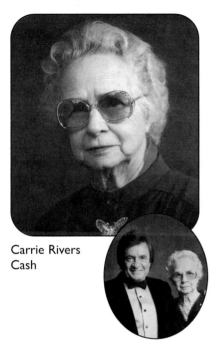

To two mothers whose legacy and unwavering love inspired their sons.

Carrie Rivers
Cash

Jackie Comer
Waddell

And to
Merle "Senator" Kilgore
1934–2005

CONTENTS

Foreword   XI

Introduction   XIII

JAY ABEND   3

CINDY CASH   6

JOHN CARTER CASH   11

MARK CASH   16

TOMMY CASH   19

JACK CLEMENT   30

GARLAND CRAFT   34

JAY DAURO   41

DENNIS DEVINE   46

LUTHER FLEANER   54

IRENE GIBBS   63

JACK HALE   68

W. S. HOLLAND   75

DMITRI KASTERINE   93

PAT KATZ   97

MERLE KILGORE   102

PENNI LANE   106

CHANCE MARTIN   113

ALAN MESSER   129

BILL MILLER   140

AL QUALLS   147

LOU ROBIN   151

DAVE ROE	155
MICHELE ROLLINS	160
TED W. ROLLINS	167
FERN SALYER	174
TARA CASH SCHWOEBEL	179
MAURY SCOBEE	181
ANTO SEPETJIAN	189
REV. JACK SHAW	193
JOHN L. SMITH	204
DUSTIN TITTLE	214
JIMMY TITTLE	218
ALMA JEAN TODD	223
HUGH WADDELL	229
BILL WALKER	258
JOHNNY WESTERN	265
REV. COURTNEY WILSON	270
NAT T. WINSTON, M.D.	272
JEANNE WITHERELL	279
BOB WOOTTON	287
DR. HARRY YATES	292
JOANNE CASH YATES	296
Acknowledgments	301
Index	303

FOREWORD

When our son Franklin was a teenager, he became very interested in the music of Johnny Cash. After he mentioned it to us, Bill made contact with people in Nashville and was able to get John's home phone number. After talking with John on the phone, we, along with Franklin, were invited to come for a visit.

Who knew that this would begin a lifelong friendship?

We had the pleasure of spending Christmas with John and June at their home in Jamaica in 1977. We came into the living room one day to find John over in a corner poring over books on Saint Paul.

He was eager to learn of other books on Paul, as he was absorbing himself in the life of Paul and his writings.

Each book we mentioned John already had. We finally thought of one he didn't have.

John's second best-selling book, *Man In White*, was the biographical story of Paul. It was an incredibly accurate history of the ministry of Paul.

We will never forget his enthusiasm for the scriptures or the thorough way he would do research. It was a part of John few in the public were aware of, but which undoubtedly accounted for a great deal of his character.

As we've said before, we often feel like the man in the South who had a mule. He decided to put his mule in the Kentucky Derby. His friends said, "You don't expect him to win, do you?" "No, but look at the company he'll be in." That's the way we feel when we are with people like John, who was so talented.

Many have also said to us that John was the kindest man they ever knew. We would have to agree.

— *RUTH AND BILLY GRAHAM*
Montreat, North Carolina

JOHNNY CASH

I have never known a greater man among men. Yet his simplicity, his common touch, his childlike compassion for his fellowman is the source of his greatness.

As a friend of mine, he is one of those in the inner-circle; those four or five friends you will only know in a lifetime of friends that come and go. He is true, He is faithful. He is what he appears to be; a dedicated vessel of Gods earthly endeavors among men. Billy Graham is my friend, and I love him.

Johnny Cash

INTRODUCTION

E RECEIVE MANY GIFTS during the course of our lives, not just on
birthdays or at Christmas, and not all are wrapped. Many gifts are
unseen, unknown, or at the time seemingly inconsequential. They are
blessings that occur when others bestow concern, or care, or grace. I have
been so blessed in this way to have known "Johnny the Cash" and to have
shared so much with him and June.

It is hard to realize that 2005 would have marked John's 50th year of
creating music since his start at Memphis's Sun Records in February 1955.
During this almost half-century, there have been so many individuals, like
myself, who were privileged to be a part of what John referred to as his
"inner circle." Some stayed in the circle longer than others.

Like moons in an orbit, we gravitated in and out of planet Johnny. All
who really knew him also knew this to be true. Although he was keen on
"out of sight, out of mind," due to the very nature of constant schedule
demands on his time, once you were in John's good graces, there you
always remained. To this day, calendars or clocks need not be consulted to
sustain a Cash family relationship.

Many books about Johnny Cash have been published recently, and all have their place in the greater repository of retrospective Cash annals. *I Still Miss Someone* is unique in that it strives only to be a respectful tribute to Johnny Cash. There are more than forty chapter contributors, none of them career writers but all of them well-versed in things Cash. There is no real way, nor would there be, to gather all of John's friends and family into a single tribute volume.

No book could be so all-encompassing, mostly because there is not, nor would there be, any reliable source who could identify each and every person who was a part of Johnny's inner circle during those fifty years. The names often changed with time, as did some of these personalities and many of their addresses. Hundreds were fortunate, or blessed, or even lucky to have known Johnny Cash outside of the sparkle and lure of celebrity. Many members of the clergy were drawn to John's honest thirst for spiritual knowledge. They were also pillars of strength during John's struggles, helping him embrace his biblical philosophy of "Never let adversity get you down, except on your knees to pray."

I Still Miss Someone is a compilation of candid and straightforward anecdotes and essays written by a token sampling of the entire sum of people, most out of the public eye, who knew Johnny Cash as a friend. Three world-renowned photographers, including two who met John only once, share their images here. Family members' chapters also are proudly included. It is an honor that they have blessed this book with viable, insightful, and heart-touching recollections that only John Cash's kin could provide.

The writers and their respective chapters in *I Still Miss Someone* are listed alphabetically. This is the book's only semblance of symmetry. Chapter length and content were determined by each of these various "Cashologists," my own term for people who knew John.

This book contains no profanity, nudity, dancing bears, or celebrity testimonials. And, as John often said onstage when describing his own concerts, it "contains no flying pigs or exploding bales of hay." However, someone in this book does refer to Johnny as "booger bear."

Several contributors here have published their own books—or should have. Some writing in these pages could fill entire volumes themselves when recalling their Johnny Cash-filled past. In addition to John's direct family, *I Still Miss Someone* presents an eclectic mix of individuals, each with their own take on whatever relationship they shared with Johnny Cash.

Luther Fleaner cared for John's grapes at Bon Aqua for more than twenty years. Bill Walker was John's only musical arranger and his conductor of choice. Michele Rollins had the pleasure of countless years of Cash Jamaican Christmas celebrations. By request, Garland Craft played piano at Mother Maybelle Carter's funeral service, at June Carter's funeral service, and, in September 2003, at John's. Pat Katz attended more than five hundred Johnny Cash concerts.

John L. Smith shared an undying love of Native Americana with John, and in addition, has published four books on Cash recordings. John once threw his younger brother Tommy off of a twelve-foot-high bridge. John hired Dave Roe as a backup musician, then asked him to play a musical style Dave didn't know on an instrument Dave didn't own. John probably didn't remember his first meeting with Dr. Nat Winston. Dennis Devine has had "Johnny Cash Is a Friend of Mine" inscribed on his tombstone for over a decade—and Dennis is still very much alive. Ted Rollins and John invented a new sport involving gallantry and golf balls.

Merle Kilgore was best man at John and June's wedding. Penni Lane chased John around the stage with hair spray. Irene Gibbs had Rev. Billy Graham and Sheriff Buford (*Walking Tall*) Pusser in her office at the same time—on her first day working for John. Alan Messer was told by John not to photograph him picking his nose. John gave his daughter Kathy a gun for a wedding present, when she married Jimmy Tittle; he gave Jimmy a book.

Chance Martin met John flipping cards. Jack Shaw met John by chance, on a prayer, a missed turn, and a fluke. W. S. "Fluke" Holland watched trucks go off cliffs and was the only road manager/drummer Johnny Cash ever had. Jay Abend shot John and Waylon Jennings and Brooke Shields together. Lou Robin could have actually been shot in Ireland. Johnny Cash and Johnny Western could shoot and got cash for being in westerns.

Jack Hale learned of French horns in England. Me, well I filled in on drums for a few Cash tours and managed not to get fired after I told John that I had pushed girls around the House of Cash building on Buddy Holly's motorcycle. (The Indian bike, on loan from Waylon after the closing of his own Nashville museum, was exhibited in Johnny's museum, and as it wouldn't start, this was the only way the girls could officially say they had ridden Buddy Holly's motorcycle.) However, John did fire me on other occasions, for other reasons. And so go the stories in *I Still Miss Someone*.

This book makes no false pretense. It only verifies that each contributor of words and photos herein, equally in their own capacity and understanding, loved and admired and respected John R. Cash. Additionally, remembrances by family members—from brother, son, and brother-in-law to grandson, sister, and daughters—reveal the passion of a man who knew well his Arkansas roots and respected his family name and legacy.

I Still Miss Someone contains no major biographical or personal Cash revelations. Those stories of fact and fiction have already been written. Actually, the only real "dirt" on Johnny Cash, other than that from his Bon Aqua garden, might be that John slipped in a cigarette here and there after telling folks he'd quit; or that, despite doctor's orders, John continued to be stealthy, not healthy, while eating fried pork rinds from the Center Point Barbecue in Hendersonville, Tennessee; or that, on "rare" occasions, he might have driven "slightly" over the posted speed limit.

However, every story inevitably weaves that perpetual Johnny Cash message of sin and redemption. Someone once asked me, "How many personalities did Johnny Cash have?" I immediately responded, "All of them!" And many of them are revealed in these pages.

John Cash had "itchy feet." He would say this on numerous occasions. Metaphorically, it was his expression for readiness and love of movement and exposure and exploration and revelation. He told me, "Everyone has itchy feet, and some scratch more than others." With few exceptions, after a couple of days in one place, Johnny Cash was ready to scratch that travel itch. In keeping with this "itchy feet" spirit of mobility, each writer's shoe size is listed at the beginning of his or her chapter.

As each new chapter debuts, there are no cumbersome, italicized paragraphs detailing the author's biography. The writers introduce themselves and reveal their relationship with Johnny Cash in any manner they wish. Holding this book together is neither glue nor thread. The force binding this book is Johnny Cash. *I Still Miss Someone* is many persons with itchy feet, all relative, and some actual relatives, whose life paths, by favorable destiny, crossed that line walked by Johnny Cash.

— *HUGH WADDELL*

I Still Miss Someone

JAY ABEND

Framingham, Massachusetts
Shoe Size 13

*I*NSPIRING. That was Johnny Cash. I met Johnny Cash on a cold and dreary Illinois afternoon. The 1988 Affordable Art Tour had pulled into Champaign, at the University of Illinois, and I had flown in after a previous weekend photo shoot in Nashville.

The day before my trip to Champaign, I was with the rock group Bon Jovi. The young New Jersey band had just notched its first No. 1 album, and though they were the opening act for Southern rock legends Molly Hatchett, the girls at the show were there for Bon Jovi. After our photo shoot, guitarist Ritchie Sambora asked where I was off to. "The Midwest," I said. "Gonna hook up with Johnny Cash." A moment of silence. "Johnny Cash, huh?" remarked Sambora. "No #@%&!"

It's tough to get a reaction out of rock stars. Johnny Cash? *He* got a reaction. As my assistant and I set up in the bowels of Illinois's 1970s poured-concrete excuse for a sports arena, word came back that Johnny was under the weather. Concerned, I poked my head in his tour bus. There he was, Johnny Cash, nursing a bad cold, casually thumbing through a dog-eared Bible. "Flew in from Boston, just for me?" he asked. "I'd fly any-where for you, Mr. Cash," I gushed. "My name's John," he replied, and his weathered face broke into a comfortable smile.

Johnny Cash was a man of his word. He felt lousy, the hall basement surroundings were a disaster, and the all-tour-bus Affordable Art Tour was taking its toll. The last thing he needed was a photo shoot. Not surprisingly, he grabbed his guitar, donned his famous black coat and followed me to our photo area. I wasn't used to celebrities treating me this way.

He posed on a stool, standing up, sitting down. With guitar and with-out. He asked me about my wife. We chatted about guitars. He asked me if I read the Bible. I told him of my experiences backstage at the Grand Ole Opry the week before. The whole while, tour co-star Brooke Shields sat on a flight case, watching the great man perform for the camera. "Do you need any more?" he asked. A gentleman.

The Affordable Art Tour cast and crew.

Just as John was pre-pared to go and catch a few hours of rest before the show, the entire Affordable Art gang showed up. A real circus at this time. June Carter, Waylon, Brooke Shields, Brooke's forceful mom, Teri, the crew, the bus drivers, the whole lot. I squeezed everyone onto my painted backdrop and tried to bang off a few frames between the good-natured jabs and uproarious laughter.

My job done, we packed up. I always

liked to grab a few live shots when shooting performers; my client always finds some use for them. I was shooting Johnny for Guild Guitars. I grabbed a Nikon body and a long lens and figured I'd shoot a few songs of the performance that night. Glad I did.

This was how a pro handled a tough day: Johnny Cash came out on stage bathed in a brilliant white spotlight. His black coat offset the stunning sunburst of his Guild GF-50 guitar. He made his way to the microphone and began really, truly forceful renditions of his best-known songs. I was amazed. I've seen weary rock stars promoting multi-platinum albums turn in half-hearted shows. Yet, here was a certified legend there to do nothing more than entertain his loyal fans, pouring every ounce of energy into his performance. Inspiring.

CINDY CASH

Jackson, Mississippi
Shoe Size 7¹/₂

I DON'T THINK I EVER realized how much pain a human heart could hold. I know I never realized the true meaning of "I miss you." Lately, my heart goes out to everyone who has felt this pain. The pain that comes to you when death takes away someone you deeply love.

When asked to write something for this book, a million different things about Dad came to mind. Dad's stamina and dedication to his career and his family was never compromised. If he was exhausted or in pain and had ten different places to go in eight days, he never complained. He just did what was expected. He was very dedicated to his fans, his career, his songwriting, his wife, and his children.

He was always aware of any pain I was in, and it was uncanny how my phone would ring just at the right moment. Just as I was planning on jumping off a bridge somewhere, he would call me and ask me what was wrong.

This was just one man, and I shared him with lots of sisters, a brother, a stepmother, aunts, uncles, grandparents, employees, band members, friends, God, and the rest of the world. Still, I always felt special. He made sure that I did. He was called upon frequently by family and friends when a crisis occurred. He was the patriarch of our family. He was so compassionate. He never judged. He was giving and he was forgiving.

Sometimes he was forgiving past the point of expectation. It kept his loved ones frustrated. He joked that once in a single year, he had to buy seventy-two hammers to continually replace the ones "borrowed" from him.

It's only been months, and I suppose denial is still my friend. I strive for acceptance, but it doesn't come as yet. My father is dead. There, I said it. My younger sister Tara had been telling me that I need to say that sentence, out loud and make it real. I have not been able to do that yet. At least not out loud.

Confrontation. Dad avoided it at any cost. He would take a loss and even allow his loved ones to take one before he would have a confrontation with a guilty party. It just wasn't worth it. Nothing was worth an argument. He did not allow people to yell or raise their voice in anger in his home. It was a rule he held strong to, along with June, their entire marriage. I can tell you, honestly, I never heard either of them yell at the other. Ever.

Airman John catches up on his reading while traveling by train from Paris to his base in Germany in 1953. The book is Dr. Eustace Chesser's *Love Without Fear.*

The demands on Dad, and his desire to keep them, made up a big part of who he was. Just one man. Committed to a choice made long ago. He never babbled on and on about anything, so when he spoke, it was worth hearing. He was knowledgeable in so many different things. He loved to read. He loved to learn. He told me that he liked to look in the dictionary every day and learn a new word to add to his vocabulary. If he learned a new word, he never forgot it. Of course, he liked to get me going by using some of them on me. Not the real words, but the ones he found just for my benefit. Words like *zygote* and *yttrium.*

He never once lost a game of Trivial Pursuit to anyone. However, he did lose a few games of dominos and horseshoes to me. He didn't care. He

Dinnertime at home with little Cindy and dad.

wasn't competitive like me. Nor did he have a huge male ego. I never said he wasn't chauvinistic. I just said he didn't have a huge ego. I believed every word he uttered. At least until I was about twenty. That was when he was teaching me how to water ski. I must have been in the water for just a few minutes when I remembered the water moccasin I had seen by the boat dock the day before.

I panicked at the thought of that snake being somewhere near me and what a sitting duck I was now. I told Dad my fears and was completely comforted by what he said: "A snake will drown instantly if he opens his mouth underwater to bite you." I think I was about twenty-three years old before someone enlightened me. He laughed about that for years.

I'm grateful to Hugh for asking me to be a part of this book, but I have struggled with what to write for days and deadline is closing in. I thought about writing a funny story or something, but not any particular one came to mind. Dad was incredibly funny. His humor was so unpredictable. He could make me laugh even when I didn't want to. Which was, of course, his favorite time to make me laugh. When I was trying to be angry.

I thought about sharing some of the lessons I learned from him, but I still couldn't think of any one particular lesson to write about. Lessons

on tolerance, patience, and love. On making
choices. Whisper or shout. Run or walk. Watch it
or read it. Say it or write it. Sing it or hum it.
Keep it or give it away. Think before you speak.
Don't be negative. Don't talk bad about other
people. Do not judge. Do not complain. Laugh
every day. Pray every day. Say "I love you" to
loved ones every day.

Dad always wrote a letter to himself every
New Year's Eve. One year I spent New Year's with
him in Jamaica. He handed me this poem at midnight. He said he wanted to write something to
me this year. This is the result. I love this and
keep it where I can see it daily.

John and granddaughter
Jessica.

    To Cindy

    Serve yourself
    For there are those
    Who'd have you held in hock
    Be your own free-flying self
    And burn the auction block
    Be the bird of beauty
    That is fighting now to fly
    Help your heart to heaven
    Don't let life go listless by
    Be whatever you are burning
    in your secret self to be
    Take what and who you're wishing
    It is quite alright with me.
    I love you.
                Daddy
         December 31, 1980
            11:50 PM

There were many lessons to learn. Overall, I believe he wanted me to know that I always had a choice. Love or hate. Choose. Study or fail. Choose. Hug or shake hands. Choose. Anger or acceptance. Choose. It's up to me. I always have a choice. That's how he always left it. Up to me.

All the lessons I learned from him and all the times he made me laugh will stay with me always. And when I miss him so much that I think I just can't stand it, I remind myself that he still lives. He lives in me and he always will. I love you, Dad.

JOHN CARTER CASH

Hendersonville, Tennessee

Shoe Size 13

*M*UCH HAS BEEN WRITTEN about my father's music, his faith, and who he was as a husband and family man; however, very little is widely known about his great adventuresome nature. As a boy, my father was my best friend. We went on fishing and hunting trips together. We hiked for miles through the Alaskan bear-infested wilderness. On numerous occasions we took our eighteen-foot skiff thirty to fifty miles out into the Gulf of Mexico.

My father, mother, and I floated an Alaskan river for five days and five nights, camping along the way. I nearly died on that trip on more than one occasion. Somehow we made it. The river had only been floated twice before. On the first trip, a man died, and only the second trip down was to retrieve the body. My father rowed continuously. If he wasn't in great shape at the beginning of the float, he was by its end. I was thirteen and my paddle seldom, if ever, touched the water, as I never ceased fishing. Dad stayed up all night one night on that trip, watching a grizzly bear eyeing us from across the river. Come sunrise, he was prepared to row all day.

11

Johnny and June celebrate John Carter's first birthday (above); John Carter at age ten (below) and in 2002 (bottom).

Perhaps my father's greatest adventure was in Jamaica in the late 1970s. Fifteen miles from our Caribbean home, Cinnamon Hill, there was a place called the Jamaican Safari Village. An American named Ross Kananga ran the place. Ross was, among many other things, a crocodile wrestler and a stunt man. If you have ever seen the 1973 James Bond film *Live and Let Die*, that was Ross running across the crocodile backs. I remember when I first saw that movie, I thought to myself, *Those can't be real crocs!* They were. Ross fell three times during the filming of those scenes, and he had to have 347 stitches. Tough guy.

As you walked through the barbwire-topped gates, the first thing you noticed were the cages along either side of the half-mile trail that led to Ross's home. They were filled with numerous panthers, lions, and apes of all sizes. The next thing you noticed was that the crocodiles were not in cages. They walked freely along the trail, right there with you. Ross would meet you at the gate with his three-legged dog, Rex. Rex seemed fearless enough. He would limp the trail ahead of the group, ever wary of the deep mangrove swamp on either side. Sadly, it was not long until I heard ol' Rex had lost another leg and retired.

Dad became good buddies with Ross and would bring his visiting friends to walk with the crocodiles. I remember being there with Waylon Jennings and Jessi Colter, and on another occasion, with Billy and Ruth Graham. My dad would be walking along with a chimpanzee on his back, singing hymns at the top of his lungs and laughing about Rex's unique hobble. The chimpanzee would jump from person to person. It was all quite a sight.

One day Ross called my father at Cinnamon Hill and told him of a rogue crocodile on the loose. It seemed that One-Eyed Jack, as he was called, was eating all the baby crocs he could get his jaws around. Ross's Safari Village was merely a high spot in the middle of a great mangrove swamp. This dangerous reptile was invading the compound at night and gorging himself on whatever he could find. Ross had lost several chickens and a spider monkey. Ross suggested a night hunt, when Jack's glaring red eye would be easy to spot with the searchlight mounted on his jet boat. Dad instantly agreed.

I was too young to go on the hunt with my father, but the story was told to me over and over. It goes like this:

My father and his friend Chance Martin went to meet Ross at 9 p.m. These three, along with Ross's assistant, Jim, left the Safari Village around 11 p.m. Jim was a giant of a man, six foot five, 325 pounds, with long, hairy arms and a short forehead. He was affectionately nicknamed "the Gorilla." The screaming jet boat flew across the shallow water of the swamp in the pitch black of the steamy Jamaican night. Our brave adventurers held on for dear life. Crocodiles were everywhere. They searched for two hours, but all of the croc eyes they spotted were in pairs, so they knew they had not seen One-Eyed Jack.

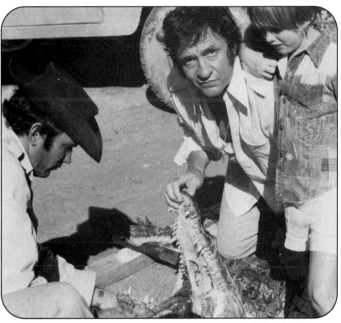

Ross Kananga, John, and John Carter examine the jaws of One-Eyed Jack.

Jim and my father were sitting toward the back of the flat, un-railed boat. Even hollering, they could not hear each other above the deafening roar of the jet engine. My father had a small but bright flashlight of his own. Suddenly he saw it: one extra-large red eye, not fifty feet from the boat. He called out, waving his arms in excitement, and somehow lost his balance. He shrieked as he fell head over heels into the shallow, muddy water, but no one heard him. The jet boat began to recede into the distance.

Back on the boat, Chance was getting tired. He decided to go talk to my father about the possibility of returning to their warm beds. When he looked to the rear of the boat, to his horror, he saw my father was not on board. Ross then turned the boat around and began to search. In a few minutes they spotted a flashlight, frantically waving in the darkness. The light appeared to be a several feet above the water. Not twenty feet from the light was one bright-red eye.

There was my father, clinging desperately to a mangrove bush he had climbed to escape the deadly jaws of Jack. Ross and the Gorilla helped him down into the boat. He was soaked to the bone, but all he could think of was the giant reptile nearby, still prowling the swamp, dangerous and hungry.

John Carter (top) and his rock band in the late 1980s.

Then Ross spotted the one red eye no more than fifteen feet away. He trained the spotlight on Jack while Dad quickly grabbed his gun. He pulled the trigger and the water exploded. The furious beast roared as my father fired again. Water and blood splashed over the boat. After some five minutes of violent, dying rage, everything became still. The massive, twelve-foot body of One-Eyed Jack floated motionless in the black water.

The next morning, I awoke to the aroma of something wonderful frying in the kitchen. I jumped out of bed, anxious to hear if Dad had shot the croc. I arrived downstairs to find family and friends already seated around the breakfast table. My father was there, bruised and tired but beaming. Ross, Chance Martin, and Jim the Gorilla were there also. My mother chatted with them excitedly as they related the tale of the previous night. I sat down between Ross and my mother, eager for food and the details of the hunt.

Father and son strike a "mad at Hugh" pose.

After serving coffee and juice, Carl, the butler, brought out a heaping plate of golden fried hunks of meat. It looked delicious. Mother asked the blessing, thanking God for the safe return of her husband and friends. She thanked God for the bountiful feast on the table, and that these brave men had brought it home.

"Amen," we all said. We ate crocodile for two years.

MARK CASH

Gallatin, Tennessee
Shoe Size 10

*N*EEDLESS TO SAY, I'VE always loved Johnny Cash. Not just as a human being, an uncle, a family member, a musician, a scholar, a songwriter or a confidant companion to talk to. I loved him because he always saw the good in me and always allowed me to learn how to live on my own two feet, without prejudice or judgment.

He allowed me to be human and make mistakes; however, not once did he stand over me and look down on me for any reason. He loved me for me, flaws and all.

I wrote this song in 1995, from a conversation I had with uncle Johnny at my grandmother Mama Cash's home during her final days in 1991. The family had gathered at her home to sing gospel songs to her. It was a sacred time I will never forget. All of our Cash family gathered around her death bed, joined hands, singing to her. She loved those songs.

This song that I wrote from that conversation when we went outside for a smoke, basically says what I want to say for this tribute book:

That family is family, and I will always miss him.

UNCLE JOHNNY

The house was built with friends and family
We stepped outside to get away
He leaned beside me on the fender
Of my Grandma's Chevrolet

He asked me, "How's your music coming?"
And "Ain't it great to stand on stage?"
It's the only time I'm happy
It's where I sing my cares away

I said, "Sometimes I think they like me
But just because of who you are
Do you know how hard it is to be
The nephew of a superstar?"

The evening air had cut right through us
As he turned to me and asked
"Have you ever once considered
How hard it is to be Johnny Cash?"

To millions he's a superstar
and a legend among men
A man in black for all the world to see
I'm just glad I've had the chance
to call him my friend
But more than any superstar could be
He's uncle Johnny to me

Now life for anyone ain't easy
And it don't matter who you are
I'd been just as proud to know him
If he'd never been a star

He was all
That any superstar could be
But always he'll be
Just uncle Johnny
To me

Kathy Cash Tittle, Mark Cash, and Cindy Cash with John.

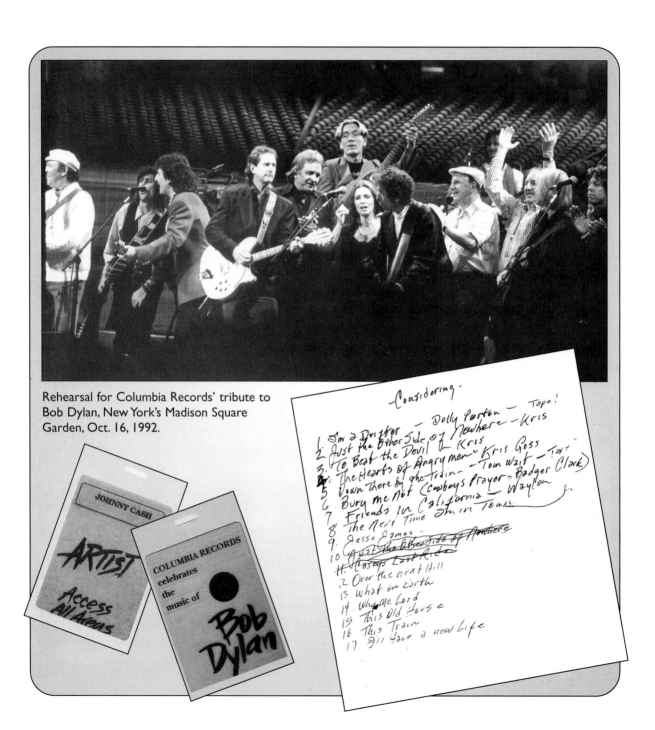

Rehearsal for Columbia Records' tribute to Bob Dylan, New York's Madison Square Garden, Oct. 16, 1992.

JOHNNY CASH

ARTIST
Access All Areas

COLUMBIA RECORDS
celebrates
the
music of
Bob Dylan

—Considering—

1. I'm a Drifter — Dolly Parton — Tape?
2. Just the Other Side of Nowhere — Kris
3. To Beat the Devil — Kris
4. The Hearts of Angry men — Kris Goss
5. Down there by the Train — Tom Wait — Tape
6. Bury me Not (Cowboys Prayer = Badger Clark)
7. Friends In California — Waylon
8. The Next Time I'm in Town
9. Jesse James
10. Just the Other Side of Nowhere
11. Casey's Last Ride
12. Over the next Hill
13. What on earth
14. Why me Lord
15. This Old House
16. This Train
17. I'll have a new life

TOMMY CASH

Hendersonville, Tennessee
Shoe Size 10½

*H*ELLO, I'M TOMMY CASH, and this is my story and I'm sticking to it. The girls called me Tommy and the boys called me Tom. When I started recording, the record company suggested I use Tommy because Tommy Cash sounded more professional to them.

Johnny Cash was the nicest, sweetest, kindest, most knowledgeable, meanest, most ornery, sweet, intelligent, hard-headedest, down-to-earth person I ever knew!

While John was in the Air Force, I worked as a projectionist for the little Dyess Theater in our hometown of Dyess, Arkansas. This was the theater where all the Cash kids ran barefoot every Saturday afternoon to see the latest western movie by Eddie Dean, Gene Autry, Lash LaRue, Al "Fuzzy" St. John, Jim Bannon, or Roy Rogers for only a quarter. It was fifteen cents to get a ticket, and you had enough left over for nickel popcorn and a nickel soda pop.

I was fourteen years old when John got out of the Air Force. I was awed by how he had changed during those four years of Air Force duty. When he went in and was sent to Germany in the spring of 1951, he was this little tall and skinny kid. He came back and got off the plane in 1954 at the

19

Memphis airport, and there was this giant of a man at six foot two or three, and 225 pounds.

Of course, I had changed, too. I had gone from nine years old to fourteen. I went back to Dyess, Arkansas, because I was a basketball player on the state championship school team that year. I made All-State, and I think we won thirty-three games that last year. John came to a few of my games, but he didn't care much for high school basketball.

The thing I remember most about him coming to Dyess after he had his first two hits—"Cry, Cry, Cry" and "Hey, Porter"—is him pulling up in our driveway in this 1954 Cadillac Coupe DeVille, and I thought that was the most amazing car I'd ever seen in my life. I'd always been crazy about cars and always spent too much money on cars, even to this day. I was more impressed with that '54 Cadillac than I was with his hit records.

His success changed my life, and it changed Mama and Daddy's lives, too, because we went from being Tom Cash, the basketball player, and Ray and Carrie Cash, the cotton farmers, to being known as Johnny Cash's family. I was very, very proud of him, but when he had "Folsom Prison Blues" a few months later, I knew he was going to be a star. It became pretty obvious.

He started taking me on the road with him on the weekends. I think the first town we ever went to together was Rhinelander, Wisconsin, and the next day we were at Buck Lake Ranch, a park in Indiana. John let me sell pictures at his concerts, and I sold them for a dollar apiece. I made $356 that first weekend selling Johnny Cash pictures. Of course, Marshall Grant and Luther Perkins sold their share and took home a gob of money from picture sales, too.

But I made $356 and I thought I was rich! Remember, this was 1956, and that was a whole lot of money then. I went home and showed it to Mama. I had it in a big wad, you know, a lot of ones, fives, and tens. I said, "Mama, it's unbelievable! Daddy, look at this. You can go out on the road and sell three hundred dollars worth of pictures. That's amazing!" John was always good to me like that.

John, for a while, however, was still just the J. R. that they knew in Mississippi County, in Dyess, Arkansas, on County Road 3, Box 238. Then he got bigger and bigger. He insisted on moving the family to Memphis in the summer of 1956, but I didn't want to go. He bought Mama and Daddy a little home on Westover Avenue in Memphis. Mama and Daddy said, "Well, Tommy, you're going to have to come with us." I said, "I can't leave my basketball team. I'm going to be a junior this coming fall, and we're going to win the state championship again."

But they talked me into coming to Memphis. There was Joanne, me, Mama, and Daddy. Everyone else was grown, moved out and gone. Joanne quickly left home later in 1956 and married her first husband and shipped out to Germany to be with him. He was in the service, in the U.S. Army.

We were no longer normal, everyday people. We were Johnny Cash's

Rustic Rhythm magazine article, May 1957.

family. When I would walk into a place, I could sit with someone and they would say, "Hey, there's Johnny Cash's brother," instead of, "It's just Tom Cash." I was always Johnny Cash's brother from then on, and people would look at me differently. They would ask, "Oh, what is he like?" You'd hear them whisper, "Does he favor Johnny?" That's been going on for almost fifty years. That's OK, because Johnny Cash was my flesh and blood.

What I miss most about my brother John is that he was always different every time you saw him. He always had something interesting to tell you, or something interesting to talk about, or something unique to ask. It was never just, "Hi, how are you? Now let's watch TV." No small talk. There was always something unusual to talk about.

Sometimes he wanted to talk quietly and just be together and be close. Sometimes he wanted to eat parched peanuts. I don't know if many people know that Johnny Cash *loved* parched peanuts. We grew up on the farm and we pulled them right out of the ground, and they would dry out, and then we would cook them up. Until the day he died, he liked parched peanuts and Breyers ice cream more than anything in the world. And of course, he loved all kinds of good food.

I've got some recorded messages saved from some of his phone calls to me. He'd always say, "Hey, Tommy, this is your brother John." Yeah, like I wouldn't recognize his voice. I've got some wonderful messages on the Code-A-Phone from him that I kept.

As far as a musical influence, he was everything. I probably would have never learned to play the guitar if it wasn't for him. Sitting around with him in 1955 and '56, you just had to pick up a guitar and try to make one of those chords to "I Walk the Line" or "Folsom Prison Blues" or "So Doggone Lonesome" or "Cry, Cry, Cry." You just had to play along.

And that's how it started for me. I wanted to be a basketball coach. That's what I wanted to be. I dreamed from the time I was ten years old and discovered basketball and a gymnasium and a basketball goal that I wanted to be a basketball coach. Why I didn't become one, I don't know, but I have had a wonderful life in the music business.

I've had more success than I deserve. I could have had a lot more if I'd been more business-minded, and my brother even told me that. He told me once, "You're not paying enough attention to business. You're trying to catch up with me. You're out being mean and disastrous." I said, "Well, I'm not doing it intentionally. It just happens." John answered, "Yeah, I know."

Our mother, Carrie, had a calming effect on me and John and all of us. I could be all to pieces over something, or happy and elated, and mother would smile at me and say, "Well, just make the best of it, son." She had a simple, spiritual way of looking at things. During my first divorce, I was totally devastated. I mean, I really was, once I realized I had lost that marriage. Mother told me, "You're going through this experience for a reason. It didn't just happen." She said, "God has better things in store for you." I couldn't see that, but she could.

The Cash family circa 1967. From left are John's sisters Reba and Louise, father Ray, John, mother Carrie, brother Roy, sister Joanne, and brother Tommy.

John had Billy Graham call me on the telephone. I was in shock! I didn't think Billy Graham would ever call *me*. I wasn't important enough to get a call from Billy Graham. I'd been drinking beer all afternoon, and John had talked to Billy Graham and said, "My brother's going through a devastating time in his life right now. Would you give him a call?"

So, Billy Graham calls me up and says, "Hello, Tommy, this is Billy Graham calling." I said, half drunk, "Yeah, sure it is! Who are you and why are you calling? What? What's your name?" I was real arrogant to the caller. However, he finally reassured me that he was Billy Graham. Then he had a really long sincere prayer with me and told me that I would get through this divorce and things would get better and that God would use me in other ways in my life.

And He did. But I couldn't see it that day. I was so full of hurt and anger and bitterness that I thought, *I don't have a chance.* But I did, and Billy Graham was right. He called me up about a month later and asked me if I remembered, and if I was working some of the principles he had taught me, like praying before I go to sleep at night and asking God to give me a sane and sober day when I wake up in the morning. Things like that.

People cared about me. I just didn't care much about myself back then. John suggested I record a new song he had just heard called "Six White Horses." Larry Murray, a television writer, brought it to town. John said, "Hey, Tommy, Larry Murray has a song that would be a great song for you." I had just signed with Epic, the biggest record label in the world!

Here's a silver platter handed to me, and I didn't see it. I thought, *That was nice, but let's go have a drink!* The day I heard the song I knew John was right. I called Glen Sutton, my producer, and Glen said, "My God, we've got to cut that song immediately and get it out before someone else." So we did. My record was out ten days later! It went No. 1 in the industry magazine charts of both *Cash Box* and *Record World.* I forgot to buy a full-page ad in *Billboard,* so it only went up to No. 2 on the *Billboard* charts.

When we first cut it in October 1969, we carried these little reel-to-reel tape recorders around with us. I played the song for John on that little player while at our mother's house in Hendersonville. He said, "Tommy, that's a number-one record. That's going to change your life." I asked him, "What do you mean, change my life?"

He told me, "You're going to be able to have whatever you need. You're going to be able to have a bus and a band. So, get yourself a really good manager, 'cause you're on your way." I thought, *Well, that's nice; that's great.* I did. I got a good manager, Buddy Lee, who booked me for almost twenty-five years, until he passed away.

So many wonderful things happened on the road with my brother. In 1976, when I was working with the Johnny Cash touring show for the whole Bicentennial year, he suggested we have clothes made with eagles on the front or back, or both. I said, "Well, that's your thing. Why don't you just have that done?" He said, "Nah, I want you to have some eagle suits, too."

So, we had Manuel make us some eagle suits. They were baby blue, with red, white, and blue eagles embroidered on the chest and a big eagle embroidered on the back. That was the big deal that year. We'd all walk out with eagle suits on. One day June Carter Cash, bless her heart and God rest her soul, came up to me and said, "Tommy, eagles is John's thing." I said, "Well, June, it might please you to know that this was John's suggestion that we all have suits made with eagles on them. It wasn't my idea." She just said, "Oh, really?" She didn't want me wearing stuff that he wore and vice versa.

I learned that year just how big Johnny was. I mean, I knew he was a giant and a legend, but I learned that year how big a celebrity and star he really was. He drew the largest crowds I've ever seen, and the most attentive. He was at his best in 1976. He was forty-four years old and was in his prime and did the best shows. He looked great, sounded great, and was at the peak of his career at that time. Yes, I learned so much from him.

We were walking through the St. Louis airport one day. I always walked about eight or ten paces behind him and June because I could hear all the comments people made about him as he passed. We would meet people coming left or right, and I'd hear people say, "Oh, there's Johnny Cash!" Then, here comes this woman with several packages in her hands, and she sees Johnny Cash coming, and she doesn't look at anything but Johnny. She walked and walked and walked, and just as she walked past him, she walked right into a post and knocked herself down.

We ran over to her to help her up and asked her, "Are you all right, ma'am? Are you hurt?" She said, "No. But I can't believe I got to see Johnny Cash in person!" She had a big knot on her head. Johnny said, "Well, ma'am, I'm really sorry. I didn't mean to startle you." And that year I realized just how big Johnny Cash really was to the public.

Walking into a hotel lobby was a marvelous experience, just watching people's reactions. It was almost like he was a god to some people. I had people approach me after shows and say, "I'll give you five hundred dollars cash if you'll let me meet your brother." I'd tell them, "He's already gone up to his room, and I don't think he'd appreciate me knocking on his door at twelve o'clock at night." But people just wanted to see him and touch him.

I'm a golfer, and I used to be a fairly good golfer. I'm just average now that I've gotten older. But back in 1976, during that year-long Cash Bicentennial Tour with John, he heard me talking about some new golf clubs called Wilson 1200s. They were the thing that year, the Cadillac of golf clubs.

He said, "Is that the kind of golf clubs you like?" I said, "Yeah!" He said, "I want to buy some for your birthday." My birthday was on April 5—and still is. I said, "You don't have to do that. I know where to buy them, like Service Merchandise or some of the stores in Nashville." So, he talked about it the whole tour. I thought, *Why would my brother be so interested in golf clubs?*

Toward the end of the tour he said, "Well, I was going to buy you a set of Wilson 1200s and a bag for your birthday, but I found out they were all sold out in Nashville. All the stores are sold out." I thought it odd, and why would he even care? I never thought much else about it and got off the plane in Nashville.

Well, there to meet me at the gate stood Armando, Johnny's security chief for twenty-plus years, with a huge golf bag full of brand-new Wilson 1200 golf clubs. I went, "Oh, my God!" I turned around and looked at John, and he had the expression of a child on his face. He was giggling and laughing and said, "I told you! I fooled you! See, I got you a set! I told you they were all sold out!" That thrilled him to death.

That made me feel really good inside, to know that my brother affected people the way he did—including me. I was in awe of him, and I wasn't intimidated by him, like some people in the family were. He used to tell me, "You're the only one in the family that will tell me like it is and shoot straight." Now, we'd argue from time to time, and we didn't always agree on everything.

Another fond memory was when I was six years old and Daddy said, "Hey, J. R., take Tommy down to the Tyronza River there in Dyess and teach him how to swim." J. R. answered him, "Oh, Daddy, my friends and buddies, we're all going to the blue hole, swimming. We don't need no kids." Daddy replied, "I said take him down there and teach him how to swim. You've been promising him you would for months." So J. R. took me down to the river, and I thought he'd just set me in the edge of the water there at the blue hole and I'd just start dog paddling.

We got to the bridge over the river, and he picked me up by the seat of the pants and threw me off the bridge. To a six-year-old, it looked like 300 feet, but it was only twelve. I didn't know how to swim, but I came up swimming real fast! I came up hollering and wailing, "Why did you do that?" He said, "I knew if I threw you in the river like that, you'd be swimming in no time. And I was right."

Then he picked me up and he hugged me and carried me down the riverbank about another couple of hundred yards to the blue hole. I was a happy little kid from then on. But when he threw me off that bridge, it was like throwing somebody off a water tank. Odd, but I recall the exact date. It was June 6, 1946, that he threw me off the bridge, and it was a warm, sunny day.

Tommy, John, and Connie Smith.

John was a person who sang and wrote about what life is, what life is all about. You know—pain, agony, joy, and sorrow. He touched on it all. He identified not only with the rich but with the poor, the downtrodden, just all the people, like he wrote in his song "Man In Black":

> *The people that never read the words that Jesus said,*
> *the prisoner who's long paid his dues,*
> *but is still there because he's the victim of the times.*

John would think way ahead of you. You had to be careful talking to him because his thought process was way above most people's. Small talk bored him because he wanted to get on to the point. Many times it was, "Yeah, yeah, yeah, but what's your point?" He wanted to get right to the meat because he had other things to think about. John was a nice man and had a huge heart. He loved everybody and everybody loved him.

I think we all have an enemy somewhere, and I think he did, too, but I think the majority loved him. They saw the love he had for others and his love of life, his love of what life is and what it means to everybody. He sang about it, talked about it, wrote about it, and lived it. He lived his songs, he absolutely lived them.

One of the last long, long, long talks I had with him was about our brother Jack. See, I was four years old when Jack died, and I did not ever know Jack or remember him. I didn't know a lot about him at all, although I had heard about him all my life and I had heard Mama and Daddy talk about Jack. I had learned little bits about Jack through snippets here and snippets there.

In the spring of 2003, four or five months before John died, he painted me a complete story of our brother Jack. He told me all about him, what he was like, and what he liked and didn't like. He just told me all about him, and I kinda got to know Jack through that long conversation I had with John.

You know, Jack had been called to the ministry even at the age of fourteen. He knew the Bible from cover to cover, and Jack could converse with adults about the Bible in a very knowledgeable fashion. It was just really good to hear that about him.

I had an album called *Special Edition*, which was a couple of years old at the time, and I took it over there to John about a year ago. I said, "I want you to hear a couple of songs on this album. I know you don't feel like listening to the whole thing." (That was because he was not well.) He said, "OK, put it on." So I put it on and played the Gordon Lightfoot song I'd recorded, "If You Could Read My Mind." I turned it off about halfway through the song.

He said, "No, no. Play it all. I want to hear it. I like the way you did that." It made me feel good. I said, "There's also a little Johnny Cash tribute medley in this album. I hope you didn't mind." He said, "Play it for me." So I played it for him, and boy, he began to squirm in his chair. He said, "Tommy, you really hooked that. You really got that. You sang those songs really good." It made me feel really good.

Instead of him saying, "Well, that's pretty good, but I don't know why you did it," he enjoyed hearing it. He really meant it; he really liked it. He liked me and I liked him. I miss him. I really miss him. I loved going over there and just sitting and watching him and listening to him, even when he was at his sickest or most ill. He was my brother. He was still so interesting, so beautiful. He just glowed with reality.

I loved him dearly and miss him terribly. Some days I'm OK with it, and some days I just feel sick inside, still, even though it's been months. A part of me is gone, and so is a huge part of the whole family. But we will go on, as John would like for us to do. He would definitely like for all of us to go on.

JACK CLEMENT

Nashville, Tennessee

Shoe Size 9½ D

I THINK I HAVE NEVER had a mortal friend better than Johnny Cash. And I know he loved me.

If anybody ever left this earthly plane owing me absolutely nothing, it's Johnny Cash.

We were great friends. We were also buddies, very much like Tom and Huck. In fact, we used to talk about who was Tom and who was Huck. We never could figure that one out because it changed all the time. Laughs? We had more than a few.

We traveled most of the world. We worked together many times and, of course, had a few musical disagreements along the way. And the friendship endured and survived because it was always honest and respectful.

I miss him every day. Do I still talk to him now and then? You bet.

My poem, "My Friend, the Famous Person," is a tribute to Johnny Cash and "buddyship" in general. Long live Tom and Huck.

MY FRIEND, THE FAMOUS PERSON

My friend, the famous person
is a barrel full of fun
a rather shy guy
in spite of all he's done

He's been around,
this friend of mine,
ten times ten
and then again

Down the river
'round the world

and up the creek times ten
but always springing forth
and back again

For springing back
brings secret laughter
and toughens up the chinny-chin
and lets the player fall down harder
just to get to bat again

To really know a fellow person
takes awhile, you know

it's seldom easy
but easily worth it
just to find a kindred soul

A kindred soul will pass the test
or flunk it just for spite
just to enjoy being a human
so let him do it
it's his right

Scold him quickly if he needs it
and never be a yesing man
tell him no
when no's the answer
or a lie he'll love and understand

A kindred soul comes back around
and never really leaves
though some time may pass
while he seems like an ass
he'll show up in one of your dreams

Just to enjoy being a human
so let him do it
it's his right

My friend, the famous person
is a pal you might know, too
for he has a lot of friends
and that's what makes him true

And true finds truth to realize
that there's more to the truth
than the absence of lies

It takes a good man to take success
and not misplace his soul
though bumbling through the facts of life
and too much rock and roll

He's a hero still drifting Huckward
ever rising from the South
ever learning
ever earning
my attention span

He gives a lot, this friend of mine
he lives a lot, this friend of mine
and loves from way within
And defeats the lust for anger
whether he needs it or not
just to enjoy being a human

But never guilt should my friend feel
that's neither good nor dignified
it's negative
wrong
and an all-round bad deal

For fame's a law
and love's a duty
and that could put one on the fence
but laughter loose and silly-hearted
makes it all make sense

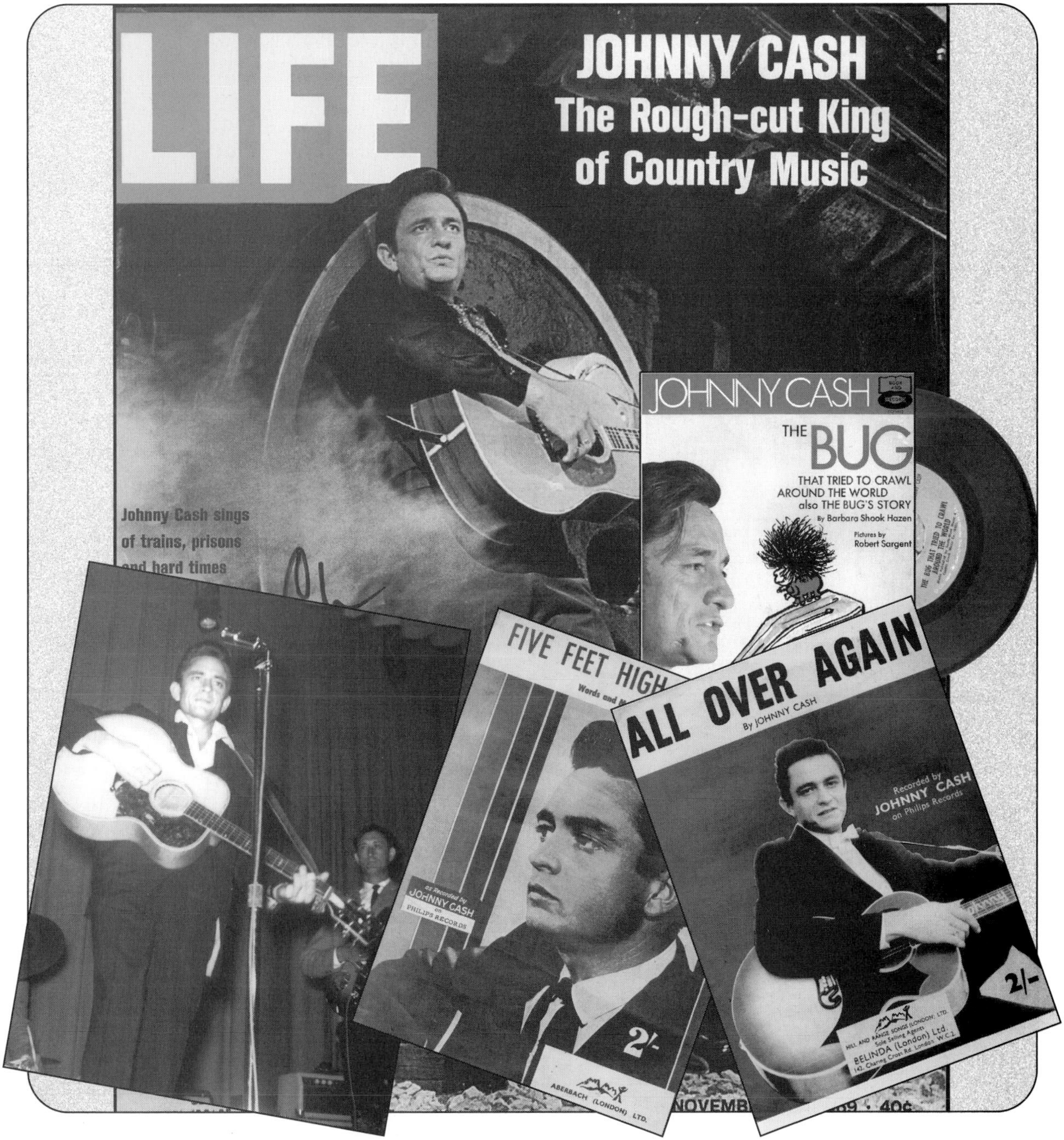

LIFE

JOHNNY CASH
The Rough-cut King
of Country Music

Johnny Cash sings
of trains, prisons
and hard times

JOHNNY CASH
THE BUG
THAT TRIED TO CRAWL
AROUND THE WORLD
also THE BUG'S STORY
By Barbara Shook Hazen

Pictures by
Robert Sargent

FIVE FEET HIGH

Words and M

as Recorded by
JOHNNY CASH
PHILIPS RECORDS

2/-

ABERBACH (LONDON) LTD.

NOVEMBER 1969 · 40¢

ALL OVER AGAIN
By JOHNNY CASH

Recorded by
JOHNNY CASH
on Philips Records

2/-

HILL AND RANGE SONGS (LONDON) LTD.
Sole Selling Agents
RELINDA (London) Ltd.
142, Charing Cross Rd, London, W.C.2.

GARLAND CRAFT

Hendersonville, Tennessee

Shoe Size 10½ WIDE

*I*T WAS 1974. I had just become a member of the Oak Ridge Boys band, playing piano. This was bigger than a dream come true, to join up with the most prestigious gospel group in America! I didn't know it at the time, but I soon found the group to be struggling to make it because of the nontraditional approach they had in their music, stagewear, and, suffice it to say, any other aspect of their presentation of the gospel.

Enter Johnny Cash. He was a friend of the Oaks, as they had appeared on his CBS-TV shows and he loved their music, as well. To help them out financially, he put them on tour with him, and besides paying a fee for their work, he paid his tithes to them from his earnings.

So, here I am, the new guy, in San Carlos, California, at the Circle Star Theater, backstage as the Man In Black strode in the back entrance. My mouth was wide open, to be sure, for I saw this bigger-than-life being that looked like the image I had of Johnny Cash, but he was so much more than what I expected.

Dressed all in black, with laced boots to his knees and a long-tailed coat. Wow! I was mesmerized. Never had anyone struck me with so much awe. I had been talking to Joe Bonsall of the Oaks, and Joe said, "Do you want to meet him?" I must have said yes, as I don't remember for certain what I said in those next few moments. I did find myself shaking hands with this walking, talking, living legend. That meeting I will always cherish.

We continued to tour with the Johnny Cash road show, which at the time included a lot of family members, including the Carter sisters as well as John's kids Rosanne, Kathy, Cindy, and John Carter. We became well-acquainted with each other, and some of my fondest memories of my thirty years touring with different acts are from this time. During this time, I also did a lot of demo-session work for Johnny's publishing companies at his House of Cash office complex in Hendersonville.

The Oaks' band with Garland Craft (top right) and the Oak Ridge Boys (front).

I became real good friends with John's daughters Kathy and Cindy, and others in the family, and, of course, I became close to June. Not too many years ago, I was shopping at K-Mart when June spotted me and pushed her basket over to where I was to say hello. It was good to see her, and we exchanged holiday pleasantries.

Then when I asked about Johnny, she said, "Honey, I'm mad at him 'cause he's gone off somewhere with some of his old cronies and he thinks I don't know where he is! He's supposed to be back by now, and I'm a little upset over it! I'm doin' this last-minute Christmas shopping to take my mind off how mad I am at him, and it ain't workin'." I could tell she was concerned with his whereabouts but not really that upset.

I recall we were working the Las Vegas Hilton in 1980, and Johnny was staying in the hotel's famed Elvis Suite. Cash had invited us up there one night for an impromptu party. The occasion was the celebration of John's bass player Marshall Grant's twenty-fifth year with Johnny.

As it turned out, there was no bartender to serve drinks and so forth for the guests, who were mostly all members of the Cash tour entourage. Somehow, I volunteered to act as bartender and had a great time picking up, serving, mixing, and everything that comes with being the bartender. At one point, Johnny asked me to call room service and ask for a very expensive bottle of wine. I did as he said.

When the wine arrived, I signed for it. A couple of days later, Johnny was in the Oaks' dressing room just chatting when someone with his entourage who I suppose kept tabs on expenditures came in and asked abruptly, "Is there a Garland Craft here?" I replied yes, not expecting the next question: "Did you sign for this extravagantly priced wine?"

Again, I replied yes. He then asked who authorized me to do that. I nodded toward Johnny and said that Cash had told me to. Johnny just looked bewildered and said, "I don't know what he's talking about!" Then I, even more bewildered, couldn't believe that I was about to have to cough up some big bucks for wine that I never tasted. It was then that Johnny broke the awkward silence by saying, "I ordered the wine and asked Garland to sign for it." He had me, and he had me good. I still to this day don't know if he set it up as a prank, or had he just seized the moment.

Sometime later, he was recording a gospel album at the House of Cash studio and I was playing piano on the session. I had the extreme pleasure of hearing him sing a song I had written, "That's Just Like Jesus" as one of the songs he had chosen for the project. The Oaks had been singing it for several years even before I joined the group. I don't suppose you can receive a better compliment than to have a prolific writer like the Man In Black find favor in words you wrote.

When June's mother, Mother Maybelle Carter, passed away, the Oak Ridge Boys were asked by the Cash family to sing "That's Just Like Jesus" at her funeral service. I accompanied them on piano as they sang it. I was so honored, I could hardly play it. The church was full, and I kept thinking the history of country music was represented that day. I recall that, as folks gathered in the church, you could hear Mother Maybelle's voice on the P.A. system recounting stories about the early days. I had gotten to know her on the road as she had traveled many dates with the Johnny Cash tour.

Of all the piano players in the world, here was I being asked to play with him and just a few other musicians recording gospel songs. We were doing tracks at his cabin studio across the street from his Hendersonville, Tennessee, home on the lake.

I remember that first session. A beautiful, sunny day, with the beginning of fall evident in the leaves on the ground. We sat outside for a while, just chatting and enjoying that crisp, clear day before going into the studio to start recording. I was sitting at a Steinway upright grand while at the same time sitting amidst historical artifacts in John's cabin, such as June's family autoharp and the bass fiddle played on many Everly Brothers classics.

There were boxes of reels stacked on a shelf to my left containing the early recordings of the Carter Family and so many other priceless pieces of musical history. It was just simply amazing. Johnny strolled over and asked if the piano would do. I told him it would certainly do just fine. I mentioned that perhaps the sustain pedal could be adjusted to work better. He told me he would have it taken care of. He did.

When it was about time to start that first session, he suggested that since the three of us—Johnny, "Cowboy" Jack Clement, and me—had not recorded together in this assemblage, we should perhaps start with a simple standard, like "Over the Next Hill," to get warmed up. He looked at me and said, "Kick it off, Garland!" This was the first time I had been in the studio with him since his 1975 gospel album that Duane Allen of the Oaks had produced.

Some of the first records I had ever heard or owned were by this man. So, when irony walks up and smacks you in the face with a "Kick it off, Garland," and your mind flashes back to the distance across that chasm from early records you heard to sitting in a studio making new ones with the same beloved artist, I was jumping up and down inside. It's moments like that you know you will never forget, and it's a mental autograph you can't show, but one you never lose. I don't take it lightly.

He had a peace about singing that song that day, although he had probably sung it a thousand times in his life. It's just that I had this feeling that it was heartfelt from him as he sang those sacred lyrics. At the same time, it was a harbinger of things to come, and not too far down the road.

Although he was sharp as a tack, witty, and at peace, Johnny knew his health was waning and that perhaps he, more than anyone, could see over that next hill. We cut about five songs over the next two weeks. Then problems began cropping up with June's health and his own frailties, and I would never speak to him again after that week in September, other than messages he sent me.

The next time I saw him, he was sitting in the front row of a church. In May of 2003, the family had asked me again to play, this time for June Carter's service. Jimmy Tittle had called me, and I returned home from a trip to Florida, where I was working. I didn't have any time to prepare anything, of course, but I did decide to play some of her favorite songs, like "Wildwood Flower" and "Jackson" and "If I Were a Carpenter." I played each number in a very soft, free-moving way, almost classical, if you will. At one point, I glanced up at Johnny, and he was listening intently to me, which made me try even harder to communicate my sorrow for this occasion and for what he was feeling.

He stared for a moment, then nodded at me, and then looked back to June. There was no fanfare around me being asked and honored to play at June's service, not even a mention, and not needed. I saw that he knew it, and I was putting my heart into it, and that nod was all I could have ever wanted.

He sent word to me that my music at June's funeral had brought everyone's hearts together for that somber occasion. He also added that he was not down for the count, and as soon as he was up and rolling, we would be back working on that spiritual CD project we had started in September of 2002.

The next time I would see Johnny Cash, I was playing at the same church, just four months later. This time, my friend John had been called

home. Again, there was no hoopla over playing piano at his service. It was
for him, and as long as he knew it, that was all that mattered. I just had
this feeling he was looking down at me from Heaven and giving me one
more nod of approval.

Whether on tour, in the studio, or at his home having dinner with those
infamous sing-along "guitar pulls" afterward, Johnny Cash never dimin-
ished in his appearance as a larger-than-life icon, even when his aged
hands trembled when reaching for a cup of coffee I handed to him at one
of our sessions.

He was, and always will be, that striking bohemian,
that one-of-a-kind personality I was fortunate to
meet thirty years ago. I told some folks recently,
"Yes, I knew Johnny Cash personally and
worked with him." I went on to say that I
considered myself on the outer periphery
of his circle of friends and I was privy to
a lot of the "goings on" in his world. I
enjoyed my acquaintance with him and
members of his family, and I did a
good job when I was asked.

If there is one thing that he taught
me, it was perseverance. He once
said, "You should never give up," and
that "one day, it will pay off." He was
right! That's what he told a fledgling
quartet called the Oak Ridge Boys, and
I'll bet he told that to a lot of artists,
like Larry Gatlin, Kris Kristofferson, and
the Statler Brothers, to name a few.

When I stop and wonder why I was one
of the people who crossed paths with this
man and got to share some of his life, I am
grateful, yet humbled. Thank you, Johnny Cash,
for showing me your path, that path less traveled.

JAY DAURO

Huntsville, Alabama

Shoe Size 17

I FIRST MET JOHN on March 15, 1977, at the Fox Theatre in Atlanta. I had been working as a computer programmer in Huntsville, Alabama, while doing community theater for fun. I purchased much of my lighting supplies from a company in Huntsville called Luna Tech. Luna Tech was approached by Lou Robin, John's booking agent, looking for a lighting director to go on the road with John. They called me and asked if I might be interested. This took a lot of consideration, but I decided to give it a try. When I discussed this with my parents, my mother's thought was that I would spend a year or so traveling and get the urge out of my system.

In preparation for going on the tour, I talked to John's bass player, Marshall Grant, and asked about a Johnny Cash concert song list so I could prepare for the show. He informed me that they didn't use a song list and that John just picked them out as he went along. He also noted that they didn't do rehearsals, so watching one was not an option. Since one of my friends was the late night deejay at our local country radio station, I spent nights for a week listening to every Johnny Cash album they had (and they had a lot), making notes on the songs.

41

Finally, the big day of my first night arrived. The night before, the owner of Luna Tech, Tom DeWille, and I drove to Atlanta and met the sound crew, Fred Smith and Mark Hunt, along with Lou's partner, Allen Tinkley, and Marshall Grant. I started setting up the show, not really knowing what was going on.

Johnny Cash tour sound crew members (from left): house mixer Larry Johnson, Jay Dauro, guitar tech Matt Garrett, and monitor man Kent Elliott.

Before the show John, June, the Carter sisters, and the band arrived. Allen introduced me to everyone. John always was an imposing figure, especially to a new employee. However, his smile and handshake made me welcome, even then.

At that time the show used a single 16mm short film from the *Ride This Train* documentary footage. Marshall explained how I would know when to start the film, as Bob Wootton kicked off the song "Hey Porter." I had set up the projector on some scaffolding at the back of the stage and hung the screen over the band. I had loaded the film and previewed it, so I would know what to expect, then cued it for the show.

Finally the show started. I was excited but disappointed that I had to work from the side of the stage. Because of the length of the projector control, I couldn't be out front to see exactly what was happening. I am there trying to keep up, learning the different voices, although there was a major difference between Anita and Helen's voices, it does take some experience before you know it. This is especially fun when all you have heard them say is "Pleased to meet you." I was managing to keep up with the songs when it came time for the film.

About an hour into the show, Bob's guitar kicked off the train segment, which was my cue, and I turned on the film. I looked up at the screen, expecting to see the train coming down the track, but instead saw numbers counting up. I had left the projector in reverse. The remote at that time did not allow me to reverse directions, so I closed the lens and went running up the scaffold. By the time I got there, the film was flapping on the front reel.

I switched the projector to forward, reloaded the film, and then had to go back down to the remote to open the lens to show the film. After some adjustments, I finally got the film going. All during this time John and the band had been playing, and as soon as they saw the film, they slid into the correct song and finished the medley as if nothing had gone wrong.

Well, I thought, *it was a nice try, but I'll be heading home tomorrow.* After the show, I met everyone and tried to apologize for the visual problem during the show. John laughed and told me that I got it running, so don't worry about it.

One time in Arizona, I managed to break my arm while running the show. It was a minor fracture. After the show, we got it checked and I ended up in a cast. The next week, while we were in San Carlos, California, I was presented with a little plaque. It says "Jay Dauro, Champion Butt-buster—Left armless" and is signed by John.

After a few years with John' traveling entourage, we were playing a concert in Canada. As the crew was leaving the hotel to go set up for the show, John pulled up in a limo. As he got out of the limo, he called me over, and had me try on a burgundy leather coat. He had been out shopping, seen a coat that he liked, and thought that it would fit me. So he had purchased it and gave it to me as a gift. I still have and treasure that coat from John.

Years later, we were working in Branson, Missouri, in the early nineties. John and June had rented a house out in the woods south of town for their stay. One day at the show, June

Jay and Cash musician Jack Hale get silly.

told of opening the door and finding a huge spider there in the doorway, which she immediately called John to come and kill. The next morning, I arrived at the theatre early to make some preparations.

Just before the show, I went up to John and June's dressing room. As June left to prepare for the show, I asked John if it would bother him if a large spider appeared while June was talking to the audience. A light came into his eyes, and he commented that he didn't think it would bother him.

Later John introduced June, and as usual they sang "Jackson." Then John took a seat while June stayed out front to talk to the audience and do some of her comedy routine. She did this every show and would tell many different stories, including the tale of the spider. While John waited, a large rubber spider descended directly behind June. When it was at her eye level, John called to her. She turned to see what he wanted, saw the spider in front of her nose, and just about jumped into the front row.

I was also privileged to go on tour with John when he went with the Highwaymen for their debut concerts as a group. This expanded my definition of family again. Watching the interaction of the four "boys" (as we called John, Waylon, Willie, and Kris Kristofferson) was always hilarious. They enjoyed performing together so much, and that showed to their audiences. John's sense of humor could blossom there also.

For many years I traveled as production manager for John's concerts along with my friends Kent Elliott, who stayed in the wings and took care of the monitor mixes, and Larry Johnson, who did the front-house sound that the audience heard. There are none better. Also in my crew for many years was Matt Garrett, who handled the stage and tuned and cared for all the many guitars. After Matt left the tour, we were joined by Brian Farmer, guitar tech extraordinaire.

The Johnny Cash production crew spent most of every day on the road together. I saw more of them than I did of my own family at home. We were all dedicated to making things work, and all got the biggest kick out of actually running the show.

I always was grateful that I could go on the road with the Cash show. John and June treated all of the folks on the road with them as family. The band, the Carters, our drivers, managers, and the many fans made being out on the road a pleasure. There were many other people involved with John and June, from the staff at the House of Cash in Nashville, Lou and Karen Robin and their staff, the many other people it took to keep the show on the road, and of course, all of John and June's family and friends.

Anyone that John worked with, toured with, or employed on the road was a friend and was treated as family by him. I met many people during my time with John and June and saw things I never could have seen any other way.

I spent twenty years on the road with John, June, and their show. I started as lighting director and ended up as production manager. When John had to retire from the road, I discovered Mom was wrong. I still don't have it out of my system.

Now that John, June, and the Carter sisters have left us, I think back on the miles and the time I spent with them and realize how lucky all of us were to be able to work with them. And in my dreams at night, I'm still doing production for the Johnny Cash Show.

DENNIS DEVINE

Council Bluffs, Iowa

Shoe Size 8 1/2 D

*J*OHNNY CASH. Just say the name and it brings back memories starting back in 1955, when we lived on a farm outside of Giltner, Nebraska, near Hastings and Grand Island. My mother, Della, had heard Johnny Cash's "Cry, Cry, Cry" and wanted me to get a 45-RPM record of it. I had just got my drivers license and jumped at the chance to drive into the big town of Hastings.

I went into the record store and laid my hands on the record for my mom. Little did I know what that day did to change my life. I took the record home, and Mom and I put it on the old record player and a voice came out that was like no other I had ever heard. I knew I had to meet this man in person someday.

This would happen when my dad, Paul, got a job in Council Bluffs, Iowa, handling mail for the post office mail terminal. It was February of 1960 when I heard on the radio that George Jones, Norman Jean, and Johnny Cash would be at the old Paramount Theatre across the river in Omaha. This was my chance to meet Johnny Cash.

My brother Norman and a friend, Bob Dangler from Giltner, and I went to see him, but the show was already sold out. They said at the ticket office we could pay and stand at the side of the stage to see the show. It was $5 to see the show, sitting or standing, so we gladly paid and went in. I didn't have a camera at that time, so I looked for someone who had one. I told him I would pay for the film. At intermission, I went to look for Johnny, to meet the man I had been listening to for five years. I went to a dressing room someone had said he was in.

John and Dennis, 1960.

He was standing there, not in black but in a western tie and a gray sports jacket. I asked for a picture and shook his hand. He had a presence about him, even then. The picture was taken.

Through the mid-1960s I would see Johnny at the Music Hall when he came to Omaha. One Saturday night I was backstage—it was February 26, 1967, to be exact. Johnny's manager at the time, Saul Holiff, asked if I would take a birthday picture of the group. I had my own camera by then and was taking slides. I went into the dressing room and could not believe my eyes. There was Johnny Cash, June Carter, Anita Carter, Helen Carter, Mother Maybelle Carter, Carl Perkins, Marshall Grant, W. S. Holland, the Statler Brothers, Luther Perkins and Saul Holiff all in a dressing room in Omaha. I could not believe my luck. I took the picture, and Saul asked me to send him some copies.

Omaha, Nebraska, February 26, 1967.

We ate cake for Johnny's birthday but that picture was the real frosting on the cake.

In 1984, I started writing for *Country Music* magazine. It was published by Russell and Helen Barnard. The first story I wrote was on Johnny Cash. I never got paid for those articles, and I have never made a dime off Johnny Cash—and I never will.

That year, we went to Des Moines, Iowa, to a concert. Johnny sang one of my favorite songs, "Orange Blossom Special," and after he finished, I left my front-row seat and approached him as he stood onstage. He smiled, looked me in the eye, and gave me his harmonica. It was the first of two we would get that night. This was the first two of a dozen harps he would give me through the years. I have them framed and labeled as to when and where I got them. I wouldn't take a million bucks for these very personal mementos from Johnny.

Through the years, I always wanted to have the chance to introduce Johnny Cash at the beginning of a concert. I would drive around practicing the words I would use to introduce my hero to my family and friends at the imaginary concert in my hometown of Council Bluffs. My brothers Norman and Joe, my sister Jean, and even my son Dennis Jr. would kid me about my dream, saying, " He will never come to perform in Council Bluffs. The closest he ever got was to sleep at the Howard Johnson motel." That was the closest motel to Johnny's concert stop in Omaha, and it is barely across the Missouri River in Council Bluffs. I know this because I took a baby present to Johnny for his son, John Carter, and they were staying at Howard Johnson.

Pride Week is a yearly celebration in Council Bluffs. It is an event to encourage a city-wide clean up and for the town to pat itself on the back for being a nice place to live, and it features other events tied to community improvement. My mother's pharmacist, Dick Miller, was one of the organizers in 1987. I went to him with the idea to bring Johnny Cash to town and have him speak on family values and how bad drug use is. I gave Dick the California phone number of Lou Robin, Johnny's agent.

Before I knew it, the Johnny Cash Show was coming to town. The Pride Week committee, the business community, and all of City Hall got on board and started the job of raising the money to pay for the concert.

The show was scheduled for May 16, 1987, at Abraham Lincoln High School right here in Council Bluffs, Iowa!

Dick Miller told me I could introduce Johnny at the concert. I could not wait to tell Mom, my doubting brothers and sisters, and even my son. My dream was coming true, and they surely would have to eat crow!

After what seemed like forever, May 16 arrived, and we all gathered at the high school for the wonderful occasion. Along with Johnny, the Carter Family with June, Helen, Anita, and June's daughter Rosey, were on the show. I went onstage with Dick Miller, and Dick said, "Della had a Devine son . . . Dennis. He is to introduce the most important person in his life, Johnny Cash."

I dedicated all of my efforts on helping with the show to my dad, Paul, and my uncle, Harold, and also to Johnny's father, Ray Cash, and June's mother, Mother Maybelle Carter, who had all passed away. I said, "I get to show the people of Council Bluffs my hero and what he is all about, and Johnny gets to see what Council Bluffs is about."

Johnny came up on stage and tried to shake my hand and tried to plug in his guitar. By then, I was in my front-row seat next to my lady friend Doris Langeneggar, my mom, and family. Johnny sang a song and a half before June came out to see what was wrong. She said, "He is having trouble with high blood pressure." They took him backstage, called an ambulance, and took him to Mercy Hospital. I went to the stage and asked for a prayer for John and his family.

The silence lasted for over five minutes. We announced, "Keep your tickets; we will reschedule the concert. I went home. John was in the hospital, in a room I could look out my back door and see.

The next morning, Sunday, the phone rang. It was Lou Robin asking if Mom and I wanted to come up to see John. He was OK. We went up early, and John came out of his room. Mom was crying. John came over to her and

To the people of Council Bluffs.

Thanks for your love, Care and Understanding.

I look forward to returning in September, with a better show than ever.

Johnny Cash

Before flying from Council Bluffs to Nashville to recuperate, doctors insisted that Johnny have an electro-cardiogram (above) before boarding the plane; Dennis introduces a hale and hearty Johnny Cash on his return to Council Bluffs (below).

said, "You are just like my mom," and gave her a kiss. We had our picture taken with June and John. John's doctor told him to go home and rest. They left early on Monday morning.

Johnny Cash gave back all the concert money, and a new concert date was set for September 12. I was going to introduce Johnny a second time to the Council Bluffs people.

He came back on September 11, and we picked him up at the Omaha airport. We went to the Finish Line Motel. Bob and Saundra Darrah let John, June, and the gang stay for free as their contribution to Pride Week. John went back to Mercy Hospital. The hospital was celebrating its 100th anniversary, and John shared some thoughts and sang. I had arranged a book signing for John's *Man In White*, and picture taking.

We then went to the Rock Island Railroad Depot. My friend Doris Langeneggar and I rode to the depot in John's limo. There were media and television press from Omaha and Council Bluffs. John was presented with a Council Bluffs key to the city, and we toured the depot. Many people got to ask him questions and take pictures, with the best yet to come: the concert at Abraham Lincoln High School.

I went onstage, and for the second time Dick Miller introduced me, and I, in turn, introduced Johnny Cash, "my hero." I went offstage to get a picture of the Carter Family coming out, and Hugh Waddell started talking to me. The next thing I knew, Johnny Cash was calling my name to come back out on the stage. I could not believe it. I cannot sing, so what did he want?

I went up to him and shook his hand. He handed me an award given by the Pride Week Committee—an award for me, presented by Johnny Cash! That has to be the best award ever given to me, but wait—something as good was about to happen. It was Helen Carter's birthday, and I got to stand between John and June and sing "Happy Birthday" to Helen. My first singing onstage was with Johnny Cash! I must have done OK, because no one in the audience left.

The show was about over, and John started singing "Orange Blossom Special," and at the end he handed me the second set of harmonicas of the year. What a perfect ending to my "Dream Concert." Council Bluffs Mayor Sam Irwin declared that day, September 12, 1987, as John and June Carter Cash Day. Two brass plaques were made, for John's Mercy Hospital room and the Finish Line Motel, which said, "Johnny Cash slept here."

In all the years I have known Johnny Cash and family, he has done special things for me. He was that kind of man. I got to know Johnny Cash upfront and personal. June, all their children, sister Reba, brother Tommy, all the band members, and the stage crew all came to know me. That is very important to me in my life.

The number of Cash concerts I went to between 1960 and 1996 totaled well over 125 shows. At most of them I was upfront and had the chance to go backstage. I have taken over 4,000 pictures, and I have suits, shirts, shoes, boots, and albums autographed by him. I have never sold any of his things and never charged for the pictures I took for other people. Once, at a party at his Hendersonville home, Johnny introduced me to the actor James Keach by saying, "This is Dennis Devine, and he is a *big* Johnny Cash collector!"

I have many personal memories, like the phone call from John when I was to have open-heart surgery in October 1995. He called and told me

Dennis and mom Della
with Johnny and June.

that June and he would pray for me. I said,
"June has an open line to God, doesn't she?"
He replied, "I believe she does." They subsequently sent me flowers while I was recovering at the Veterans Hospital in Wisconsin.

I guess I could write an entire book about
me, the "Johnny Cash Number One Fan,"
but Hugh Waddell has given me this opportunity to share some of my many stories
about J. R., as his mother called him.

When Abe Lincoln died, they said, "And
now he belongs to the ages." That also
applies to Johnny Cash. I am glad I lived in
his time and knew Johnny Cash, the man.
He is, and will always be, "my hero."

The last words I spoke to Johnny were at his beloved wife June's
funeral. I had just shared some remembrances of June
and was returning to my seat from the pul-
pit. I walked up to John in the
front pew, and he said,
"Thank you, Dennis." I told
him I loved him and sat
down with tears in my eyes.

I thought about that
moment a few short months
later, while sitting in the same
church at John's funeral. How
blessed I was to have known this
man. God has surely blessed me.
My favorite Johnny Cash song is "I
Still Miss Someone," and, yes, we
all will.

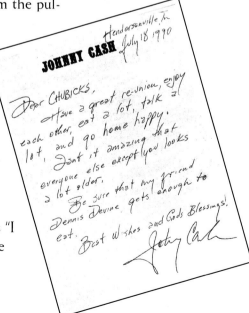

JOHNNY CASH   Hendersonville, Tn
July 18 1990

Dear CHUBICKS,
Have a great re-union, enjoy
each other, eat a lot, talk a
lot, and go home happy.
Isn't it amazing that
everyone else except you looks
a lot older.
Be sure that my friend
Dennis Devine gets enough to
eat. Best Wishes and Gods Blessings!
Johnny Cash

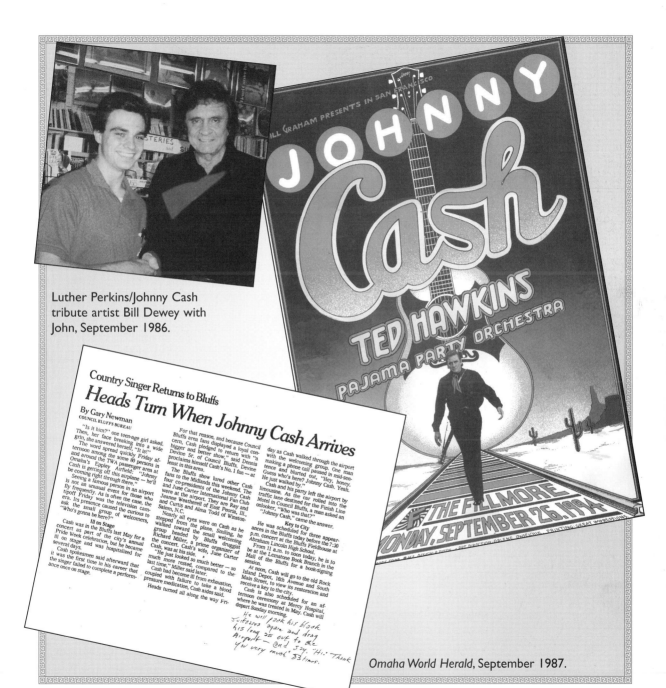

Luther Perkins/Johnny Cash tribute artist Bill Dewey with John, September 1986.

BILL GRAHAM PRESENTS IN SAN FRANCISCO

JOHNNY Cash

TED HAWKINS

PAJAMA PARTY ORCHESTRA

THE FILLMORE
MONDAY, SEPTEMBER 26, 1994

Country Singer Returns to Bluffs
Heads Turn When Johnny Cash Arrives

By Gary Newman
COUNCIL BLUFFS BUREAU

"Is it him?" one teen-age girl asked. Then, her face breaking into a wide grin, she answered herself, "It is."

The word spread quickly Friday afternoon among the some 80 persons in and around the TWA passenger area at Omaha's Eppley Airfield. "Johnny Cash is getting off this airplane — he'll be coming right through there."

Seeing a famous person in an airport is not an unusual event for those who fly frequently. As is often the case, the tipoff Friday was the television cameras. Its presence caused the curious to ask the small group of welcomers, "Who's gonna be here?"

Ill on Stage

Cash was in the Bluffs last May for a concert as part of the city's annual Pride week celebration, but he became ill on stage and was hospitalized for several days.

Cash spokesmen said afterward that it was the first time in his career that the singer failed to complete a performance once on stage.

For that reason, and because Council Bluffs area fans displayed a loyal concern, Cash pledged to return with "a bigger and better show," said Dennis Devine Sr. of Council Bluffs. Devine proclaims himself Cash's No. 1 fan — at least in this area.

The Bluffs show lured other Cash fans to the Midlands this weekend. The four co-presidents of the Johnny Cash and June Carter International Fan Club were at the airport. They are Ray and Jeanne Weatherell of East Peoria, Ill., and Curtis and Alma Todd of Winston-Salem, N.C.

Nearly all eyes were on Cash as he stepped from the plane. Smiling, he walked toward the small welcoming group headed by Bluffs druggist Richard Miller, a prime organizer of the concert. Cash's wife, June Carter Cash, was at his side.

"He just looked so much better — so much more rested, compared to the last time," Miller said later.

Cash had become ill from exhaustion, coupled with failure to take a blood pressure medication, Cash aides said.

Heads turned all along the way Fri-

day as Cash walked through the airport with the welcoming group. One man making a phone call paused in mid-sentence and blurted out, "Hey, honey. Guess who's here? Johnny Cash. Yeah. He just walked by."

Cash and his party left the airport by limousine. As the car rolled into the traffic lane destined for the Finish Line Motel in Council Bluffs, a man asked an onlooker, "Who was that?"

"Johnny Cash," came the answer.

Key to City

He was scheduled for three appearances in the Bluffs today before the 7:30 p.m. concert at the Bluffs Fieldhouse at Abraham Lincoln High School.

From 11 a.m. to noon today, he is to be at the Lemstone Book Branch in the Mall of the Bluffs for a book-signing session.

At noon, Cash will go to the old Rock Island Depot, 16th Avenue and South Main Street, to view its restoration and receive a key to the city.

Cash is also scheduled for an afternoon ceremony at Mercy Hospital, where he was treated in May. Cash will depart Sunday morning.

He will pack his black suitcases again and drag his long ass out to the Airport — and say "Hi!" Thank you very much 83 times.

Omaha World Herald, September 1987.

LUTHER FLEANER

Bon Aqua, Tennessee
Shoe Size 10

*T*HE FIRST TIME I met Johnny Cash I was working a farm about five miles from my home in Hickman County, located between Centerville and Dickson in western Middle Tennessee. I was keeping cattle and horses on this old place in Bon Aqua, when John acquired the farm in 1971, in a business deal. He immediately put this 107 acres and its 1850s-built log house up for sale.

In the spring of '72, Johnny and June came down to look at their property for the first time and decided right then and there that they didn't want to sell it. He fell in love with it on first sight. Johnny, June, and John Carter all sat out in the front yard and had a picnic that very same day they first came down.

Shortly after, Johnny called me back and wanted to know if I would continue working up here at Bon Aqua, taking care of it for him. I've been here ever since. The first I knew of Johnny Cash was on the radio. I had always liked his songs. But from that day I first met him, I thought I'd died and went to heaven. I worked for him at Bon Aqua for thirty years.

Johnny would come to Bon Aqua every chance he'd get. They would call me from his office and say he was coming, and I'd make sure the house was cleaned. I made sure the lawn was mowed every week. I wouldn't ever bother him when he was at the house in Bon Aqua. If he needed me, he had my phone number, and anyway, I was in and out all the time. Most of the time when he came to Bon Aqua, he was by himself.

He loved this place. He'd sit right out there on that front porch in his rocking chair. Nobody would bother him. People didn't come up here like they did in Hendersonville. He would go to the grocery store, the hardware store, anywhere, and not be bothered because he was a star.

John's Bon Aqua cabin.

As time went on, I put some beagle hounds at Bon Aqua, and I'd leave them up here so Johnny could listen to them run. If I knew he was coming down, I would make sure and have the dogs there. He'd turn them out and listen to them run. He loved the sound of them beagle hounds out in the field behind the house, running a rabbit. I just kept them on the place so that John could turn them loose, and later on I'd come back, put them up, and feed them.

Johnny wouldn't ever put them up. He'd say, "I'm done," and feed them baloney and weenies. He just never ran a dog off, or anything. If an old stray dog came up to the house, he'd feed it. When I got coon hounds in the mid-1980s, Johnny decided he wanted to go coon huntin'. So I took him coon huntin', and on that first hunt on his farm, we killed us a coon.

I dressed the coon for him, and he took it back to his house in Hendersonville and had them cook it for him. The house staff up there thought it was the awfulest thing they'd ever seen, and yes, he cooked that coon and ate it. We got him two or three more coons that he took back to Hendersonville over the years.

He liked hunting so much that he wanted him a coon dog. Tom T. Hall's wife knew someone, I believe in Wyoming, that raised black and tan coon dogs. She had a registered black and tan breed flown in here on a plane. The dog's name was Molly. John wanted to raise some pups then, and he bred her to my coon dog. He fell in love with that dog and kept her at his house in Hendersonville until she died.

Johnny had grapevines and muscadines growing at his house in Hendersonville, and he decided he wanted some at Bon Aqua. About 1983, he said "Luther, I want to get some started down here." I said, "Well, where do you want 'em? I'll help you put some out." He had somebody at his Hendersonville house go get and bring down to Bon Aqua some crossties to make a place to hold the vines.

We dug the holes and set 'em out, and he said he was going to order some grapevines, I think it was out of Georgia. He had 'em sent to me, and I brought 'em up here and set 'em out. I kept them watered, fertilized, and he would call me, or have his sister Reba to call me, and ask how his grapevines were doin'.

When they got to runnin' good, he said, "I've got to put some wire up for them." So, John went to the store and bought some wire, right up there at the Ace Hardware on 46 Highway. We strung it up, started stringing the vines, and got it like he wanted and got the vines all across the top. He was so thrilled over those grapes.

When they were traveling, or if he was gone for several months, we'd make a picture of his grapes and send it him. I would send John pictures of his grapevines like I would pictures of children. When he would call, he'd ask, "How's my grape vines?" He

Wanda,
Thank you for the Pictures. They're beautiful. I'll see ya'll in about three weeks
John

wouldn't ask about how you were doing or is the house still all right, but instead he'd ask, "How's my grapevines?"

As they grew and started bearing grapes, he'd come down and eat a few and say, "Now, get them grapes and muscadines and use them." He had the white grapes, the purple grapes, the white muscadines, and the red muscadines. He put them all together and had them all mixed up.

And when one of his grapevines died, he ordered a whole bunch and told me, "You set out some at your house and replace that one in my vineyard." He'd give everybody that he knew grapevines. Them vines growing out there at Bon Aqua have been planted now for about ten years. It's just something like an apple tree. They grow, but sometimes one will die with cold weather or disease.

Luther Fleaner with sons Jeff and Chad.

It was about 1985, I guess, when he come down and said, "You need to get these grapevines trimmed." I answered him, "Johnny, I don't know where to start, but I'll call county extension offices and see if anybody knows." Well, you don't just start cutting grapevines, because you got to know which stems to leave to produce the grapes. But nobody knew how to trim a grapevine when I called in Dickson County and Hickman County.

So, John come down with somebody for a day or two. I drove up, and it really looked like a storm had hit those grapevines. There was grapevine cuttings so high I sure enough couldn't step over them. I came in the house and said, "Well, I see you trimmed them grapevines." Johnny answered back, "Hell yeah, I couldn't get no one else to do it, so I did it myself." Next year, though, we didn't have a single grape, or no muscadine or nothing else. It took a couple of years for them to finally grow out. Johnny told me, "We'll set out more vines, and I'm not sure they won't die, but we'll set out some more if they do."

January 6, 1997

Mr. and Mrs. Luther Fleaner
9433 Big Spring Creek Road
Bon Aqua, Tennessee 37025

Dear Luther & Wanda:

June and I have discussed it, and we have decided what we want to give you as a wedding present. Two round trip airline tickets, anywhere in the United States you wish to go, your hotel room, all meals and a rental car for the length of your trip.

You cannot turn down this gift. Please call Karen, once you make your decision as to where and when you can go.

Hope you have a nice honeymoon. See you in a couple of weeks.

Your Friend,

John

Johnny Cash
200 Caudill Drive
Hendersonville, Tn.
37075

In 1990, we had a good year and the vines were loaded with grapes. Johnny called, and I told him, "This thing's loaded. You need to send and get 'em." He said, "Well, I got plenty up here. You take 'em and make wine out of 'em." I said OK. I picked the grapes and made five gallons of grape wine and five or six gallons of muscadine wine and really took pains with making it, you know?

And anytime anybody would come down, they'd ask me, "You got any wine? You got any wine?" Well, I wouldn't give just anyone much, 'cause I was saving it for Johnny. When he'd come in, he'd ask, "Where's the wine?" I'd tell him where I had it hid in the house. He'd drink a glass of wine, and that's all he'd drink.

Every time he'd come down here to Bon Aqua, Johnny would buy a new tool. He might have two or three of some tool in the garage, but he'd forgot about them and go buy a new one. When the summertime or early spring got here, he'd get garden fever. He'd go buy okra seeds, tomato seeds, cucumber seeds, and he'd go out there in that old hard yard and dig it up. I'd help him, but mostly it was my job to keep it watered and take care of it.

Sometimes we'd have big tomatoes sitting on the ground. I wouldn't pick 'em, because I'd be afraid he'd come down and I wanted him to have them. I'd cut the okra, though, 'cause if you didn't keep the okra cut, it'd ruin. But if he'd come in, and he got two or three okra pods or tomatoes, it was the greatest thing in the world to him, because it come off this farm and he grew it. There's still seed over there in the kitchen right now. I imagine that he bought them. He'd just buy big packs of seed with no particular place to put them, unless he dug up a place.

There is a recipe that John came up with right after he had open-heart surgery. He was going to quit eating all red meat, so they came up with his special veggie burgers. He wrote the recipe down and gave it to us sitting right there at the kitchen table in Bon Aqua.

When I'd come up here, if that door was shut and his truck was here, I didn't knock. If he wanted to see me, he'd call me or he'd come outside the log house. I didn't bother him. I was the only one who had the keys to the house, besides John Carter, just like I do now. John didn't even have a key. I had to actually open the door for him, because I bet I had no tellin' how many keys made for Johnny and he'd lose them or he'd forget 'em. He called me up one time and said, "I didn't have my keys and I wanted in right then, so I just kicked the door in. Get it fixed." I said, "OK, it's your door!" And that's just the way he was.

My most favorite times with John was the coon huntin' and our mule wagon rides. He loved to go, 'cause when he was young he worked mules. He liked taking those rides through his property. I also loved being with him in the woods, 'cause he loved nature so much. We even had many picnics out in the yard at Bon Aqua. One Fourth of July, Johnny brought his whole family, his sisters, everybody, to share the beauty of this place.

In the early '70s, when he was doing a Dean Martin TV show, he taped a segment up here. He had several celebrities up here when he'd tape parts of his TV specials. They once had a big yellow ribbon tied around the huge oak tree in the front yard for Tony Orlando. Some of the production company tied the ribbon, and Tony Orlando sang there by it.

Johnny would call me if he needed anything. When he first got the place, he didn't have a phone. He'd be down here, and he wouldn't call to check in with nobody. His office would call me and want to know how he was doing. They'd ask if I'd seen him, and I'd say, "Yeah, seen him a while ago." One time, Waylon called trying to get hold of him.

They all had my phone number. Emmylou Harris called me one time trying to get hold of him. John would come down to my house to call them. He'd have a mobile phone, go to a pay phone, or come to my house and call them. He finally got a phone up there, but then he'd put the phone off the hook or not answer, so they were still calling me!

Johnny loved the property and he loved the people around it. He would come down here in the middle of the day and would stop by and see my mama and daddy. He'd pull in their driveway and just walk right in their house and talk to them. Mother would make him a chocolate pie sometimes, or send him cornbread or a green-bean dinner. I've seen my mother go in her kitchen and have a pan of cornbread and a pot of turnip greens and bring them up here to him. He loved it and would say, "That's just like Mother would make."

He loved that old log house at Bon Aqua, and he loved its old fire-places. The place is hard to heat, and you can't hardly heat without the fireplaces. So they had put a damper in it, because when you got a fire-place, if you don't keep the damper cut off, it sucks all the heat out. Johnny would come down here and light a fire, and he wouldn't open the damper. And here would come smoke rolling out!

He'd call me and say, "This damn fireplace is stopped up!" I'd ask, "Did you put the damper on?" He'd then say, "Oh, well, I forgot it." So one day he told me, "I want that damn thing took out." I didn't ask him why or nothin' else. When he told you he wanted something done, he wanted it done right then. I crawled up in that cockeyed thing and worked half a day yanking that damper out. He was something.

Back in the 1970s, when he first got his place, Johnny bought an old abandoned store by the railroad tracks in Bon Aqua, and he'd put on shows, with him and the family. Marty Stuart came down and so did Jim Varney and others, and they'd have old-fashioned picking sessions with acoustic guitars. The doors were open to everyone. They had a surprise birthday party for Johnny there around 1973. His sister Reba was the head of it. We worked up there all day getting it ready. We had to get all the cars back so Johnny could pull his big Cadillac up and get out. He didn't know what to think!

Merle Kilgore was down for it, and he sang and talked. There was more food than you could imagine because the whole town brought food. The people who weren't invited came in, because in Bon Aqua word travels like wildfire. Everybody was welcome.

He would ride the back roads and stop and talk to people. He loved people! There is a guy, Mike Barnhill, over at Lyles, Tennessee, and John loved his barbecue. I took him over there to Mike's place one day, and you could have heard a needle drop. The place was full of folks, but you could have heard a needle drop. When Johnny was in Australia, he sent Mike a cap, and it about tickled Mike to death. I would go out to Mike's, and he'd ask about Johnny. I'd say, "Johnny's out there in Bon Aqua right now," and Mike would send John some chicken. Everybody loved John!

When he'd come to Bon Aqua, he might be in his underwear, you know? He came here to relax. I pulled up in the driveway one day and my wife was with me (this was before we got married). Johnny was standing out on the front porch, and all he had on was a pair of black boxer shorts and a smile! Lord, she got out of the truck and he hit that front door like a groundhog hits a hole. That embarrassed my future wife and him, too. He didn't know she was in the truck, and she didn't realize he would only have on his underwear. That morning, he really was the Man In Black!

Johnny had a small lake out on his property, and he wanted it stocked with fish. He was acquainted with Sterling Holt, so Sterling told him to come down to his place and seine some fish. Sterling lowered his pond, and John, June, and I, along with Sterling, got in there and seined that pond. I bet we got about a half-barrel of fish! We brought them up here to Bon Aqua and put the fish in Johnny's pond. Anything like that, he was all for. Johnny caught a lot of fish out of it. He'd come up here with his fishing poles, and the last fish Johnny caught at Bon Aqua was a big one-pound brim.

He loved Bon Aqua, even if he was only going to be here four or five hours. He told me once, "Luther, I can come down here, take a nap, and walk around the yard, and it's like being in another world." He wanted his private time just like everyone else, but he couldn't get it till he came down here. He also read his Bible a lot while he was at Bon Aqua, and you would see the Bible laying around in different spots, where he'd carry it from room to room.

The Cash group was in Wales in the late 1980s doing one of his Christmas programs, and Johnny brought me back a watch. I never seen one like it in my life. It had a hole in the face of it. Johnny said it was a design Napoleon had come up with. He told me Napoleon was a big hunter and could pull that watch out and tell time without having to open the face up.

He was fond of giving people stuff, like in the early 1990s, when Johnny went to Australia and brought me back a bullwhip made out of kangaroo hide. He also brought my wife a little beaver hat. He had a big gun collection, and when he sold it, he brought me a centennial-edition, gold-plated .50-caliber rifle and gave my sister a pistol.

You wouldn't know John had a dime when he was down here. There was a junk store over on Highway 100 where they sold secondhand clothes. I've seen him go in there and buy clothes and come home and wear them. He would go to the store, and he didn't care what he looked like—hair all messed up, with his beard grown out. He never mentioned his wealth, and I never heard Johnny brag.

I could just sit at Bon Aqua, day in and day out, and tell great Johnny Cash things. This was his heaven. Bon Aqua *is* Johnny Cash. He didn't want nobody to know about it, as this was all his. The last time Johnny was down here, I came up to see him. It was in the spring, about six months before he died. He had waited until it got warm enough for him. He'd come and sit on the front porch. He'd stay as long as he could, maybe two or three days, until he had to go back to Hendersonville with his worsening health.

I made a statement to myself when he was getting sicker. I said, "Well if John ever passes away, I'll just quit, 'cause I just don't want to come back up here to Bon Aqua." But I can't keep away. This is me. I was born and raised right up the hill from his place.

I still come up here to Bon Aqua a lot and just sit in the driveway. To me, it feels like he's still here. He's everywhere. Johnny Cash was the best friend I ever had, and he was more like my family. There will never be another Johnny Cash. No, there will never be another Johnny Cash.

IRENE GIBBS

Nashville, Tennessee

Shoe Size 8¹/₂

*L*ITTLE DID I KNOW that the tall, skinny man who came running into my sister's club yelling, "Hide me, Dottie, hide me!" would someday become a part of my future. This was in 1965, and the Dottie he was calling happened to be Dottie Swan, my sister, and her club was the Professional Club on Music Row in Nashville. It was located in one of the old homes on Sixteenth Avenue South and was beautifully decorated with a very large round table in the center of the room.

The club served as a meeting place for songwriters, artists, and other members of the music industry. Several hit songs were written on that round table. I was visiting Dot when this man came in. I don't know who he was hiding from, it could have been anybody. She explained to me that he was Johnny Cash, the singer. Having just moved to Nashville from Pennsylvania, I had heard of Johnny Cash but knew very little about him. All I could tell then was that he was one really wild man.

A few years later, in 1969, I was to see this man again. I had just recently started attending church at Evangel Temple, where Hank Snow's son, Jimmy Snow, was the pastor. It seemed that Johnny Cash had also started attending Evangel Temple. I was in the choir, along with John's sister

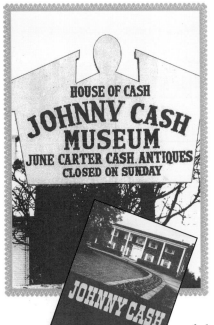

Joanne. John liked listening to the choir, and soon we were asked to sing backup on a couple of songs on his upcoming album, *A Thing Called Love.*

The entire Evangel Temple choir went to the CBS studio, where Larry Butler was producing the album. We sang on the title track, "A Thing Called Love" and the song "Papa Was a Good Man." We had a fantastic time, and a few years later our Evangel Temple choir appeared in a national Amoco Oil television commercial with John.

In October 1973, either by accident or on purpose, John's sister Joanne told me that John was looking for a new secretary, so I decided that I would apply for the job. As I pulled into the House of Cash parking lot, the first thing I noticed was this beautiful Colonial-style building with big white pillars on the front. I opened the door and saw the lobby with the huge pieces of antique furniture.

I was ushered up the staircase to a large office in the back of the House of Cash. It also was furnished with beautiful antique furniture. This was the office of Reba Hancock, manager of House of Cash and John's sister. After we talked for a while, she took me to John's office for a personal interview. John's office was very large, with dark paneling and beautiful antique furnishings. The focal point of the office was a very large, ornately carved antique partner's desk.

After he asked me a few questions, he dictated a new gospel song to me that he had just written, "Over the Next Hill," and he dictated a letter. I was then taken into an office where I was to type the lyrics and letter. The first thing I discovered was that this was a new kind of typewriter for me. It had proportional spacing, and I had never used one like that. So I proceeded to mess up royally. To top it off, the ribbon ran out, and I had no idea how to change it.

His accountant, Maribeth Wendt, brought me a new ribbon and installed it for me. After about thirty minutes, John came in and told me I didn't have to finish typing, but I was determined. I felt this would be the only time I would get to do any work for John. So, after I finished typing (no mistakes, either), I took the papers and put them on John's desk. He told me to go to Reba's office and she would talk to me further. I was all set to hear "Sorry, but no thanks." Instead, Reba asked me, "When can you start?" I was to work as John's executive secretary for the next fifteen years.

On my first day, as I walked into the House of Cash, I saw two very well-known men standing there with John. He called me over and introduced me to them, Billy Graham and Sheriff Buford Pusser. I could not believe that on my first day at work, I had met these two important people. John told me we would be having morning devotions when the other girls got there.

This was to be a regular event before we started to work each day. There was a beautifully furnished room on the side of the lobby that was our prayer room. It was a very small, quiet room with chairs, a couch, and a Bible. If we had problems at any time, we could go in there and pray. I came to use that room quite often.

There are many stories I can tell about my years working with Johnny Cash. I must say they were some of the happiest years of my life. One of my favorite stories took place in October 1978, when Mother Maybelle Carter died. I loved my job so much that I was usually the first one in the office and the last one to leave every day. I came in early that particular morning and found John sitting on the steps alone. He asked me to sit down there with him so he could talk.

He loved Maybelle so much, and he just wanted to talk about happy times. He told me several funny stories about her, about them fishing together and other things. He also had some sad tales, and he cried. He was going to miss her so very much. I sat there and listened for about thirty minutes. He finally got up and left. I felt so honored that he had chosen to share such a sad time in his life with me.

John gets "arrested" at the House of Cash during a Jail-a-thon benefiting the American Cancer Society.

Another incident occurred in my office. It was the middle of the morning when John came into my office. I was a little down that day, and of course John noticed. He asked me what was wrong, but I couldn't tell him because I didn't know. He left the office, and a little later he came back, bringing me a beautiful turquoise and silver ring. He said, "Just thought this might cheer you up a little." Shortly after that, June came in.

She said, "Honey, Johnny tells me you're feelin' kinda puny, so I brought something to help cheer you up." She gave me a bottle of Shalimar perfume and a very long, green necklace. Needless to say, I felt very pampered that day, and the blues left me as fast as they had come on. John and June were both so thoughtful and always made me feel good about working for them, or as they used to say, "You work *with* me, not *for* me."

John had started writing his autobiography, *Man In Black*, and I had the privilege of typing the book. John wrote the entire book by hand, and believe me, there were times when it was hard to decipher. Every time John would edit the book, I would have to retype the whole thing. He didn't like adding pages or pasting changes. I lost count of the number of times I typed *Man In Black*. When it was finally published, John gave me a special bonus. He sent me to Israel with my church group and gave me money to spend on the trip. What a thrill that was for me! I had a wonderful time and would never have been able to make that trip on my own. This was just one more little perk from working with John Cash.

John's faith in God was very strong. At one time he bought all of his staff new Bibles and started us on a Bible study. He would assign a chapter for us to study, then work up a test on the chapter. I would type it, and each person would receive a copy. We had to answer the questions, and John would check them the next time he was in the office.

Johnny Cash was to write another book, called *Man In White*, also entirely handwritten. This was his novel based on the story of the Apostle Paul. John started this book three different times before he finally came up with what he was looking for. This book reflects John's vast knowledge of the Bible. He studied for hours at a time before writing a chapter. John spent about two years writing that book. I also had the privilege of typing *Man In White*, and it is a wonderful story about Saul and his conversion to Christianity.

These are just a few of my pleasant memories of those fifteen years I spent at House of Cash. Johnny Cash was a great person to work for, as it never seemed like work. I felt like I was getting paid for enjoying myself and doing things that I would never have been able to do on my own. There was a new experience every day, places to go, people to meet, and things to do. John and June were wonderful people, and I miss them very much. But, as Bob Hope always said, "Thanks for the memories."

JACK HALE

Hendersonville, Tennessee
Shoe Size 10 D

*O*NE DAY IN 1987, I was in my room, practicing on my trumpet. At that time, I was the trumpet player for the Memphis Horns, a very well-known horn section whose credits range from Aretha Franklin to the Doobie Brothers. This was quite an honor (and a lot of fun), so when it appeared we had quite a bit of time off coming up, I was wondering if I should go back and finish my last year of college. I was twenty-two years old and full of ambition and drive and did not want to go back to school!

During my practice session that day, I received a call from the House of Cash, Johnny Cash's business office. The Johnny Cash Show was going on a ten-day concert tour of California in the month of June, which also coincided with June Carter's birthday. As part of her birthday presents, John decided to give her, for that tour, real trumpets to play on the song "Ring of Fire," which she had co-written with Merle Kilgore. The money offered was fine, and it sounded like the easiest job I'd ever had.

Without hesitation I agreed, called my friend Bob Lewin, and the next thing you know, we were flying out to meet the Johnny Cash band. Now I must digress. My father and uncle are very well known in the field of music—especially by their peers. My father, (the original) Jack Hale, was a child prodigy on trombone. He began his career during the big-band era, playing principal trombone with the Memphis Symphony and had his own jazz band, the Memphians. My father later became one of the most famous rock 'n' roll trombonists in history while with the Memphis Horns.

Jack Hale (left) and Bob Lewin.

My uncle, Ralph Hale, is in the American Bandmasters Hall of Fame, with the likes of John Phillip Sousa, for accomplishments in the music education field. When I was fourteen, I told my father I wanted to be a musician. His exact words of reply shouldn't be repeated, but it can be said that I was told to follow the instructions given by my uncle and my father.

I could not have a summer job like my friends such as sacking groceries. I was to practice and study music for my generous allowance. I even remember my father and uncle debating about letting me watch the Beatles' debut on Ed Sullivan. I did get to, thanks to my uncle! Only later did I realize how fortunate I had been and how correct my father was.

The reason for my family history here is to explain the reason I did not know who Johnny Cash was. Totally ignorant of country music, I literally had never heard his music. I thought he was an actor or some other kind of celebrity. The only country music I ever remember hearing was my friend's father's Jim Reeves 8-track tape. I thought it was a comedy album for about the first twenty minutes! Only later did I become appreciative of country music as an art form. As you will see, ignorance can be bliss.

The opening concert for us was at the Los Angeles Forum. Bob Lewin and I showed up at the sound check in rock 'n' roll-type outfits, and Goldie, John's wardrobe lady, asked if we had brought anything black to wear. We had not, and she explained that John was known as the Man In Black, and after sound check we should get some black stage clothes. We were puzzled, but it was fine.

We went on out to the stage where the band and Johnny Cash waited for sound check, looked at the charts that had been brought out for us to play, and the band kicked off "Ring of Fire." We began to play and, being excellent readers, didn't miss a note. The problem was that the chart had been written for some televised Johnny Cash special and it was in the wrong key and had the wrong number of bars, etc. I did not know the song but knew what we were playing was horribly incorrect.

John would stop the band and then restart the song from the top—he did this several times. Finally he said to me, "Something doesn't sound right." Being overly confident (after all, I was the youngest musician on stage and had the Memphis Horns credentials/ego), I snapped back, "These charts are what's wrong—if you can get someone to play me a record or even just sing the parts to me, I'll correctly write it and we'll come out and play it—we don't need to rehearse!"

John, Reverend Billy Graham, and Jack Hale.

He replied, "Son, the show tonight is sold out, and we'll have many Hollywood celebrities in the audience (many who were John's friends, I would find out later, as I came to know more about him) as well as critics from the papers." I replied it didn't matter who was going to be there, we would be fine once I had correct charts. My first lesson in John's humility was when he said "All right, son" and walked off calmly.

Bob and I got with one of the sound engineers, not anyone from the band, and put together the chart. It was a funny vibe in the backstage area compared to the rock 'n' roll-type scene I was more accustomed to. I remember they were discussing the Carter Family's part of the show and were talking about the song "Wildwood Flower." To show how sheltered I had been from country music and its history, I honestly confused the song with "Wildwood Weed," a well-known anti-establishment song—I'm totally serious! I was trying to picture these beautiful dignified ladies singing it!

We finally went to the stage and the band kicked off "Ring of Fire." Bob and I started into it, and then John came out. Everything went perfectly, proving God watches over children and idiots! John looked at us and gave us his two-thumbs-up approval and a huge smile! I still didn't see what the big deal was, but I was glad that we played well. At intermission, many celebrities came backstage, arousing my suspicions as to who this Johnny Cash really was.

I'm a little fuzzy about this, but somewhere during the ten-day-only tour, John gave us a raise and asked if we'd like to continue on for a few months. Our job at the time was to play "Ring of Fire," go backstage and eat, relax, then go out and play "When the Saints Go Marching In." We only played the first and last song of the concert show. Needless to say, we said great! That three months turned into ten years, during which time I became his musical director, among other things.

Sometime during my first year with John, we went on tour to Europe, where playing with Johnny Cash was the equivalent of a Rolling Stones tour, I'd have to say. While we were in London, John informed us that he was planning on recording "Ghost Riders in the Sky" and wanted us to play French horns on the record. I tried to explain that trumpet and French horn were very much different, but he said he believed we could do it, and besides, how much were French horns, anyway? I was given a pillowcase full of English pounds (about $6,000 U.S.) and told to go get them.

Thanks again to my family contacts, I was able to call Julian Baker, one of the most famous horn players in the world. Bob and I met this legendary musician at the Paxman Horn Shop in downtown London. Since we could not make sounds that were pleasing to the ear, he had to pick out the French horns he felt were the best! Out came the pillowcase of dough, and I remember the stacks of currency on the store's glass counter top. We left with two of the finest French horns money could buy.

Back at the hotel, we were trying hard to make them sound good and had the tape of "Ghost Riders" to practice to. It was bad. That night, in concert with John at London's Royal Albert Hall, we were going to debut our virtuosity on French horn when John debuted live, his next hit, "Ghost Riders in the Sky." I secretly got together with the stage mixer—the one who is responsible for what the musicians hear on stage, as opposed to the house mixer who is responsible for what the audience out front hears. I told him to keep us out of the monitor mix—no matter what! We were not ready, and I'd treat him to refreshments later.

That night we "played" the French horns, and John kept looking at the stage mixer, indicating he couldn't hear us! Every now and then I'd catch some blast out in the concert hall that sounded awful—it was us. When we finished the song, John once again gave us double thumbs-up but had a puzzled look on his face. By the next evening's show, we were able to pull it off without too much embarrassment.

As I mentioned earlier, I had become his musical director, since I was able to write music notation, conduct an orchestra, etc. This was a very exciting thing for me in more ways than one. John had a band that could "turn on a dime." If he decided to change something in a song, the band was right there, which always made the shows spontaneous and fun to play. There was never a "song set list" like most artists and bands have. John went with his instincts and did whatever he wanted.

However, when you are conducting a large symphonic orchestra, who are all reading written music, you are pretty well forced to stay the course of the musical arrangement. The conductor is the bridge between the artist and the orchestra, combining the two as a seamless unit. As a conductor, the biggest things to stay on top of are dynamics, tempo, and pitch from the orchestra. Their responsibility is to pay close attention to the conductor and not get buried in the written-score chart.

I would stress this to the musicians when I'd rehearse an orchestra without John's presence, and most of the time I was given minimal attention. Guest conductors (young ones, at that) can get a bit disrespected. One evening, while conducting the Houston Symphony, we were into a piece scored by Bill Walker. I think it was a patriotic trilogy. There were the usual tempo changes, pauses, so on. All was going well, although the musicians really were not watching me too closely, when we came to a pause in the music.

John was supposed to sing a few lines of the song "Shenandoah" a cappella, then I would bring the orchestra back in. I had my baton up, the orchestra was quiet, when John started singing some other song! You could hear the orchestra's necks snapping up from the music stands. Talk about paying attention! I was frozen, as nothing in music school will ever prepare you for a moment like this. I looked over my shoulder and John was just singing a chorus of some other song.

Then he looked at me and started into "Shenandoah"—perfectly. The orchestra came in and we finished the concert. The "addition" John had added was actually nice, and it sounded like it should have been there. The audience did not have a clue as to what almost happened. John left to thunderous applause, I left the conductor's podium, and the orchestra was dismissed. I was still trying to regain my composure when John walked by. He said, "I scared you, didn't I, son?" with a slight smile as he walked away.

Later, I was handed an envelope with my name on it, and it contained a bonus check for a thousand dollars. I thanked him but never had the nerve to ask if he meant to do that unexpected extra song in that trilogy or not. Knowing John, it is quite possible he was just having fun with me.

I would like to express an example of how sincerely compassionate and thoughtful Johnny Cash was. We would play Trivial Pursuit on his bus (he usually won), and that's when I found out how well read he was. There was a question about the authorship of *The Rubaiyat*—none of us had even heard of it—and he answered Omar Khayyam correctly. I was particularly amazed and asked about the book and the author.

A few months later, my mother passed away completely unexpected. I was at home when it happened, and John was one of the first to call and check up on me. Months later, around Christmastime, I got a package that had been sent from New York City. Inside was *The Rubaiyat of Omar Khayyam*, with the handwritten inscription on the inside, "May you know no more sorrow, Your Friend, John Cash."

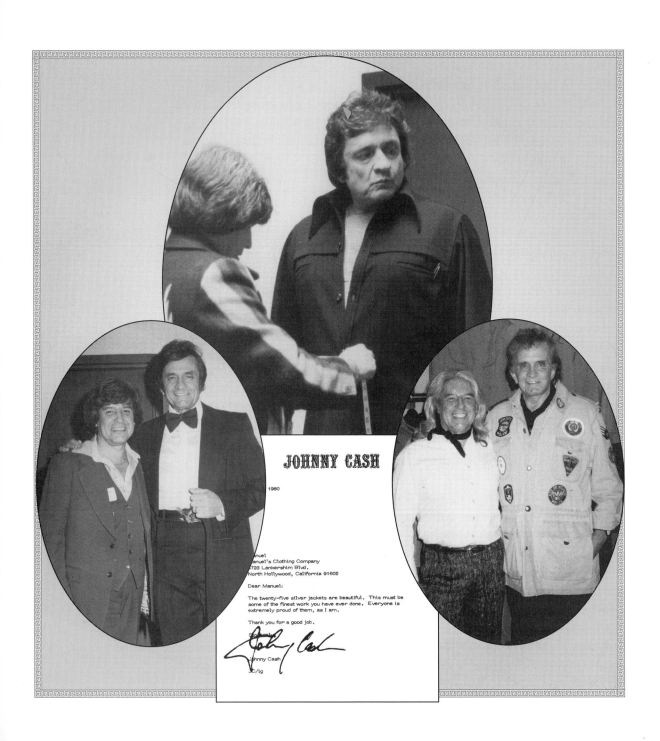

JOHNNY CASH

1980

Manuel
Manuel's Clothing Company
723 Lankershim Blvd.
North Hollywood, California 91602

Dear Manuel:

The twenty-five silver jackets are beautiful. This must be some of the finest work you have ever done. Everyone is extremely proud of them, as I am.

Thank you for a good job.

Sincerely,

Johnny Cash

Johnny Cash

JC/jg

W. S. HOLLAND

Jackson, Tennessee
Shoe Size 11 D

*T*HE FIRST TIME I ever met Johnny Cash was in 1955 at Sun Records studio in Memphis, Tennessee. I was drumming with Carl Perkins at that time, and we were doing a recording session. That was a time period when people like Elvis, John, and Jerry Lee had just gotten into the business. They would drop by the studio to hang out and listen to each other record. John, Warren Smith, Bud Deckerman, and all the Sun Records artists would come hang at the studio. Even Elvis. *The Million Dollar Quartet* photo and recording session happened during one of these times.

But when John came by the Sun studios that day, I didn't think a lot about it. He was just another guy to drop by. It wasn't something that I made a big deal about at the time. Years later, it was a different deal.

Carl Perkins, his two brothers Clayton and J. B., and myself were all from Jackson, Tennessee. We'd been playing together since 1954. At a point in 1955, when John had come along, rock-'n'-rollers Sonny Burgess & The Pacers, Jerry Lee Lewis, Roy Orbison, Billy Reilly, and other future Hall of Famers were all recording for Sun Records. Sam Phillips, who owned Sun, and Bob Neil, a disc jockey in Memphis, had set up a little booking agency called Stars Incorporated. They would just book Sun

Records artists, and bookings were always in like a 150- to 200-mile radius of Memphis. We played in all the little towns around Memphis, and we all worked together. Sometimes it would be three or four different groups on the same show. We were out roughly a hundred days a year.

Carl Perkins onstage with W. S. Holland and Johnny Cash.

The first thing Sam Phillips would do when he cut a song on any of the Sun Records guys was to get it to Memphis disc jockey Dewey Phillips for his show, *Red, Hot & Blue.* He played everything from new records to chart-topper hits. He helped break many of the national hits from Sun. He broke more Sun Records singles than anybody.

So, we're all playing music, but a lot of us still have full-time jobs so we can afford to work at night playing music. I still had a job at this time working at the S. M. Lawrence Company here in Jackson. If I needed off early, they'd let me off. If I was up late, they'd let me come in late the next morning. They were real nice about it. I put up metal awnings and worked on coal-loading equipment. Back then, a lot of homes had furnaces in the basement, called stokers. They had all this equipment that hauled the coal, and I helped keep the trucks going.

In addition to hanging at the studio, we all traveled together. It just happened that Carl, Clayton, J. B., and me—the Perkins Band—kinda got real close to John and his bandmates, bass player Marshall Grant and guitarist Luther Perkins. We all became real close friends and just kinda really bonded together real early. They were from Memphis, and when we went on tour, we were the ones that buddied up together. In other words, we would ride together to shows. I liked speedboats, and Marshall Grant liked them, so we had something in common to talk about.

Fact of it is, that is how the "Blue Suede Shoes" song was born. Carl had three single releases out, and we were touring now in two cars. I was in John's car, a '53 Plymouth. Luther, Clayton, and Jay were in my 1948 four-door

Cadillac. Me and Marshall would be driving, and John and Carl would be in the back seat. John had just come out of the Air Force. John stuck his foot up, resting it on the back of the front seat and noticed his shoe. He had a flashback of being in the Air Force and having to keep his shoes shined. He made a statement: "Carl, we ought to write a song about some shoes." We rode on a few more miles, and they started talking about it again. John told Carl they should write a song about suede shoes, blue shoes, or something like that. There wasn't anything else said about it.

Later on, we're playing at a little club out here in Jackson called Tommy's Drive-in on Highway 45 South. They didn't have a bandstand, and so we just set up in the corner. That night, Carl heard this boy say to his girl as they were dancing, "Don't step on my new shoes." Obviously, the boy had gotten some new shoes. Carl heard that, remembered what John had said in the car, and goes home and writes "Blue Suede Shoes" late that night. That's how that song was born. You'll hear the story fifty different ways, but that's the way it was. John helped plant that shoe idea.

So, we're all traveling together on the road. In 1958, John and Carl went to the Columbia Records label, so we all started recording in Nashville. It was now just about over for Sun Records; just a couple or three years is all that it lasted. It was something everybody talked about. I remember one conversation. It was the day Elvis bought Graceland. We were all in the Sun studios in Memphis talking about it, and I remember Sam saying, "Man, I don't know why Elvis spent that kind of money. How will he ever pay for it? He spent a hundred three, a hundred four thousand dollars for that place."

All this time passed and John had moved out to California in 1957 or '58. At that time, the biggest engagement for John to date was a week at the Steel Pier in Atlantic City and a week at the Three Rivers Club in Syracuse, New York. John had never used a drummer, as it had always been the Tennessee Two and himself. I think John and everybody he knew figured this booking was a big deal, or maybe Marshall and Luther couldn't make enough noise. Johnny Cash called me and wanted me to go for two weeks on this trip.

I guess I just happened to be the best drummer they knew. I had already quit playing with Carl. I had recorded this hit song called "Mona Lisa" with Carl Mann. After that, I was going to quit the business in 1960, because me and Joyce got married. I was tired of it. I was going to get a regular job. I told him I couldn't go. I told him, "John, I have already got a job lined up to start to work Monday working for the City of Jackson, helping out a surveying engineer." I guess I was going to go hold survey sticks or something, or stick them in the ground. So, I told him I'd call him back.

I called Jerry, the guy at the city department I was going to go work for,

and I told him I would like to go up there with these boys and play drums for the two weeks. Jerry told me to go ahead and to give him a call when I got back. The first week was at the club in Syracuse. While I was with Carl, I played a full set of drums, but when I went with them to New York, this spring of 1960, I just carried a snare drum, a stool, and high hat, or as we called them, sock cymbals. No bass drum. For one thing, we didn't have room in the car for anything else.

That was really weird to me, sitting there with just a snare drum and brushes after playing a whole set of drums with Carl. That sound that I developed was a weird thing. Normally, you'll accent the snare drum on the two and the four beats in a measure of 4/4 time. Your one beat will be louder than the two beat. But I didn't know what I was doing, so I started playing galloping triplets like John had been doing on his guitar with a piece of paper stuck in the strings to mute the ring. And for some reason, I would make all three of the beats the same loudness. The first couple of songs at that show, you have the Tennessee Two, and all of a sudden there's this guy on snare drum and everybody thought it was good. Hell, it was great! I was doing something that nobody had done, while playing with Johnny Cash on the stage anyway. Playing a drum. It was one of the greatest things that happened.

Johnny Cash and the Tennessee Three (from left): Luther Perkins, W. S. Holland, John, and Marshall Grant.

Then I learned to close the high hat and play on the side of it doing the same lick. I could play something up-tempo, and it worked really good. The style that Luther was playing, the style that Marshall was playing, and the style that John was singing, not knowing what I was doing drum playing-wise, just happened to work perfect. If I had been somebody who really knew music and knew exactly one way to play something, like you're supposed to know, it wouldn't have happened. I was just doing the only thing I knew to do. Syracuse worked out great, and we moved on to Atlantic City.

We had so much fun in the Atlantic City dressing room it was unreal. Teen idol Fabian was coming in to play the Steel Pier Club the week after us. Well, the guy wasn't exactly a great singer, but it didn't stop him from having a dozen hits in the '50s. In our dressing room there was an indirect lighting system. We all thought it would be funny, and with John prompting us, Marshall Grant and me went and bought eggs in the middle of the week. We took these eggs and broke them all in the dressing room's indirect lighting system so that when Fabian got there the following week, they'd be smelling real good. Our tribute to teen idols. We were doing this in just our second week together, and John was right in the middle of it all.

Another thing we'd do a lot, was me and Marshall went and bought a box of 10-gauge shotgun shells. We'd open the door to the tiled restroom and I would get on the other side of the door. I would get some pliers and hold the shotgun shells and Marshall would take a hammer and a hole punch and hit the shotgun shell and fire it. The shot would go all over the room. We shot a whole box of shells that way. You couldn't walk. You had to hold onto something to walk in the dressing room, 'cause the shots were like BBs all over the floor and your feet would fly out from under you. John was egging us on and having a big time right with us.

So, that's when I decided I wanted to do this! Johnny asked me about money, and he just wanted me to work occasionally. I told him I had to have a regular full-time job. He said, "I want you to work every show I work, as long as I'm in the business." I said, "Well, that sounds like a regular job to me." I come home and told Jerry I was going to stay in the music business, so I wouldn't be working for him and the City of Jackson.

Shortly after that, we went out to California in a brand-new 1960 model Cadillac. John, married with daughters at this time, lived in the corner-lot house on Havenhurst Street in North Hollywood that Johnny Carson had once owned. John had moved his parents out to Ojai, California, from Memphis, and they managed a trailer park there. So, we drove out to Ojai, located in Ventura County, north of Los Angeles, to see them. John had a friend named Curly Lewis, a contractor who later would build John's new house in Ojai after he moved from North Hollywood. Curly had an old '57 Ford Ranchero that was just plumb wore out.

On the way to John's parents, we stopped for a bit of sightseeing at a cliff. We were sitting on the side of this mountain, and Curly said, "Man, if that truck was to roll off here, I would collect insurance." John said, "Curly, we can get it off here." And for some reason, it started rolling, and we sat there and watched it tumble. Tumble, tumble, and tumble. We all thought that was funny. It never caught fire or blowed up, but it looked like an oil can an elephant had trampled. I don't know if the statute of limitations for insurance fraud is out yet, so "officially" the truck rolled off the cliff!

For a time, we four, John and the Tennessee Three, traveled in one car and stayed in one room with two beds. We were traveling on the Pennsylvania Turnpike and got stopped by a policeman, and we pulled over at a coffee-shop kind of rest area. He walks up to our car and asks, "Whose car is this?" One of us said, "It belongs to Johnny Cash." And of course at this time, he didn't know who Johnny Cash was. Well, John was in the back seat asleep, so we woke him up and got him out of the car. He had that Johnny Cash style working for him real good there.

W. S. Holland and John, 1960.

The cop asked him for the car's registration. John fumbled around in the glove box and couldn't find it. Then, John walks around to the front of the car, reaches down and rubs the bottom of the front tire with his hand and says to the policeman, "You know what? That registration was stamped on this tire right here and it must of worn off, I'm pretty sure." John then turned and walked into the coffee shop. The policeman said nothing, got in his car, and drove away. When people saw something that unusual happen, they'd just drive away stunned.

We were in Hammond, Indiana, doing three shows a day. We were standing out back of this theater and got some slingshots and marbles and started shooting the windows out of this old warehouse across the street. We graduated from that to where Marshall and I would play with cherry bombs, those little red balls with the green fuses. Did you know they would stay lit underwater? Well, Marshall and I would flush these down the commode in our hotel.

These things would go down to the next floor before they would explode, but when they did, they'd blow a hole in the sewer pipes and just tear stuff up. The hotel would have to call the plumbers to fix it. We nicknamed Marshall "the Mad Bomber" because of this. Even Lester Flatt called him that. We had to stop, though, because we started taking the cherry bombs into the dressing rooms. We'd lay one of them at somebody's heels and light it. It'd go off, and they'd holler and jump a mile. Well, we were someplace in Iowa and lit one at a lady's high heel. It went off and it really hurt her leg. Hurt her pretty bad. If it was today, John and all of us would have been sued for a hundred million each. We quit then and there with the cherry bombs.

Johnny, why, he'd do anything. We went up in the mountains in Ventura County, California, near John's house, to zero-in the scopes on some of John's rifles. We had about four .30-06 rifles between us. While we were sighting in the scopes, we saw that there were some game wardens up there, also playing with their guns. Anyway, John is shooting around at nothing in particular. From his rifle scope, John sees a deer standing way up on the side of the mountain. He wanted to shoot that deer.

So, he goes to the game wardens. He says, "I want to shoot that deer standing up there. What will be the deal if I shoot him?" They answered, "Well, it's not deer season, and you will be shooting across two roads. If the deer isn't a legal deer, we'd take all your guns." John said, "Well, about what do you figure the fine will be?" They kinda guessed and said, "Well, with what your guns are worth and the fines, no license, out of season and all, it'd be about three thousand dollars, probably."

I said, "John, you don't have to worry about paying a fine. Just shoot that deer, 'cause you can't hit the damn thing. You or nobody else!"

Without saying a word, he stretched out on his stomach on the ground in the dirt and propped up on his elbow and pulled the trigger. If the moon had fallen on that deer, it wouldn't have knocked it down any more! It was unreal. That deer was so far away you couldn't see it with your naked eye. The game wardens just stood there watching us.

We jumped in the car, rode to the next road up, and stopped. Luther stayed in the car. You can't imagine how hard it was to climb up that mountainside to get that deer. We get up there, drag the bloody deer down the steep slope, and throw him in the trunk of that Cadillac—with the game wardens watching all this happening. We then drove back down to Ojai, to his parent's trailer park. John goes around the back to a little shed and hangs the deer up. I was in shock watching all this, as I didn't know anything about all this deer hunting.

They hang the deer up and dress it, then carry it to John's parent's house and cook it. A damn alligator couldn't have eaten it, that deer meat was so tough! See, Johnny wanted to shoot that deer. He didn't care what it cost, so he did. That was vintage Johnny Cash. That was just another thing that made him so unique.

We felt like we could do anything and get away with it. And we usually did! If people today did some of the things we did back then, they'd be in jail the first night, prison the first week. By this time, you began to realize that Johnny Cash was somebody different. Not just as an entertainer, but as a man, also. For him to do something like shooting that deer in front of the game wardens, he had to be different and had to have some guts. He was someone I wanted to be associated with!

Johnny Cash was a funny guy. He liked to cut up and have fun. That's a part of him that a lot of people didn't know. As far as just getting upset or just worrying about anything, he didn't do that. He was a happy-go-lucky fellow. It seemed like he only worked on writing his songs.

We were on a tour one time, and Faron Young was on the same tour. Now, Faron was the type of guy that worried about everything and had to know all about everything. In fact, he fired Gordon Terry off of his show when Gordon was one of his band members because Gordon showed up with a shirt on that cost six dollars.

Faron told him he didn't need to wear a six-dollar shirt, he ought to have a two-dollar shirt. After the show, Faron rides to the hotel with us. In the car it's me, John, Marshall, and Faron with Luther, who is driving. We pull up in front of the hotel, and Luther says, "We're at the hotel. If anybody wants to eat, stay in the car; if they don't, get out."

There were no restaurants in the hotel, so John starts getting out of the car, and Faron says, "John, you mean to tell me this is the way ya'll do? And John says, "Yeah, what's wrong with that?"

Faron says, "You mean you let these boys have this freedom over you and have your car to go out doing what they want to do? They tell you to get out?" John says to Faron, "Yeah, I don't care what they do. We played the show and now I'm going to bed. They can go eat if they want to. If I wanted to go eat, I would. If you want to go eat, stay in the car; if not, just get out." Faron was caught off guard by John's answers and how John supported his band. Johnny Cash just didn't sweat things like that.

Later on, there was so much big stuff and so much happening by him being the big star that he was, I can't really pinpoint any one thing that is better than the other. The whole career with Johnny Cash felt like one big tour. He had a lot of ideas that was weird, like putting trumpets on his "Ring of Fire" record that Anita Carter had put out as a single a year or two before. Her real pretty singing voice on that song, and Johnny Cash had a vision of putting trumpets on his new version of that record and making it different. And trumpets is what made the record be a big hit.

John at Folsom Prison, January 13, 1968.

I'm pretty sure it was John's idea to record live prison concerts. I don't know if he was smart enough to realize the huge audience reaction he'd get, or if there would even be a reaction. The main thing I remember about it was how it wasn't anything anybody was scared to do. We never thought we were in any danger, because of all the guards. But the thing I remember them talking about was recording it. I remember saying, "Man, we record that stuff in that prison, it won't sell enough records to pay for the tape."

It turned out to be the thing that skyrocketed Johnny Cash to stardom. The audience sound and all on the prison albums is what made it so big. That proved how wrong I was right there. I began to realize I would just play the drums and not predict how to make records. If you'll listen to the song "San Quentin" from those prison concerts, the words to that song he did in front of that prison audience, and you watch the video now and see the reaction of the prison audience, he was saying exactly what they wanted to hear. Like, "San Quentin, I hate every inch of you," and "San Quentin, I hope you burn in hell." That's how smart he was at that time.

Now, the wardens and all the people who worked there didn't like it. It was almost to the point it could have caused a riot. When Johnny would sing about burning San Quentin, the prisoners were ready to burn it! But we never felt like we were in danger. Johnny Cash was in total control of that prison crowd.

We didn't have any monitor system, so we couldn't hear John singing. At that time, we didn't even know he was saying all that stuff. Like on "A Boy Named Sue," that song was cut and we never heard the words to it, only saw the audience reaction to it. When we were on stage playing those two songs, we really never heard the words. I remember how we got through "A Boy Named Sue," as it was a poem that Shel Silverstein wrote.

John decided he wanted to do it, so he fumbles through his briefcase on stage and comes out with this poem, unfolds the paper, and walks up to the microphone. Nobody in the band had ever heard it, and we didn't know it even existed. By now, Carl Perkins is playing guitar with us, and he's standing up close to John so he can hear his voice. John just starts reading "A Boy Named Sue."

Carl walks right up to John and just kicks off a lead rhythm thing. When he starts playing, we can hear his amplifier, so we start playing some. So, me, Marshall, and Luther are playing along to the rhythm. I don't know if we all ended together or what. If you listen, you can hear how raw it was musically. We couldn't follow John because we couldn't hear the lyrics he was saying. We could hear the crowd's reaction but didn't have a clue why they were reacting like that.

The first time I actually heard the lyrics of the song was after it was cut and we were in the studio playing it, trying to get some kind of mix to make it good enough to release, which we never did. It never was good. But, there again, it proves that I didn't know much about the music business. I said, "Man, that's awful." "A Boy Named Sue" was one of the biggest things John ever did and the one thing everybody made the least effort to do.

That's when I did begin to realize a person like Johnny Cash or Willie Nelson don't need anyone to tell them how to do things. They're going to do what they're going to do. That's what made that record so exciting. We didn't have any idea what was happening. It just happened. That's another thing that was so unique about John. Who else would have done that?

I don't ever remember having a rehearsal or anything when we'd get a call to go to a recording session. When we'd leave home, none of us had any idea what we were going to record. When we'd get to the studio, we never heard the song until the tape was rolling and we'd just cut it. We didn't know how to play anything real good or how to make a mistake! I guess I had to be a genius, when I look back on it, because John never told me how to play or what to play on drums.

I made a joke once. I said, "Man, it's really good to be working for a man who don't know anything about music either." He didn't know how to tell you what to do. There were some times I would have liked for someone to tell us what to do. Like when we were doing a session, I would like to have had somebody give me a cue or a stop or something. John couldn't really do that. It wasn't his thing. He knew what he wanted, but he left it up to the people in the group to figure out what to do and then let us do it.

Recording with Bob Dylan, we began to realize that Johnny Cash was a big star. No, nobody knew what was going to happen a few years later, how popular those Nashville Dylan sessions would become. It was just something we did and didn't think anything about it at the time. I look back at it now and think something had to be wrong with me. I was more concerned with getting home and making my boat go faster. I now realize how important it was.

It was an honor for somebody like me to be able to work and be around John and people like Dylan. As far as I was concerned, John was it. There was nobody else. I'd sit on that drum stool and from there, he was a giant of a man. No matter who else was around, he was it. In all the time we worked together, almost forty years, we never had a cross word or an argument. Not one, in all that time. What employee can say that about their boss of almost forty years?

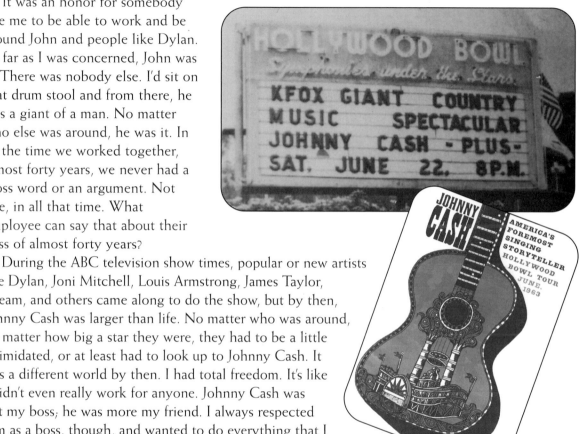

During the ABC television show times, popular or new artists like Dylan, Joni Mitchell, Louis Armstrong, James Taylor, Cream, and others came along to do the show, but by then, Johnny Cash was larger than life. No matter who was around, no matter how big a star they were, they had to be a little intimidated, or at least had to look up to Johnny Cash. It was a different world by then. I had total freedom. It's like I didn't even really work for anyone. Johnny Cash was not my boss; he was more my friend. I always respected him as a boss, though, and wanted to do everything that I could that he wanted done. Trouble was, most of the time John didn't know exactly what he wanted done.

Another thing that was unique about Johnny Cash is that he would hardly ever ask you to do something. For example, backstage before a show he never would say, "Go get me a cup of coffee," or "Go get me a hotdog." He never one time said that to me, not in the whole forty years I worked for him. I don't know why. I don't know if I looked too mean or something. He didn't boss anyone around like that. Now, later years, when he got, well . . . I can't say old, I don't think he ever got old, but I think he may have got a little cranky some. I know I have.

Besides playing the music and working for him, there was a time when me and Johnny Cash got really close. We'd talk about things that he wouldn't talk about to anybody else. Like after the show, I'd call him and congratulate him on doing a good show. He liked that. It got to be a joke between me and him. On stage before a show, he'd drag a chair over to me

and set down by me. He'd say, "We've got to talk for a minute, and I've got to get over here where Lou can't hear us or he will try to stop us." Just making a joke like that. We were pretty close buddies.

One of the greatest times of my life was in 1975, when we were in Las Vegas and John came to me and said, "Go tomorrow and buy a new Mercedes. I want to give Marshall a new Mercedes." I had such a big time. Man, I got me a cab and went all over Las Vegas to some of the highest-priced car dealers to buy a new Mercedes. I bought it and had it delivered to the hotel. You think that wasn't fun?

I didn't want it to happen when John finally fired Marshall Grant in 1980, after they had been together for years. I knew it was going to happen a little while before it happened. There were things going on that didn't make John happy. John was his own boss and was having a little trouble being his own boss, so he wanted to make some changes. In his mind, he visualized doing some music stuff that required some musicians that would play a little different than what we had been playing. You kinda realized around 1980 that that Tennessee Three sound was over with for Johnny Cash.

John wanted a little different sound, and for some reason I made it a point to be able to play a few different styles. Anyway, he wanted to make this change, and I tried to keep him from it. I remember saying, "You'll never find anybody to do what Marshall does." I made a joke: "He does a great job at everything except play the bass." Knowing Johnny Cash, I don't think if someone had come along that wanted to tell Johnny Cash what to do and what to wear, he would have lasted, because John wouldn't take orders.

I remember I thought that when Luther died in 1968, it was all over then. I thought, *There goes our sound. It can't be duplicated; we're out of business.* A few of us thought that. But by that time, Carl Perkins had joined us, and a few years before that, the Statler Brothers had joined us. Bob Wootton came along, and he did Luther's style good enough to not miss a beat. Then, in 1980, here comes Joe Allen playing bass for us and we keep going!

It just felt so weird not having Marshall around that I said, "You'll never find anyone to replace him." John replied, "Yep, yep, I already found some-one." I said, "Well, who is it?" He said, "He sits on the drum stool behind me every night." I said, "Oh, no. No, no. That's all I want to do, is sit on the drum stool every night behind you." John was persuasive, so I became John's road manager after that.

We got to having so much fun again, and every-thing seemed to be getting bigger. Instead of worry-ing about it going away and not having it, we were doing it. That band was unreal, and we were having a big time. We just said, "We're moving on," and it worked great.

Johnny got his first tour bus in 1980. The crew came on and the group got so big that I remember there were something like ninety-three pieces of per-sonal baggage that we checked in at airports to go on the airplane. We had the wardrobe lady, the makeup lady, the hairdresser. It got to be almost more than one man could handle.

W. S. Holland "on the road again."

I always made a joke out of it. I said John was smart enough to hire people he did not have to worry about. Just do your own thing and let them do theirs. And in a sense that's how it was. He didn't take time to be concerned with things that he didn't need to be concerned with.

I never will forget, we were hiring a truck driver, and John said, "I don't need to be concerned about it. You get one." I said, "Well, let me tell you how I'd go about hiring one. We'll get a driver and we'll let him drive." I said, "Let me get somebody and let me do it this way." He said, "Do it the way you want to. I don't want to be bothered with it."

If a driver couldn't be on time in four or five trips, then my deal was to get one that could. That saved everyone a lot of trouble. John Cash was that way. He didn't want to have the problem of having to tell someone how to do or what to do, he just wanted to get the people to do it. And it worked so good in our organization. It relieved the headaches for everybody.

Johnny Cash was several different people. He was one person on the stage, then when the show was over, the next day he was another person, and the next day he was another person. He was more than one or two different people. Everybody who's written a book or made a documentary about him, well, they just want to talk about the great Johnny Cash that was on stage. The great entertainer Johnny Cash.

I don't know if it's because they have too much respect, or what. I always said that if I was going to write a book, I want to put all the Johnny Cashes in it. I want to put the great ones in it and the not-so-greats, along with the super-entertainer Johnny Cash. I would list several different kinds of Johnny Cashes. It would take ten books just to list all the funny things he did.

I remember getting my Lincoln Mark V, I think in 1977, and before I even knew anything about getting one, I thought it was one of the prettiest cars I'd ever seen. I'd mentioned it a couple of times to John in the dressing room. I didn't think anything else about it. We finished a tour and drove into Nashville, and we were going to have a birthday party for me at John's Hendersonville house. When we got there, John said, "Look, yonder comes Joyce and your kids from Jackson." Now, this 1977 Bill Blass Edition Mark V Lincoln was coming up my driveway. I answered him, "That's not Joyce. That's not my car." John said, "Yeah, that's your car. That's them."

John had bought me that new Lincoln for my birthday present and had them to bring it up there. I still have it, and it still looks like it did the day it rolled up the drive. Now, the next year for my birthday he bought me a fine watch I still have, and it's worth a lot of money. The next year, he gave me a picture of Abe Lincoln in a wood frame, and the next year I got nothing. I don't know what happened! I went wrong somewhere there on getting the birthday gifts.

But, Johnny Cash didn't sweat the small stuff. He got people to do that for him. People say to me even now, "Man, old John sure had a rough life, didn't he?" I say, "Let me tell you something. Of all the people that I have known, I don't know of anyone who had an easier life than Johnny Cash." He never had to do anything that he didn't want to do.

Now, I don't mean that he didn't have things in his personal life that he didn't like or things that were tough on

Avid racer W. S. Holland and the Johnny Cash show boat.

him, like we all have. But as far as his working conditions and his traveling, nobody had it easier. He had somebody to carry his luggage, open the doors for him—he never even had to go up to a desk and check into a hotel. When he arrived, they had the key ready, and somebody would take him to his room. It's not necessarily that he had it so easy but that he was smart enough to hire people who knew how to do these jobs and he'd let them do them. So then, it could be said he had it easy.

I think it was in Czechoslovakia, where there were all these real pretty skins and furs on the wall at our restaurant. They were unusual-looking, and none of us could tell what they were. I called the waiter and finally made him understand what I was asking: "What are these skins on the wall?" He replied in broken English, "They were dogs!" They skinned dogs and put them on the wall. Countless laughs like that.

It's weird to look back on it now and realize that we just didn't know what we were really doing. The music, to me, all through these years, besides being a business, was a fun thing. It could not have been that way for me with anyone other than Johnny Cash. The only reason I've been able to deal with [his passing] is being able to still get out and play drums.

I always said, "I never could play very good, so I play as good as I ever could." If I hadn't been able to keep on playing my drums, I would have had a hard time with losing John.

I want to tell you, when it's sad is when we get out the videos and we look at all the old footage. It is a good feeling to have been with Johnny Cash all those years and set all the records that we set. We filled every building in the United States, Canada, and Europe. Because of fire codes now, the only way some of our records of standing-room-only concerts will be broken is when enough time passes and the old buildings are torn down and new ones are built. I won't be around to see that happen.

It's a great feeling, and it would never have happened to me if it hadn't been with somebody like Johnny Cash. I am so fortunate in this hard music industry to know and to have been a member of the Johnny Cash band. That was a big honor for something like that to happen to me. The band made a unique sound, and it fit what Johnny Cash did so much, and nobody else could do it. It had nothing to do with being that good. It's just that nobody else could do it. To be part of that sound the Tennessee Three made is just something that I have a hard time describing. It was something that was meant to be.

No one will top Johnny Cash's record that we will ever see. There's not enough time. From 1955 to 2003, when he died, think about what he did. Nobody will do that. It can't happen. Everybody else will get to a point when they think they are old, whether it's age fifty-five, sixty-five, or seventy, and they'll drop out. But he never dropped out. Just like the "Hurt" video, his last big record. That was something that was meant to happen. It was like John wrote that song himself and told the story of his life in it. He never let up. No one has done the things he did for that long a period of time.

There's two people that hardly a day ever passes that I don't think about or see. One of them died in 1945, and that was my dad. After all these years, hardly a day goes by that I don't visualize him. The other is John Cash. I guarantee you, there's hardly ever a night that I don't lay down and see something about Johnny Cash. There's probably a lot of people who didn't even know him well that are the same way. He was such a unique guy, that Johnny Cash.

DMITRI KASTERINE

Garrison, New York

Shoe Size 11 1/2

ℐN 1987, THE CAMERA manufacturer Hasselblad asked me to photograph a singer of my choice for their advertising campaign. I chose Johnny Cash. After a few telephone calls to Johnny's office at the House of Cash, I took a flight to Nashville, and my assistant Caroline and I drove out to Hendersonville, a comfortable suburb north of Nashville.

We set up a seamless background in one of the offices and waited for our subject, or "sitter," who would soon be heading for Jamaica for the holidays. The first thing that struck me, because I had never seen Johnny Cash in the flesh, was how tall he was. With a very slight stoop, he towered over you, and then you heard the voice, exactly how you remembered it. It wrapped around you.

He sat down where I asked him to, and straightaway my troubles started. Of course, this is the moment when all photographers' troubles start; it is a leap into the unknown: those first few minutes when you are watching for something the sitter does, or something you can ask him to do that is not out of character, but you don't know what that is because you don't really know the person you're photographing.

I soothe, reassure and steer, praise, murmur and ask for a move here and a move there, hoping for a spontaneous pose. But none of this put Mr. Cash at ease or allowed him to forget the camera's presence. All my efforts were useless; I was making him more and more nervous. He just sat there with an expression of boredom and discomfort, and he blinked. He blinked and he blinked. Occasionally I knew that I had caught him between blinks, but these pictures just would not do. I turned to Caroline, my assistant, and whispered, "Talk to him."

"Mr. Cash," said Caroline, "tell us about that beautiful ring you have on your finger." He looked down at it and was immediately and totally absorbed in the ring, its history, and its meaning. Caroline, standing behind me but keeping her eyes on Mr. Cash, continued the conversation that she had begun. He had been given the ring by his Bible class.

This led to more talk of God, how he was going to shoot pictures on the beach with his new camera that Hasselblad had given him, and how much he was looking forward to a pedicure at the hotel. His face now wore an expression of nature and his own act. Caroline had brought this about with conversation, and not long after our trip to Nashville, Caroline and I got married.

I am very proud that one of my photographs of Johnny Cash, taken on that December day that started so shakily and ended so happily was chosen for use on the cover of this *I Still Miss Someone* Johnny Cash tribute book.

I mentioned to my photography students at Vassar College (in Poughkeepsie, New York, a small city on the Hudson River, seventy-five miles north of New York City) that I was writing this, and they cried, "You photographed Johnny Cash? Oh! my God, we love him!" And Caroline and I and our twelve-year-old son, Nicholas, loved him, too.

122287-2

Cash to open Hall of Fame exhibit

This year's tourism season in Nashville will be highlighted by a Country Music Hall of Fame exhibit devoted to the life and career of the legendary Johnny Cash.

The facility, which bills itself as the most visited of all halls of fame," announced yesterday that it will open a $70,000, 2,000 square-foot salute to Cash March 23. "The Johnny Cash Exhibit" will be the first and most elaborate biographical salute in the museum's history.

...collection provides unprecedented documentation of music's most distinguished said Hall of Fame director in making the announcement. "It is extraordinarily Cash's unusual level of ...mation and interest, and the ...ty of his extensive performances."

...indicated that many of the ...facts and memorabilia planned ...lusion in the multimedia exhibit have never been publicly displayed before. Cash personally ...the majority of the items included.

...suggestion, the entire ...being mounted and displayed in black, white and silver

...will be in seven ...first will be devoted ...s" as a boy in Ar...kabilly" section ...way to Memphis ...ng career. The ...sizes his emer...an troubadour. ...s called "Bal...

...an will de...that sur...k in the ...reen," in ...his ...ances. ...eer to ...vi...

Superstar Johnny Cash poses with a few of the items he's selected for the Country Music Hall of Fame exhibit in his honor. The $70,000 display will be the museum's largest-ever biographical salute and will open at the end of this month.

John Guider ● Country Music Foundation

...sored by the Holiday Inn Worldwide Hotel System.

The museum is operated as a division of the non-profit educational institution the Country Music Foundation (CMF). It has an average annual attendance of 400,000 and has been visited by more than ...en million since its opening in

Sources of Country Music.
It operates two historic sites in Nashville, RCA's Studio B and Hatch Show Print.

The CMF's Li... Cent... um, h... cordin... films,... period... tion au... The C... ...ity cen...

With a staff of 32 the Country Music Foundation is the non-...

Holiday Inn presents

The Johnny Cash Exhibit

Holiday Inn presents

The Johnny Cash Exhibit

New for 1988
At The Country Music Hall of Fame and Museum

Opened in 1988, the Johnny Cash exhibit at the former site of the Country Music Hall of Fame and Museum was a mecca for Cash fans for several years.

Jonas

Johnny Cash

To Jonas,
Good Luck and best Wishes
Johnny Cash

JOHNNY CASH

Hendersonville, TN.
Jan 11 1991

Thanks Jonas,
For the picture you drew
of me. I'm happy to autograph
it for you.
I'm glad you liked my exhibit
at the Hall of Fame.

Sincerely
Johnny Cash

PAT KATZ

St. Croix Falls, Wisconsin

Shoe Size 6 WIDE

I RECALL HEARING JOHNNY Cash when his first record of "Cry, Cry, Cry" and "Hey Porter" was released and thinking, "Hey, this guy is really good!" It was a rare treat at that time to find country music played in our area.

I had a few favorite artists, but Johnny Cash was instantly placed at the top of my favorites. Then came "Ring of Fire," and I was more than "solidly hooked."

I started going to all the Johnny Cash shows that I could, and my desire to meet the man was overwhelming. I became the Minnesota representative of the Johnny and June Cash International Fan Club and figured only certain people would get access to John and June.

Through a letter written by a friend, my wish came true. On Feb. 17, 1997, Lou Robin escorted my father, my son, and me backstage in Madison, Wisconsin. I was ecstatic as I watched a tall, slender man all dressed in black emerge from a dressing room down the hall and walk toward me.

97

My mind went wild! Half was saying, *Here he comes! I am actually going to meet Johnny Cash!* The other half was saying, *Don't be silly. That's not actually Johnny Cash.* All questions and doubts vanished quickly as John came over and shook hands with us. He was joking and chatting with us and made me feel as if I'd known him for years. After photos and autographs, the three of us left backstage, and I can recall Lou warning me, "Don't trip on the cables." I answered, "Right now, Mr. Robin, I am so far above the earth I couldn't trip if I tried."

From then on, I felt privileged to be allowed backstage visits with John and June at most shows, and they were always friendly and happy to see me. Our friendship and my love and respect grew with each visit and concert.

Several friends met in Green Bay, Wisconsin, and went to De Pere, Wisconsin, for an outdoor concert. We were sitting on the ground in front of the stage when, about halfway through the show, it began to rain. Soon it was pouring and we were drenched. John was laughing at us (he was nice and dry, of course) and commented to the audience, "I've never had to cancel a show because of rain, but I have drowned a few fans!"

His sense of humor was what made each show unique. At another outdoor concert, we were sitting on the ground in front of the stage. John was in rare form that night and was joking with us from the stage. He'd make a comment to the audience, and then look at us for confirmation or denial. At one point, he stuck out his tongue at us.

He told the audience, "That's my fan club down there." He paused. "All seven of them!" Then, as if an afterthought, he said, "International." The audience went wild!

Six of us fans flew to Las Vegas, rented a van, and drove to Sun City, Nevada, for a show before continuing on to Laughlin, Nevada, for four more shows. I would just as soon forget the trip, as our driver was going ninety miles an hour over steep mountains so we wouldn't be late for the show. Despite pleas and threats from us passengers, our driver continued at that speed, but we did indeed arrive just in time for the show. I had been asked to find Lou Robin and let him know that we had arrived.

As soon as I went backstage to look for him, I ran into John. He said he was sure glad to see us, and added, "Now I can relax." Apparently, Lou had told him our plans, and John was concerned for our safety. John was about to . . . "turn me over his knee" when I said how fast we drove, until I assured him I was not the driver.

Pat and John backstage.

The next night in Laughlin, we were all supposed to go backstage for a brief visit. As we were anxiously waiting, Lou came to us with a message from John. Lou said John would rather we didn't go backstage that night. Our faces fell as we said, "That's okay." Then, with a twinkle in his eyes, Lou completed the message by saying, "John thought that maybe you'd rather have breakfast with him tomorrow morning, instead." Would we? I recall telling Lou, "It's a tough job, but somebody has to do it, so it might as well be us."

Both John and June came to breakfast and greeted each fan club member personally, making everyone feel extra special. When he informed us that he had stopped smoking, everyone applauded. John and June took time for breakfast with fan club members several times over the years and always made each member feel special.

A very special personal event for me took place in Minneapolis, Minnesota. My husband, the assistant police chief of our small town, had recently passed away. Sorting through his closet, I came across his police gun. After checking on legalities with our police chief, I wrote to John and asked him if he would like to have the gun as part of his private collection. I was given permission to present the gun to John in Minneapolis. John was thrilled when I gave him the gun and a gunbelt backstage that evening.

I can't talk about John without including June, as she was also special to me. Because of dense fog and limited visibility, June told me to follow the bus from Minneapolis to Ames, Iowa. So, keeping the taillights in sight, we started out. Later the bus driver told me that June had made him slow down and keep me in sight. He also missed the exit for the motel and had to go to the next overpass and turn back. We followed, and at the motel June gave me a big hug and said, "We made it! Ya'll hung right in there, even when we missed the turn."

I recall a fan club membership contest where the fifteen people who signed up the most new members were invited to a party at the Cash home. John and June greeted every person and spent quality time with them. After a banquet fit for a king, June and John and the Carter family treated us to in impromptu concert. We were then given a tour of their home.

During Fan Fair week in Nashville, I would spend a majority of my time helping out in our fan club booth. John made an unexpected visit to the booth, and his fan club members had no more than a ten-minute notice to secure the booth for John to sign autographs. All the fan club members linked hands to form a human chain keeping the huge crowd back enough to allow room.

John was escorted to the booth by a security guard escort, but when he saw his fan club members, he left them and quickly came to greet us. Then he continued on into the booth, where he shook hands, had photos taken, and gave autographs to those lucky enough to catch him there.

Alma Todd, Jeanne Witherell, and I each held our breath and prayed that the table in front of the booth wouldn't give way as John leaned way over it to pick up a baby, approximately one and a half years old. The baby had cerebral palsy and appeared to be blind. But when John held her and she heard his voice, she smiled one of the biggest, prettiest smiles I have ever seen and nuzzled her face into his neck. Her mother had tears of joy when John handed her the baby. She commented later that she couldn't believe that someone as big a star as Johnny Cash would take special time to hold her baby.

I have been with the Cashes when both were exhausted from a lengthy tour, yet they would stop to greet fans, give autographs, and have photos taken. With them, the fans always seemed to come first. And, I have over the years heard numerous comments such as, "I can't believe how nice they are," "I didn't realize what a great Christian he is; it shows, " and "I hadn't heard him before, but when's the next show, because I'm going!"

John and Pat at the head of the table during a breakfast for fan club members.

About four years prior to their deaths, I had driven by myself to Hendersonville on the slim chance that I could see John and June to say hi. When June heard I was in town, a friend who worked for them called to tell me to stop by the Cash house. I had the opportunity to chat with them both and was about to leave when June stopped me with, "We are about to have lunch." I didn't want to be in the way, so I tried again to tell her I was leaving, saying, "I don't want to be a bother." But in no time I was sitting down to lunch with John and June. It was well worth my 1,800-mile round-trip.

I have attended over 500 Johnny Cash concerts, and each one was special. I have never gotten tired of what June called "those same old songs." I have been to concerts coast to coast and even a few in Canada. John was never surprised to see me. As he once told me, "I expect you to show up most anywhere." Never have I seen or heard John be rude or short with any fan, and he treated everyone he met with love and respect.

Johnny and June Cash were the most gracious Christian people I have ever met, and I am very proud to be able to say Johnny and June Cash were personal friends of mine. I miss them so much, and I am looking forward to my next Johnny Cash show in Heaven.

MERLE KILGORE

Paris, Tennessee

Shoe Size 13 D

*T*HE INTERNATIONAL ENTERTAINMENT BUYERS Association honored Johnny Cash in 2002 with their prestigious Pioneer Award. After being approached by his booking agent, Bonnie Sugarman, with a list of possible presenters for this award, Johnny requested that I do the honors. Following is the speech I gave at the Sheraton Hotel in Nashville during the annual IEBA awards banquet on October 10, 2002:

Good evening, ladies and gentlemen. It is my honor to share with you some glances from the past and some of my golden memories of the man we honor tonight—Johnny Cash.

Johnny Cash once said to me that as a young boy growing up in the farming community of Dyess, Arkansas, his family owned a battery-operated radio and that it was one of the most cherished items they had in the house. He said that for a few minutes in the mornings before they would go to the fields or to school, they would listen to the live country music broadcasts on the radio station out of Memphis, Tennessee. And every day at noon, his mama would listen to the *Gospel Quartet Hour*.

Those songs he heard stayed in his heart, setting the pattern for the many hits he would write—hits that the whole world would someday know and love.

Johnny Cash and I first met around 1956 at the Louisiana Hayride show in Shreveport. And then, later, at my neighbor's house in Bossier City, Louisiana—that neighbor was the great Johnny Horton.

Johnny Cash asked to be invited over, not for any showbiz talk, but to hear about Johnny Horton's experiences as a professional fisherman (the rod and reel type, of course).

As soon as he came in and we all shook hands, he said, "Mr. Horton I am sure proud to be here." Then John said, "I understand you're called the 'Singing Fisherman.'" And Johnny Horton laughed and said, "Yeah, that's right."

John said, "Is it true that you can cast a lump of sugar twenty yards into a coffee cup?"

Johnny got up, got his rod and reel, and we all went outside. He threw that lump of sugar into that coffee cup, and Johnny Cash and I slapped our leg. . . and couldn't believe it.

Then, the three of us went on the first of many fishing trips together. Johnny Cash kept coming back, and the two Johnnys formed such a close friendship. On one of those fishing trips we took, they asked me to stay on the bank—they were afraid they were going to lose an ear or an eye with the "angle of the dangle" of my casting.

It was so great to see those two together. They were always laughing. They even became business partners by forming the Natchitoches Red River Bait Company. Johnny Horton had designed an artificial lure he named the Old Fireball.

Johnny Cash told everyone, "Anyone can catch a fish with the Old Fireball."

They went on the market with this beautiful lure, but they had a problem. After the first sales, people wanted their money back. It *would not* catch a fish.

Horton said, "I think when we transformed it from wood to plastic, it lost that magic action."

A worse tragedy happened, and they never came out with a second Old Fireball.

Johnny Horton was killed in a head-on automobile collision November 5, 1960.

At the funeral, I remember Johnny Cash reading one of the most beautiful things a man could say about a close friend. And he wept—as we all did.

But Johnny and I kept in contact with each other, and when he heard I had moved to Nashville in 1962, he said, "Kilgore, I want you to do some road shows with me. I want you to let me polish you up for the big time."

And I said, "Oh, the big time!"

It was on one of these shows that I met June Carter. And like Johnny always said, "Meeting June Carter *was* the big time!" And I certainly agree.

In 1968, I was honored to be the best man at their wedding. I was so nervous.

I had on one of those sharkskin tuxedos (that was the big thing at that time), and I stuck the ring in the ring box in my pocket. Johnny said, "When I nudge you, give me the ring."

It would not come out, and Johnny liked to have beaten my arm off nudging me. . . ump, ump, ump! I had to rip my pants to get it out. Then I forgot to pay the preacher . . . but I went back later to pay him—I think.

You know, one of the great things that June and I did was to write songs together. We were performing on the shows with Johnny, and she said, "Kilgore, let's get together and write some songs when we're not on the road." And we did.

Her sister Anita recorded one of our songs, the "Ring of Fire." She sang it so beautifully, like an angel. But it didn't sell.

One morning at breakfast, Johnny said, "You know, I had a dream last night. I dreamt that I heard the "Ring of Fire" and it had Mexican trumpets in it."

I said, "Mexican trumpets?" And he said, "Uh-huh."

I said, "Man, you know I always liked Mexico and Mexican food. Record it, do it, do it!" June smiled at me and winked. They had already set up the session for it.

Well, I want to tell you ladies and gentlemen that was one of the greatest thrills of my life. That was back in 1963. First, it made the Top 10, and then it popped to No. 1 on the country music charts for ten weeks!

The "Ring of Fire," the original recording by Johnny, is still played on radio, television, and movies. And it's featured on all kinds of commercials, from Microsoft to soft drinks—and now Applebee's! . . . one of my favorite restaurants.

You know what? The "Ring of Fire" is still burning brightly, and Johnny Cash is still burning brightly. He's done it all. He's been honored by all.

From his induction into the Country Music Hall of Fame, the Rock and Roll Hall of Fame, and receiving the Kennedy Center's Award for Lifetime Achievement that includes 130 hits on the *Billboard* Country Singles Chart. His records have sold over 50 million copies and have won eleven Grammys.

Although Johnny Cash is country, he has tallied more hits than Michael Jackson, Barbara Streisand, and Elton John, just to name a few.

Ladies and gentlemen, as Eddy Arnold said in song, "There never was a hoss like the Tennessee Stud," and I say to you tonight, there never was a man like Johnny Cash.

Ladies and gentlemen, the International Entertainment Buyers Association salutes and bestows the prestigious Pioneer Award to John R. Cash.

At the end of my speech, Johnny made his way to the stage, shook my hand and said, "Thank you, my dear friend." He then turned to the crowd, stepped up to the podium, and said, "HELLO, I'M JOHNNY CASH."

PENNI LANE

Nashville, Tennessee

Shoe Size 10 MEDIUM

*E*VERY TIME I HEAR "A Boy Named Sue" my mind moves back in time to the night that Johnny Cash recorded that song at San Quentin Prison, and where I was at that time. I was flying on a Japan Air Lines flight 30,000 feet in the air above the ocean on my way from Tokyo to San Francisco. I was missing the Johnny Cash concert at San Quentin Prison. I had just spent two months in the Far East with Grand Ole Opry star Jeannie Seely and was asleep in a luxury hotel in Tokyo when I received a call from the United States. Johnny Cash was wanting me to join his show in California and stay out on tour with the Cash show during the filming of *Johnny Cash—The Man, His World, His Music.*

Jeannie Seely had just finished her Far Eastern tour of Japan, Taiwan, and Thailand. It's funny, because we were days right behind the Johnny Cash Show at many of these concert venues, but we didn't catch up with one another. Anyway, we were on a layover in Tokyo, ready to come home, when I got that unexpected call from the Cash show, asking could I join them. Wow! You bet I could, and would! Yeah, right away.

Unfortunately, there was no flight out of Tokyo to California until the following day, so I missed that historic San Quentin Prison concert and the

live album recording. It wasn't
so important to me at the time,
my missing the prison show,
till later, when "A Boy Named
Sue" became such a national
hit. I would be constantly
reminded that I had missed the
actual moments of that hit
recording at the prison every
time I would hear John sing it
on stage.

I think that call to join the
Johnny Cash Show was the
beginning of the best of the
rest of the coming years for
me. Certainly, it was starting a
new career experience in my life that this Kentucky girl had never
dreamed of, and a fifteen-year journey with Johnny Cash.

The previous summer I had been out on tour with the Carter Family,
who were part of John's road show. We were doing the last show at the
Friday night Opry at the Ryman Auditorium, and I had done the Carter
family's hair. Anita Carter asked, "You ever been to Texas, Penni?" I
answered no, and she asked, "Well, you want to go to Texas with us and do
our hair?" I said yeah, as I didn't have anything else to do for a while, since
the Ryman shows had stopped for the season.

Actually, I jumped at the invitation. Mother Maybelle Carter had bought
a new white Cadillac, and Helen, Anita, and I left Nashville headed west
as fast as I could drive! Mother Maybelle traveled with John and June, so it
was just Helen, Anita, and I in that long white Cadillac. What fun!!

That's how I got connected with the Johnny Cash group and went out
on the road with them. After we got back from Texas, the Carter sisters
took me on to different places with them for several months.

That's how John knew that he wanted to call me and ask would I work
for him. I'd never even seen a Johnny Cash concert at the time, but I knew

he was a stallion on stage. He had a bit of mystery about his presence. He was quite awesome! I had heard stories about him, but I wasn't afraid of him and talked to him a little while myself. Along the way, he began to compliment me on the girls' hairdos and how good I had them looking.

And I recall the first time I touched his hair. We were in San Antonio, and just he and I were in the dressing room. The Carter Family was already

on stage, and he was getting ready. He had brushed his hair and couldn't get it to stand up the way he wanted. In other words, he was having a bad hair day! Now, I watched from across the room for a few moments and finally asked, "You want me to give you a hand with your hair?" Johnny replied, "Yes, if you think you can do better!"

Well, I could and I did! I teased it up on top and hit it with my Spray Net hair spray. That impressed him so much that he said to me, "Hell, I'll just hire you for my very own." That was the beginning of a lifelong friendship that has taken me on a journey that will last into eternity.

Now back to my California gig. First there was a wild ride in a helicopter going under the Golden Gate Bridge on our way to Santa Barbara after our flight from Japan had landed in San Francisco. Thus began the most exciting journeys of my life as hairdresser for *The Johnny Cash Show*.

For one thing, I didn't really know or understand the magnitude of the man Johnny Cash. It was a few years later that it began to register with me, the importance of the Man In Black. During my first days with him, he told me about the summer ABC-TV show he was going to be taping when we got back home, and he asked me if I would work for him exclusively. We worked out the details, and I was thrilled, to say the least! John was fun to work with during that time.

As serious as he was, and as concerned as he was about his TV show, he could still find time to cut up some. He found it funny to have me chase him around the stage to check his hair in front of the audience, just before and during the taping times. We made a joke of me chasing him around to fix his hair, and he'd laugh that hearty laugh he had and fling his arms while running to get away. Chasing him around the stage before the taping began was our little act that warmed the audience up every week. I can still see those long legs loping across the stage of the Ryman, John looking over his shoulder to see if I was about to catch him with my comb and can of hair spray. The audience ate it up.

Lord, he loved that hair spray stuff! I'd splash his hair with spray just enough and have it looking great. But as I'd be leaving the dressing room, I'd hear that can of hair spray just a-hissing. He had to have more of that spray.

I mentioned the helicopter ride as my first experience, and there were so many more. The prison concerts in California at Folsom and others in Arkansas, Kansas, and Tennessee. We were hours behind the earthquakes in Los Angeles in the early '70s . We were out in California when Charles Manson and his group murdered actress Sharon Tate and others. We were at Knott's Berry Farm for a television taping, with fires from the Watts riots burning all around us so close that we had to stop cameras because of the smoke.

Johnny Cash's image and stature were huge and awesome to most, but I knew him to be a "booger bear." That's what I called him. I treasure the memories of his bearhugs. I was his hairdresser even off the road for all of Johnny's album covers and his CBS specials and CMA show appearances. While we were taping the ABC-TV show in Nashville, John had an assortment of musical styles and artists performing from all genres.

I remember the week we had Linda Ronstadt as a musical guest, and she came out on stage during rehearsal with a short minidress barely covering her bottom. And she was wearing no underwear! Backstage, June Carter was beside herself. She said, "She's out there with my Johnny without any bloomers on. Somebody go get her some bloomers. She can't act like that on this show!"

Linda, when told that she had to put on underwear, retorted, "But I sing better bare-assed." "Not with my Johnny, she don't!" came back June. Linda did wear underwear that night. We all laughed about that. Johnny said he didn't even know she was showing her tootie. We all found it hard to believe that he didn't peek!

I recall some scary threats we had while out on the road with Johnny Cash. Calling in bomb threats was a horrible fad at the time; however, you took each one very serious. When the threats started, we had security guards travel with us on the tour. We kept guards posted in the hotel hallways, above the hotel on the roof, and outside our dressing rooms. One time there was a bomb threat at the fairgrounds, and when we arrived, our bus was sent to the far end of the field while the stage and grandstands were searched.

When we were finally cleared and the show began, I went onstage and declared, "If anything is going to happen to them, then I am going to go with them." It got a bit spooky at times. I knew John was pretty shook about the threats when they occurred, though he tried to always play it cool. On one Midwest trip, a small bomb actually went off in a hotel where we had stayed. It actually exploded just a few minutes after we all had checked out and were on our way to the airport. That period of threats was a tense and scary time for us all.

But life was a hoot out there with Johnny Cash most of the time. He was the most popular celebrity in America during his superstar days. I remember when we went to the White House as guests of President Nixon. Johnny laughed while I did his hair, saying, "Can you imagine me—*me!*—telling the president I ain't singing Merle Haggard's songs." I remembered how hard we laughed.

Like all those that knew him as a friend, I have so many memories of my friend Johnny Cash. Johnny was a giver. He knew that I collected telephone insulators, and he gave me an old wooden insulator from Death

Valley. He got it out West somewhere and brought that little 100-year-old insulator back to me.

I owe him so much for joys I would never have known had I not been a part of his organization for those years. I traveled to places I had only read about, tasted food I would have never tasted, such as escargots and kangaroo while we were in Australia. Yes, I did eat kangaroo soup.

I used to cry as he started aging because I knew how vain he was, and not in an egotistical way. He cared about his appearance and everything. In his heyday, the press was everywhere all the time, and he always looked good, knowing that his picture might be snapped any time. I knew how particular he was about how he looked as he aged, with his hair thinning.

Chet Atkins presents Johnny and June with a CMA Award.

My heart just cried. Actually, my whole being cried, because I was watching the man that I had chased around the stage with a can of hair spray. He became so fragile, and I had known him as so strong a man (hence, the statement where I called him a stallion on stage).

When I see that "Hurt" video, with its montage of old film and photos during his career, I say to myself, *I did his hair there, I did his hair here, I did his hair there.* When he died and the media had all of his many different pictures in the newspaper, I took some of the articles and pictures and wrote to my family members. I wrote telling them I did Johnny's hair here in this picture and that picture. I want them to always be able to say, "Aunt Penni was Johnny Cash's hairdresser."

He is a piece of American musical history, and I was making history with this giant of a man. I do have beautiful memories of him and fondness of him. I have to say that, indeed, Johnny Cash was soup for my soul.

KODAK TX 6043
TX▷1
TX▷2
TX▷3
TX▷4
TX▷5
TX▷6
TX▷7
TX▷8
TX▷9
TX▷10
TX▷11
TX▷12
TX▷13
TX▷14
TX▷15
TX▷16
TX▷17
TX▷18

CHANCE MARTIN

Nashville, Tennessee
Shoe Size 12

*H*ELLO, I'M CHANCE MARTIN. I was raised in Nashville and graduated in 1966 from high school. After radio broadcasting school, I went to Atlanta and got my then-required FCC Third Class Broadcaster's License. When I got back to Nashville, I taught at a new broadcasting school run by local radio air personalities from Nashville. I also took some classes at the University of Tennessee and was hanging out with some dee-jay friends from the Nashville Top 40 AM radio station WMAK.

If someone didn't know Johnny Cash, I'd have to say you're going to have to close your eyes and imagine something as big as the universe. Something that you relate to. Something that you look up to. Something that you start to love and draw near to. Then you start hearing the music. Then, if you see the man and hear the music at the same time, you realize that Johnny Cash is and was one of the greatest performers that ever lived. He started everything. He was the master of mayhem, and all the rock stars copied him. That's one thing about him, he's not a copy. The Man In Black was the real deal. How many real deals do you really know?

113

He could walk into a room with a thousand people and he'd be the only one in the room. So, that was some kind of magic. Now, this was when the word *superstar* was invented, during this time when Johnny Cash was on TV and on the radio and selling a bunch of records and selling out concerts. Popular entertainers were called stars, but the word *superstar* was kinda born and first used in the media to describe him. Did you know that?

Chance Martin, in a "Johnny Cash black" jumpsuit, watches a *Johnny Cash Show* rehearsal from the stage of the Ryman Auditorium in 1969.

One afternoon in 1969, while I was at WMAK, my mother called and said that my dad was at the Nashville Ramada Inn downtown on James Robertson Parkway and had found a job for me and that I needed to come in and audition for it. I asked my mother what it was about. She said it was working on a summer replacement television show for ABC network. By this time, I was twenty-three years old and looking for a job.

Momma said it was to be hosted by Johnny Cash. I said, "Who is that?" She said, "He's a singer who sang the song 'Johnny Yuma' on that Nick Adams western program on TV that I like called *The Rebel.* I was on my way to the audition right then! The TV show's producer and director were in a room that had been converted into an office in the hotel. They had several people who tried out for the job of cue card handler and still hadn't found the right person, thank God.

Apparently, they liked what I did and said, so I started that very day. They gave me a room to print in, and the cards, and they gave me a room to sleep in after I worked all night. The next day, they called a staff meeting, and lo and behold, Johnny Cash himself came strolling in—and my life has never been the same. When he picked my mama and daddy up and took me to a church on Music Row, I got baptized. Then he said, "It's going to really get tough now, Chance." I didn't know what he meant, I really didn't. But I do now.

Taped at the Ryman Auditorium, the "Mother Church of Country Music," this variety show called *The Johnny Cash Show* kicked off thirteen one-hour shows. The people and ratings loved it so much that it was picked up by ABC and went two more seasons. The cue card person always had to be there, next to John and all the other performers that were guests on his show. So I became dependent on him and him on me, because it was a very personal relationship we developed. He was hollering for cue cards, always ready to go over something.

So anyway, me and John got to become good friends. There was one time, by accident, during the live tapings that I had this cue card upside down. All of the songs performed on the show had cue cards with the lyrics. It was like real critical, and John didn't know these particular lyrics and I didn't have time to flip it over 'cause there were a lot of cards. John proceeded to read it upside down—which would have been upside down and backwards—without any hesitation. Afterwards, I went up to him and told him that was an accident.

He said, "Well, that's good, Chance. I noticed that everybody was panicking when the card was upside down; you know, the producers." They were all standing around and getting ready to nail me to the wall. John decided after that one time that every now and then we would get the producers and the staff all bent out of shape. He would come and tell me, "Flip a couple over tonight." Because he could read them upside down or backwards, he didn't care. I'd ask, "Well, John, do you know this song?" He'd say, "No, but flip one over—your choice." I thought, "Boy, this is nerve, but I'm not going to get fired, 'cause Johnny Cash told me to do it."

I remember one time I got fired and I went and told John what they did. I think I got fired a couple of times, but this once John said, "Chance, you go back and tell them you want a raise and a retraction in the newspaper." I thought at my age of twenty-three, this was cool. Johnny Cash was like a daddy to me and meanwhile like an icon person. He was in his early forties by this time and was like a friend, who later became a mentor of spiritual words.

We were in rehearsal in the Ryman Auditorium and Linda Ronstadt was one of the special guests on *The Johnny Cash Show*. I'm in there and I'm running down the cards. So, they're in the den set; you know, the home area. I'm down on my knees. We're doing a real close thing, and there's another set of cards, and John, my buddy, is holding Linda's. She was quite an attractive young lady, and she had a real pretty sundress on. And she didn't have on any undergarments. I thought, *I'm the only one seeing this?* Anyhow, my cards started to shake, they were trembling. I thought, *I feel guilty. What have I done?*

You can hear the cameramen sometimes when they're talking low and also hear their headsets if the director is screaming. And he was. He was going, "Go to camera three. Over at two. Zoom in!" And then, "Oh, no! Oh, my God! This is just what I thought!" He said, "Let's break for lunch—and get wardrobe in here!" So, nobody really suspected nothing, but all of a sudden they all come out from wardrobe. Linda said, "I don't have any panties." The wardrobe guy was sent to get some.

So, after lunch everyone has come back onstage, and they're all milling around, getting in their positions. In the meantime, Linda is walking around the Ryman in the stage wings and in the dressing room, pulling her little sundress up and showing her new panties to everybody. It's like she never ever had a pair! That was the real hoot of the day.

Anyway, John and I developed a close friendship at this point. I heard that John hired me because I could make him laugh. I thought that's really good. I didn't want to be famous for lighting or photography, but to make somebody feel good. John was the kind of person that had a lot of gesticulation—movements with his body and hands. He had a ton of them in the beginning, in 1969, and he never lost all of them. He had some really cool ones that only John could do.

Backstage behind his back, I started copying John's mannerisms, even the special cough and where you lift your leg up before speaking. I wasn't doing his voice at this time. I'd get up close to my friends and do a little John impersonation. They were all laughing and loving it. I was really nervous about it because I thought that if he found out, I could lose my job. I thought, *I've never impersonated anybody and I'm not sure I am now. I just like doing John impersonations.* Even if it was picking at my nose or playing with invisible spiderwebs on my face like John did, there was something about it that I liked.

So, we went to a wrap party after the first season of the TV show, out at John's house, with all kinds of entertainers and stars, plus the crew and the ABC Hollywood people. After you eat, you pay for your dinner by

A rare photo of the entire *Johnny Cash Show* cast and crew.

singing a song you wrote or a story you've heard. You have to do some-thing as you sit in the high-back seat. At the end of it, I thought I had gotten out of having to do anything at this "guitar pull." Then one of the stagehands in the back hollered, "We want to see Chance Martin do Johnny Cash."

John said, "I do, too." I thought, *Uh-oh, John has heard about it.* Oh, man, I needed Preparation H. What was I going to do? So I got up and got his sister Reba, who was like an assistant on the stage, and she brought a mag-azine that I pretended was a script. I read it and flipped through it like Johnny did. I did the shirt-collar pull and the cough and got it going, look-ing for the invisible spiderwebs on my face. They all loved it and John laughed. I thought, *Oh, man, that's butterflies.*

I went to radio school, so voice was something I appreciated. Naturally, I just started picking up words John would say. Over the years, the voice impersonations I did just got better, according to everybody that heard them. Me and John would get together and do dueling Cashes. One time in Jack Clement's studio, the "Cowboy Arms Hotel & Recording Spa," John was in the kitchen and he turned to me and said, "Chance, why don't you go ahead and take my band out on the road and do the

Johnny Cash Show? Now remember, I'm the Man In Black, but you can be the Legend in Black."

So I came back with, "Well, you know I'm going to need your Amoco credit card and your bus. Of course, you know I'm going to be playing in Holiday Inn lounges, not huge concert halls." John got a kick out of that.

By 1971, John's fifty-eight shows had changed television and country music history as we know it. The night of the taping of the last show, Johnny Cash presented me with his Martin guitar that he played during the second and third seasons of the television shows, as a token of appreciation. I was beside myself with excitement and failed to realize that, due to the show being over, I was suddenly unemployed. I went to John's studio, the House of Cash, and was hired to listen to tapes from J. R.'s publishing company.

I had been living in the House of Cash in those early stages when they still had some cots and single beds in there. Cash was getting ready to go to Spain to do a motion picture with Kirk Douglas called *A Gunfight*. John asked me to live in his Hendersonville home on the lake, as the man of the house, while he was in Spain. I was to watch over the family—John's four daughters and June Carter's two daughters. The girls were all young.

I'm laying in John's master bedroom with an eight-foot round bed and

I get a call from the intercom from the girls saying, "Chance, there's somebody on the roof peeking in our window." Well, yes there were a couple of people on John's roof. So, I went down, and it's daytime too, and there's this sword in the lower level of the house sticking in this beam. A sword stuck in a ceiling beam was typical at John's house. Anyway, I worked the sword out of the beam and put it behind my back and went and asked these people, "What are ya'll doing?" They said, "We're looking for Johnny Cash." They were die-hard Johnny Cash fans, and I emphasize that the word *fan* comes from *fanatic*. But they're up on his roof, so I said, "Well, he's in Spain and you're on his roof. You need to come down right now. The girls have called, and you've got them all tore up by looking in the window. So, come on down."

The man started walking down, and his wife was still up there taking pictures. So I said, "Ma'am, you're going to have to come down right now." The husband said, "Don't you talk to my wife that way!" So, they're both off the roof now, but he's still giving me a lot of problems. I promised him John wasn't there. I told him they could take pictures standing here right now, but they'd have to get on the other side of the fence. He kept getting pushy about that wife thing. So, I just pulled the sword out from behind my back like Zorro and kinda made cutting motions in the air. Savvy?

They started sashaying away from me and all the while picking up a little speed. So am I, and I'm going behind them swishing the air behind their rear ends. They left, and what a story they'll tell their grandkids about their Johnny Cash house visit. John came home from filming the movie and heard about the fiddlers on his roof and thought it was great. There again, I could have gotten fired.

In 1975, I wanted to see a Johnny Cash concert. I was jones-ing! I'd done fifty-eight TV shows and John's gone on the road and I'm still working for him, but I haven't seen him in concert except for one other time at Madison Square Garden in New York. So, I went down to Florida. I called the House of Cash and asked Reba where he would be, and she said I could catch him in Lakeland. So, I went down there and checked into a hotel. I was standing in the front of my room, and they pulled up. I had no idea they were staying in that hotel. I thought, *This is really weird, and this is meant to be.* I had been there a couple of days there in the hotel and they just pulled up at my hotel. I walked out and they're pulling in.

So, that night I went to the show and got to see the concert. I was sitting out in the audience watching the concert and thought, *You know, I've been working in TV and rock concerts for years on and off doing lighting, and that John deserves better.* I'm thinking, *What are you thinking now, son?* I made some notes from the audience and after the show I went up to John. He said, "What are you doing, Chance, wandering around in the wilderness?" I said, "Nah, I just wanted to come and see you. I was jones-ing and wanted to see a Johnny Cash concert and came here to see a show. But while I was here, I decided I'd like to go to work on your tour and do your lighting."

He replied, " Well, I have a light director." I said, "Oh, yeah? Well, I'd like to meet him." See, I knew something that John didn't know. The real light director that he was expecting to be there wasn't really there. He'd gone to Vegas to do a show for another entertainer. That put a stranger in charge of John's production, which could have been why the lighting wasn't good that night. I said, "Well, Marshall Grant couldn't come up with this guy." Then I said, "John, your man is in Vegas. He's not here, and he's got a rookie running your show. That just don't seem right." He said, "It doesn't seem right either, Chance. Why don't you ride up to Georgia with us to the next show? We'll talk about it some more."

That night he hired me. He said, "Your first show will be in Hershey, Pennsylvania." The tour was over, so I came home and panicked. Now I had to really do this. My next magic trick! So, I brought in real locomotive lights. I had to make some special thing to run them, to power them from DC current to AC, complete with a big dimmer. One of the lights would sweep right over the people's heads. That's scary anyway, especially when there's a huge stage-rear screen with footage of trains getting ready to slam head-on into each other. I had another train light that did a figure eight in front of Johnny's feet. I also had a brand-new mirror ball, the biggest I could find, and I put it on an eight-foot chain and hung it in the middle of the auditorium. I wanted like six Super Trooper spotlights to shine on the ball and have a couple preset for a full body shot on John. The stage goes black and I had put amber gels in all the spotlights.

So now, just imagine there are like 10,000 to 20,000 people in the dark. Then you see these gold dots from the amber spots and the disco ball, all over the building. What I'd noticed, as I came from doing tightly scheduled Broadway shows and rock concerts, was that John's shows weren't really like that. It was like John would just kinda come out when he was ready, you know? I thought, *We've got to get this down to a science or all these gimmicks ain't gonna work.* John asked, "What's them dots for?" I said, "John, we're standing in the wings and the music's playing. When them amber dots start moving, you go to center stage."

When you turn the mirror ball on, it takes a while for the chain to catch up, and the amber dots would start real slow and pull you in. And, man, by the time John got out there to center stage, the mirror ball still wasn't wide open. It like swept him out there, and then that mirror ball would go off and he'd say, "Hello, I'm Johnny Cash." I covered the stage in white carpet and put a six-foot black carpet in the middle for the Man In Black. And then, when you had the red stage lights coming down, and you focused them just outside the black carpet dot on the outsides, you had "Ring of Fire" lighting.

Back to the trains. In the overhead stage footage, the trains slam into each other head-on, and I have the locomotive lights going. This is all building and John's really got it going, singing a medley of train songs to screen, like a movie score. The trains slam and the lights are going and then *boom!*, it hits. And when it does, here come the pyrotechnics with the explosions.

One time, we were playing Prince Edward Island in Canada, and when we got up there we didn't have the pyro stuff I needed, so I asked the stagehands, "You guys got any shotguns in your trucks?" They said, "Oh, yeah." I said, "Well, have you got any bullets?" They said, "Yeah." I said, "Well, bring some shells in and let's empty the powder out." I took black gunpowder and put it in a quad box and then plugged it in and *Whooom!* It was a bit much that night, and the explosion sent a smoke ring, and God,

it looked like an atomic bomb! It shook the building and blew part of the front of the stage off. The audience loved that.

I did the lights for John's Bicentennial Tour. At this time, during the whole thing, I was taking pictures with my Nikon camera because I had seen John's souvenir book that he had. I think it had been around the world with him three times—it's a black-and-white dollar book. So I thought, *I'm going to put a two-dollar book together and give people some colored pictures and some personal stuff on the whole show and make it worth their money, and even put red, white, and blue in there but not really date it.*

When I first brought it to John on the airplane going to Europe, he said it was too fancy for him. It was only a mock-up copy, and June said, "Oh, that sounds good." She liked the idea. I said, "Well, what's so fancy about a couple of hundred thousand dollars from the book sales in the next six months?" So, I got to do the book, and then I put a slide show together to get everything under control before the concert started. At the beginning of the show, you bring the house lights to half and then you start the slide show.

Everybody on the show was photographed for this, and they'd be in their dress clothes, then they'd be doing what they do at home. If they had a tractor, they were photographed on a tractor. If they had a speedboat, like W. S. Holland, then I had them with their boat. So I would get the audience to know everybody in the show just before it started.

We got to England and John was recording a live album at the London Palladium. It was released under the title *Strawberry Cake*. We had a big bomb threat. That was weird because people came in and snatched the microphones out of their hands and shut the show down. They brought us all outside and we stood right beside the Palladium, which is kinda like the mother church of English music performance, all brick and stuff. I thought to myself, *Here is John signing autographs of his San Quentin album.* I got pictures of that, and he's standing next to the building that supposedly may blow up any minute. There wasn't a bomb, and we got to keep on doing the show. John finished the show.

At this point the tour ended, and I went over to John's house and he said, "Let's go crocodile hunting in Jamaica, and you can bring that souvenir book when you get it finished over there." I was all excited that I was going to get to go to Jamaica and hang out with John and his great Caribbean house. I thought, *This is great!* I didn't know about the crocodile hunting.

The thing I liked best is that John discovered what he called his first hobby, besides the entertainment business. It was looking through the lens of a camera. We shot all day and afternoon, nothing but closeups, micro-shots of flowers. He had all the flowers in the world to photograph there in Jamaica. I said, "We'll get up early in the morning and you can get a star filter. We'll go down to the store and get one, and you can catch a little morning dew on the petal of the flower and get a four-point star." He said, "Well, what time do we have to get up?"

I said, "Well, let's just do it now." And I pulled out a spray bottle and sprayed a little mist on the flower, and when the sun hit it, he just loved all that. So, he found the world through his camera lenses, and as you know, he went on to take pictures, pictures, and more pictures all over the world. We used to go shopping for cameras in Germany. That was a lot of fun.

I was lying on the beach in Jamaica and he walks up with a sack. People are all lying on the beach. Here comes John with that stroll, that Johnny Cash walk that nobody's got one like, on the beach fully dressed, with a grocery bag. He comes up to me and blocks the sun-light. It's just a big silhouette of this man with this sack, and he says,

John, Chance, and the late One-Eyed Jack.

"Chance, this is your new camera. You can throw your old one in the Caribbean. You can just sling it out there."

It was a new Nikon, and I said, "Well, I've got two now, John, and I can get in other shows free." Back in those days, if you had two cameras, you were a photographer and could get into concerts free. So then he told me when we went back to the house that he was canceling the New York photographer for that *Strawberry Cake* album cover and that he wanted this picture he saw in the souvenir book, that I took in Colorado. It really thrilled me to get an album cover, you know? So now I had the album cover, the souvenir book, and I got to go to Jamaica.

Now, we're talking about this crocodile, the big One-Eyed Jack. That John—man, he was a fantastic shot, an expert! Besides reading cue cards upside down and backwards, he nailed that crocodile with his first shot at over one hundred feet away, at night. When we got him on the dock that night I said, "John, that sure would make a cool-looking guitar strap, some of that croc hide." He said, "I think it'd make a nice set of boots for you, Chance. What size foot do you have?"

I thought, *What have I got myself into now?* They had tanned it and put it on the wall. They had a lot of trouble getting those beautiful teeth out of that jaw, but they got them out and John gave me two of them. He took the rest them and had a necklace made. It's just awesome, partly because of the story behind it. I heard that Steve McQueen and Roger Moore had been there trying to get One-Eyed Jack, and it had eluded them. So, you take someone like Johnny Cash to make that story come true.

I was staying in Jamaica for fourteen days at Cinnamon Hill in 1976. One night, I went down to the nearby hotel to listen to some entertainment. I met a cute stewardess in there and got to talking to her. I said, "You want to go up on the big Cinnamon Hill and check out the view?" Of course it's midnight, not much of a view. We get up there, and I never said it was my house, but she thought it was. We were sitting out on the porch that went all the way around the house. We'd been out there quite a while when all of a sudden Johnny Cash appears in the doorway and says, "Hey Chance, how are ya'll doing this evening?"

The stewardess didn't know anything about Johnny Cash being there at all, let alone the fact that we were at Johnny Cash's house. Then John says to me, "I sure am enjoying my stay here, Chance. I'll leave ya'll alone." He went in and she said, "That's Johnny Cash!" I said, "Yeah, he likes to drop by and stay here at my house once in a while." She fell in love with me immediately!

We were in the Midwest on tour somewhere and got up one morning, came out of the hotel, and John said, "Chance, can I ride with you?" Besides just ride with me, he got behind the wheel. After we get on the interstate, he pulls off into a truck stop, gets out, and we go in. He got some candy and stuff and bought about ten magazines, the latest magazines. We got back in the car, and he said, "Chance, you drive."

John, wearing the necklace made from One-Eyed Jack's choppers.

At this point, we're back on the interstate and he's got those magazines in his lap riding shotgun there, and if you've ever seen John read a script or anything, he can read one quicker than anybody. It took him probably about five or six minutes to read all ten of those magazines. He turns the radio on and scans all the channels, then turns it off and says, " I'm going to take a little nap now, Chance. You can drive as fast as you want to."

So, we get into the next town, where the gig is that night. Here's the other rental cars, and the first one in the line as we come around the corner is Bob Wootton's. He was right in front of the hotel sitting in his rental car. We're coming like sideways into him, pulling into the hotel. John looks over and says, "Run into Bob Wootton; run into that car he's driving." So, I'm heading into the side of his car. I wasn't going fast, probably five miles and hour. I yelled, "I'm going in, John!"

Bob wasn't paying any attention. John takes his left foot, that big black boot, and puts it over on my foot and punches it to the floorboard. The front end of this rental car lifted up. I was probably twenty-five feet away and we slammed into Bob's door and destroyed the whole thing. Immediately, John got out and said, "Good job, Chance. I'll see you at the show," and leaves me there with Wootton, who was in kind of a shock.

I would be on an elevator in a hotel with just Johnny Cash and me, and there'd be a couple of good-looking ladies on there. I was young and a bachelor. They knew he was in there. The vibrations were just rattling the cables on this elevator. They were wanting to say something to him, you could tell. So John would break the ice. He'd reach up and push another button so he could stop it and he'd turn around and say, "Girls, have ya'll met Chance Martin?" And then he'd get off the elevator and leave me with them and shut the door. He'd be on the wrong floor. He'd have to catch another elevator. You don't expect stuff like that, but you could take advantage of it. The thing about it is, if the girls were at the show, backstage with me that night, then he knew it had worked.

John had a way of lifting your energy. He had so much energy that if you didn't know him, he could make you uneasy and nervous because of his charisma. If you knew him personally, and was his friend, and loved him, and he loved you, there was just something about that charisma that would transfer over to you and lift you up no matter how down you were, immediately. That was hard for me to understand at that time. But then, once I realized it was really real, it was something every day to look forward to being around Johnny Cash, because he would put you right there at a level that you wanted to be. He used to read the Bible to me while we were on the road.

One time he'd just got his first cell phone, one of the first cell phones I'd ever seen in a car, a hard-wired telephone. He called me up and said, "Hey, Chance, I got a new cell phone in my car. I'm going to give you my number. You wait about ten minutes, I'm out in the country in the field in the woods. I'm going to go off from the car. My horn is supposed to blow and my lights are supposed to flash when I get a call. I want to see if it really works."

So, I said, "OK, John." I'm at home and I'm thinking, *This is really funny.* So, I look at the clock, and ten minutes later I called him. It took him about five minutes to come to the phone. I guess he was enjoying the horn blowing. I thought, *I hope he hurries up before his battery goes dead.* He finally picked up the phone and answered, "It works, Chance," and he hung up. That was it.

One day I came home and had a message on the Code-A-Phone. I hit the play button and this voice—nobody else in the world had a voice like that, you know—and he said, "Hello, this is Chance Martin. I'm looking for Johnny Cash," and hung up. He did hundreds of things like that, not just one or two, that I remember. It was like an everyday thing. I know he was stationed in Germany with the Air Force in the early '50s. We were on tour in Germany, and I think it was in Berlin where I came in and there was a bunch of German francs in an envelope and a note from John. It said, "Chance, here's some German francs. Have a good time." So I did.

These stories and memories and the pictures, records, and music will always be with us. Not a day goes by that I don't think about John and miss him. Whether you knew him or not, I think he was one of the truest clowns. His humor was right up there with any comedian. Everybody saw him as serious, and he was, but yet he had a sense of humor that astounded me and rubbed off on me. Like I said, I've never been right since the first time I saw him. It changed my life, and it changed it for the better.

John took this snapshot of Old Glory through the screen door of his room while performing for U.S. troops at Guantanamo Bay, Cuba, in 1987.

ALAN MESSER

Nashville, Tennessee
Shoe Size 12

*S*HOOT ME ANY WHICH way you want, never when I'm picking my nose, and never in a limo. Good morning, Alan, I just wrote this song," said Johnny Cash on the curbside at Nashville Airport. It was 1987. We were about to take an early morning flight to Florida. I loved John's forthright way of getting to the point. From the start he allowed me to photograph Johnny Cash and June Carter without being intrusive or embarrassed.

The day before, I had received a phone call at my Nashville studio from Hugh Waddell. He called to inform me that I was going on the road with Cash the next day to start work on a tour book. I didn't believe him and thought it was a joke. Then an unmistakable voice said, "Hello, Alan, this is John Cash. I look forward to working with you tomorrow. Here's Hugh. . . ."

During the first show, while June and the Carter Family played their set, John came backstage and we went to his dressing room, where he picked up some oranges from the fruit bowl and juggled them for me.

I worked with Johnny Cash during the period between record labels Columbia and American Recordings, when he was signed to Polygram. I first met Cash in 1976; we were introduced by his musical director, Bill Walker, at the Grand Ole Opry during rehearsals for a Johnny Cash TV special. I was on assignment in Nashville for an English magazine, and I didn't see him again until 1987.

John and June get ready to go onstage with Waylon at Rock for the Animals.

Hugh brought me in to photograph Johnny Cash in a more casual and European way, because of my history of photographing the British rock and pop scene; which included the Beatles, Rolling Stones, and Iggy Pop.

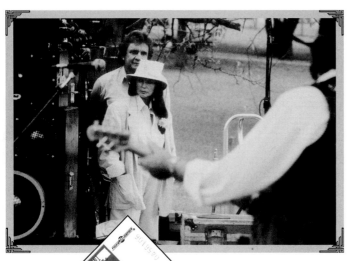

Cash was unenthused by the traditional photographs originating from Nashville during the '80s. These traditional, boring Nashville images were a far cry from Jim Marshall's renowned classic photographs of him at San Quentin Prison in 1969.

In September of 1987, Hugh invited me to photograph the Rock for the Animals music marathon. John was headlining this twelve-hour festival, which Hugh produced to raise money for local charities. The event was held at Monthaven, the Waddell family farm in Hendersonville. This show also featured June, Waylon, Tony Joe White, John Carter, Rosey Carter, Stella Parton, Townes Van Zandt, Aashid Himons, and Guy Clark. The show was emceed by radio disc jockey Wolfman Jack. John sat in with Waylon during the afternoon.

It was after dark when Johnny Cash finally took the stage with his band. They launched into "Ring of Fire" with that all so familiar boom-chicka-boom sound. I was on stage next to drummer W. S. Holland, photographing John with his audience, when suddenly the electrical power failed and the band were silenced. John continued playing acoustic guitar and singing unamplified. I got my electronic flash out of my camera bag, went over to John and started to flash repeatedly to illuminate him. Wolfman Jack joined me to John's right and lit him with a flashlight.

Johnny Cash never stopped singing or playing. I jumped off the front of the stage into the audience. June came out and yelled, "If everyone would like to move closer to the stage and be quiet, the show will go on without electricity." Then John and June launched into a rip-roaring acoustic performance of "Jackson." A staggering, beer-sodden biker to my right exclaimed in the Southern American vernacular, "#*$@%!&-A. This is the real thing!"

He was absolutely right, it didn't get much better than that raw performance. Johnny and June sang for thirty minutes to several thousand people, many of whom crammed up to the front of the stage to hear them, while the stage crew lit them with hand-held flashlights until the power was restored. These were two supreme performers who could hold an audience without gimmicks. As John often said, "I don't use flying pigs or exploding bales of hay in my concerts."

John had many sayings, witticisms and countryisms. He once told me that when a dog is sick, he lays down by water and drinks. The next day I went to stay at John and June's Virginia home to photograph June for her *Wildwood Flower* movie storyboard. I was unwell, and so the day before June arrived, I took John's advice and drank long and hard from the stream that runs through the property. Then I hiked up the hill behind the house and felt better. But then I remembered something else that John had told me: "Never drink downstream from the herd!"

After the photo session, I returned to Nashville and immediately flew out to Columbia, South Carolina, to photograph John at the Billy Graham Crusade. June was tired and stayed over at her family home. The trip was John and June's gift to me in return for the favour of shooting the session without payment.

Before breakfast on the morning of the Crusade, John phoned me in my room to ask me to bring my cassette player over to his suite. He was excited about some new back-to-basics tracks he had recorded with producer Bob Moore. What I heard there was the foundation for the new wave of Johnny Cash music.

Several weeks later, I was invited to dinner at their Hendersonville home. June and I showed the storyboard photographs to Robert Duvall, who was to co-star with her in the film as Jim Laughner. Johnny Cash was to have played A. P. Carter, and June, Vancie Laughner. After dinner, John wanted to play Duvall a cassette tape of his latest song. Unable to get the cassette player to work, he decided to pick up his guitar and proudly delivered his song. Then I took a photograph. (Incidentally, the *Wildwood Flower* movie was never been made, due to June's unfailing commitment to her husband's health in his later years.)

Robert Duvall was researching characters for his film *The Apostle*, in which he would play a preacher and June would play his mother. One Sunday, John decided to drive Duvall out to the Millersville Pentecostal Church to experience the preacher, Reverend Baggett, whom I think was an influence on Duvall's character in *The Apostle*. John and Waylon had introduced Robert Duvall to their producer, Chips Moman, having seen him play a country singer in *Tender Mercies*. I was working with Duvall's album as I was the art director and photographer for Chips's record label, Triad.

I arrived at the house, that Sunday, John greeted me in his usual way at the front door, invited me in, and excused himself as June was complaining about his trousers and he decided to change! When the Sunday church-going clothes were sorted out, we left in John's black Mercedes. John drove, June was in the front seat, and Bobby, Gayle Duvall, and I were in the back seat. Bobby said he felt like we were the children driving with our parents!

I persuaded John to pose in a swimsuit after *Spin* magazine's owner/editor, Bob Guccioni, phoned me to see if I could get Johnny Cash to pose for the lead page of their summer of '88 Swimsuit Edition. It took weeks of coercion for me to get John to pose in a swimsuit, because he didn't think he had the legs or the body for it! Eventually he consented to do the photograph.

The evening before the session, I went to see John with my brother David, who was visiting from England. We arrived late in the afternoon after a wedding for one of his daughters. We apologised for missing the wedding, and John said, "Don't worry, there will be another!"

Next morning, we arrived at John and June's home at eight o'clock. The great Johnny Cash appeared at the photo session dressed in knee-high socks, flame-embossed cowboy boots, boxer shorts, a white Caribbean shirt, and a large-brimmed black hat. Cash jumped up onto the diving board of his swimming pool and started posing. After the session, my film was couriered to New York, where *Spin* were holding the page on press deadline. John told me later that he had a good laugh with his office staff over that photograph.

In January 1999, I flew to Jamaica to photograph June for her album *Press On*. John greeted me at the front door of their house, Cinnamon Hill, and led me to the "Billy Graham Suite" guest quarters, situated downstairs next to the kitchen. John had placed several books in the room for me that proved interesting reading over the next week. One was *The Hidden Jesus*, another, *The White Witch of Rose Hall*, and he also gave me a book about the Polish holocaust that he and June had just finished reading.

The Rose Hall Great House at Cinnamon Hill.

"Meet me at 4:30, Alan," said John. I was ready at 4:15. So was he. John was always punctual and had no patience for lateness. "June says I drive this golf cart too fast," he chuckled, as we sped down a hill on the golf course to the hotel to buy the latest world newspapers. "Am I scaring you, Alan?" That day we talked about women, love, our families, and Jamaica. We went to the beach and we shopped for hot sauce, shirts, and a dress for my mother.

John gave me several shirts during his semi-retirement in 1998, when he was diagnosed as terminally ill with Shy-Drager syndrome. To occupy his time, he said he would sit at home and shop compulsively from catalogues. John always liked to wear a fresh, well-starched shirt. Geraldine, one of his housekeepers at Cinnamon Hill, is the best ironer I have ever seen!

I had a great time with John and June in Jamaica. We had many wonderful talks and meals together. As long as I had known them, it was mostly around business, and in Jamaica they were relaxed and away from the pressures of being celebrities. Since my room was next to the kitchen, I delighted in having coffee with John at daybreak, which was usually about 5:30 a.m. It was a good time to talk and spend time with my host. He would then go back upstairs to read and watch TV with June.

John would pick bunches of flowers for his wife each morning and arrange them in a vase before breakfast, which was always on one of the porches, as was lunch. Dinner was formally set in the dining room, and meals were announced by a hand bell. Before each meal we would join hands and one of my hosts would say grace, which was always heartfelt and relevant to the day. John liked to play dominos, and after dinner he and I sat for several evenings playing. He would shake the dice and mutter, "Come on, Johnny!"

John and June would drive a golf cart down from Cinnamon Hill to the seafront to pick up stray golf balls that the hotel guests had lost over the tall chain-link fence. They were champions at collecting stray golf balls, and when they had a plastic shopping bag full, would return them to the clubhouse. Because they liked the echo, John and June would stop to sing gospel songs when they rode their golf cart through the tunnels under the golf course. One day I shot some video footage of John singing the Edward Perronet hymn "All Hail the Power of Jesus' Name . . . And Crown Him Lord of All."

John asked me one morning in Jamaica if I had seen Hugh in a while, which I had not. He asked me to give him a message that he still loved him and missed him. John disliked being surrounded by "hangers on" and "yes" people, which is why I believe he was so fond of Hugh.

One evening as we stood on "Pee Hill," (so nicknamed by he and John Carter) John described in detail the proposed Johnny Cash WaterWorld undersea park that would stretch from Rose Hall into the Caribbean! Such was his wacky sense of humour.

John was a great practical joker and a prankster. He could run a joke for days, weeks, or even years! He was playful with his friends; his capacity for humour was infectious and charming. Every time he saw me during one of those early road trips he would go into a silly joke about Carlene. He was a man of extremes who was always serious about humour, religion, family, and music.

When John Carter was a teenager, he was in a rock band that would play loud hell-raising music in his room. His father would entertain shaken "muso biz" guests in the lakeside room below, who would have trouble hearing Johnny Cash speak. I remember John taking a group of them upstairs to hear the band. He, the proud father, said, "Hey, that's my son's music."

After one of those music business gatherings, John asked his guests if John Carter could sing them a song. I think the guests were expecting a Johnny clone, but instead they got an acoustic anti-establishment punk song, and then another! They all politely left, thanking the Man In Black for his hospitality. John Carter was upset that they didn't seem to like his music. John turned to his son and said, "I know how you feel son. . . ." That moment has always touched me deeply. It was a loving and truthful supportive statement, not just from an experienced artist but from a loving dad.

In December 1992, John hand wrote the sleeve notes for my brother Michael Messer's collaborative album *Rhythm Oil—The Sessions with Terry Clarke and Jesse "Guitar" Taylor.* Michael and Terry met John in 1994, after a Johnny Cash show in London, and thanked him for his contribution. John was flattered and asked if it had helped sales, because as much as he loved the music, he was aware that the bottom line was about record sales and that young artists need all the help and encouragement they can get. John was always willing to help his fellow man, just as long as they were willing to help themselves.

Jammin' at John Carter Cash's 21st Birthday Bash (from left): Alan Messer, June, John Carter and sister Cindy, Bell Cove Club owner Joy Ford, and guitarist Michael.

"A man can't help falling over, but he can help laying there," said the wise dad on stage at "John Carter's 21st Birthday Bash and Musical Bar Mitzvah" that Hugh arranged at the Bell Cove Club on Old Hickory Lake. I played congas and my zydeco rub board and took some photographs. After playing a big jam version of Dylan's "The Weight," I went outside to cool off in the night air. John was there and gave me a cigarette. He said, "I know how you feel," referring to that click-clack rhythm. Then we smoked. John Carter's twenty-first birthday party jam session continued into the March night.

"Alan, would you buy me some cigarettes? Get me a carton of Marlboro and a carton of Pall Mall. Here's some 'Cash' money!" That John Cash would really smoke when he smoked. He did everything in excess. Big John would consume a cigarette in a couple of draws! There we were during the Billy Graham Crusade in Columbia, South Carolina—John, Hugh, Jack Hale, and me sitting in John's hotel suite with two hundred cigarettes, practically chain-smoking. Jack didn't smoke; he just breathed the air. John eventually stopped smoking after his heart by-pass surgery, but even then it took an English hypnotist and a persuasive wife for him to stop.

June didn't like cigarette smoke and frowned upon marijuana even more. We were on tour with the Highwaymen, I think it was in Minnesota, during the sub-zero depths of winter. Willie's bus drove into the backstage area, the door opened, and Willie stepped out in a cloud of smoke, just as John, June, and I were walking by on the way to the dressing room. This didn't exactly please June.

I had lent John my Nikon "point-and-shoot" camera that afternoon, which he took onstage, and at times during the show he would pull that little camera out from his long black stage coat and photo- graph Waylon, Willie, and Kris. After the show, when I followed John back to the dressing room to get my cam- era, the first thing he said was, "I don't know what Willie was smoking tonight, but he sure did sound good!"

In 1988, Hugh suggested that I fly to New York to pho- tograph Johnny Cash. I was very broke at the time. But I scraped together every last dollar I could find, bought a plane ticket and some film, and slept on the floor of Hugh's hotel room. With little sleep, the following morning, we went over to John and June's apartment on Central Park South.

John didn't know that I would be there and didn't want to shoot a photo session. Although pleased to see me, he suggested that I photograph him "casually" as he moved through his morning in New York. He shopped and posed for pictures in the street. One of those photographs won an editorial award in New York's *Art Direction Magazine* later that year and then in 1991 became the cover of John's Mercury album *The Mystery of Life*.

We walked over to one of John's favourite New York shops, Banana Republic, where he wanted to buy me a present of a photographer's khaki jacket. I urged him not to, explaining that it wasn't my style, and thanked

him for the offer of the gift, saying that the gesture was worth more than the gift itself, but that I really wouldn't wear it. So John said he liked the jacket anyway and bought one for himself and one for Hugh. Later that day, I bought John some black silk socks. He was always buying presents for others, so I wanted to get him something for a change.

A few months later I was meeting with John and June in their back office at the House of Cash, showing them my photographs from the Billy Graham Crusade in Denver. John was wearing that Banana Republic jacket and a lot of One Man Show cologne. He looked over the pictures which were spread out on a light box on June's desk, marked his choice of the contact sheets and slides with his usual shaky X, then left me with June to finish editing the pictures. He was restless and said he was late for a meeting in Nashville and had to leave.

One minute later, he was back in the room, those long legs striding and a "hey, caught you with my wife!" look upon his face. "I am well pleased with those photographs, Alan," he said, at which point John ceremoniously took off that photographer's jacket and handed it to me. I could not refuse him. That's the type of man that he was.

The last time I saw John and June together was in August of 2002. I
went over to their house to discuss my proposed book of Johnny Cash
photographs. John sat in his armchair, unable to get up. We discussed our
business and then we spoke of his recent hospital visit. He said the latest
near-death experience had really scared June, who had rescued him, got
him into Baptist Hospital, and successfully prayed for him. I gave them
one of my signed photographs of Billy Graham for the Cinnamon Hill
guest suite, and another print of June dancing on the porch at their
Virginia home.

We shared some happy memories. We spoke about my father's health,
of our families, and then about Steve Earle, whom I was about to see later
that evening at the Belcourt Theater. John gave me a message for Steve,
complimenting him on his performance of his song, "Hardin Wouldn't
Run," on the recent Sony tribute album *Kindred Spirits*. Steve was ecstatic
with J. R.'s compliment (he called him J. R.), and we reminisced about the
time Johnny had asked him to start "Will the Circle Be Unbroken" on his
mandolin on that same stage, fifteen years earlier, during a songwriters
matinee concert.

I have many photographs from the two decades I knew John Cash.
John and June were like my American aunt and uncle. When they died it
ended an era. It is with sadness and fond memories that I will always miss
John. I consider him to have been a wealthy man, not just financially, or as
a land owner, but in his heart and wisdom. He shall always be a brilliant
star to light my path.

BILL MILLER

Corona, California

Shoe Size 11

*H*ERO. A big word with a lot of meaning to those lucky enough to have one. Unfortunately for kids these days, not many heroes are being made.

In the old days, young boys had plenty of heroes to admire. There were John Wayne, Gene Autry, Roy Rogers, and all the good guys on the big screen who represented bravery, idealism, and integrity. A good hero is hard to find these days, for sure, and, on September 12, 2003, the world lost its last true hero, Johnny Cash.

John fit the definition of the word and its meaning to a T. He was a good guy; he had more integrity than anyone I've ever known and he was a kind and gentle soul. There's no question that he was and will always be my hero.

I discovered Johnny Cash for the first time quite by accident. It was 1968, and I was a typical kid in the third grade with typical interests. Living in a small town in the Southern California desert, I chased lizards and snakes, played with my G.I. Joe, and hung out with my fellow third-graders. Music was never an interest. My brother was into Jimi Hendrix, the Doors, and other big rock acts of the time, and my parents' tastes ran to Bing Crosby (Dad) and Wayne Newton (Mom). That all changed one fateful day in my elementary school during the show-and-tell portion of class.

A fellow third-grader, Lanette Nelson, a cute little girl whom I had my first schoolboy crush on, brought the album *Johnny Cash at Folsom Prison* to share with the class. The teacher put the record on the turntable, and the very minute Johnny proclaimed "Hello, I'm Johnny Cash" and went into "Folsom Prison Blues," my life changed. Forever. The voice and accompanying instrumentation

John with Shannon and Bill Miller.

was unlike anything I'd ever heard. It was electric and it captured my full attention. Unfortunately, in those days, John used some salty language, and as soon as the first uncensored cuss word was uttered, our teacher ran to the record player, grabbed the disc, and returned it to its sleeve.

Regardless of that unhappy ending, my hiatus from Johnny Cash was very short-lived. I begged my parents to take me to a record store so I could buy my very own Johnny Cash record. My family was akin to the Cleavers of *Leave It to Beaver* fame, but my parents tolerated the questionable language and themes on my records because they could see that I had a real connection to the music.

As fate would have it, Johnny Cash immediately became the biggest recording artist in the world. You couldn't go anywhere without hearing one of his songs, seeing his face on a magazine cover, or turning on the TV and seeing something about him. He was huge. I bought every magazine, poster, and record I could find. I couldn't get enough of this magic, larger-than-life man, and soon the walls of my room were covered with Johnny Cash posters. I was hooked.

In 1969, Johnny got his own weekly TV series on ABC, and I was able to see him in motion for the first time. He appeared even bigger and more awesome than he did in the posters and magazines, and his presence on that little black-and-white screen captivated me every week. I lived for those dates with Johnny and with each episode my admiration for and interest in him grew. I had become Johnny Cash's biggest fan.

It wasn't until 1973, when I was thirteen years old, that I was able to see John in concert for the first time. By then my family had moved to New Mexico and I'd heard that the Johnny Cash Show was coming to Denver, Colorado, which was some five hours away (each way) from our town. By the time I finally got up the nerve to ask my dad if he'd make the drive to Denver, only the cheapest, worst nosebleed seats were available. But I would have stood outside the arena just to hear his voice in person if that were the only way, so Dad agreed and we made the trek to Denver.

In those days, Johnny carried a large troupe with him comprised of Carl Perkins, the Statler Brothers, and the Carter Family. While the others warmed the audience up, I couldn't really focus on their talents, since all I could think of was Johnny's arrival. And when he walked onto that stage, the crowd went wild. It was a large arena, and from my perspective, Johnny looked as large as a small ant. I asked my dad if I could go down and get closer to the stage and he allowed me. I walked around the circular arena for what seemed like a day, and when I finally reached the floor, Johnny was doing "Orange Blossom Special." The song was nearing its finale, and as I raised my two-dollar Kodak Instamatic to take my first picture of him, Johnny made eye contact with me and tossed me one of his harmonicas. Needless to say, I had all but died and gone to heaven. If there ever was a Nirvana, to this thirteen-year-old kid, that moment was it.

With my treasure in hand, I made my way to the lobby to see it in the light. When I raised my head after a thorough examination of it, I saw June Carter standing right next to me, awaiting her cue to join Johnny onstage. I made my way over to her, and she greeted me before I could open my mouth. "Well hi, son, what's your name?" I'm sure she could tell I was a bona fide fan by the four-inch fan club button I had pinned to my shirt. I

BILLY MILLER
P. O. Box 725
Eagle Mountain, California 92241

REPRESENTING
JOHNNY & JUNE CASH
International Fan Club
YOUTH EDITOR, OVERSEAS REPRESENTATIVE

TEL. (714) 227-3225

recall telling her my name and asked her if she'd sign my button, which she graciously did. I had my picture taken with her, and as soon as the flash cube went off, she left to join Johnny for her part of the show. Nirvana had just gotten better.

When the show was over, I dashed out to the front lobby as Johnny left the stage. As he approached the exit, I realized just how big and imposing he was. Surrounded by six uniformed police officers, Johnny's stride resembled that of the legendary creature Bigfoot in the famed video taken many years ago. I walked quickly ahead and placed myself between the door and the approaching group. Johnny stopped briefly, stuck out his hand, and said, "Hi, son." With that, he was escorted to the awaiting limousine and was off into the night.

From that seemingly routine fan encounter, our relationship deepened and strengthened over the ensuing thirty years. As a kid, I continued to attend concerts and was eventually granted a backstage pass for each and every show I attended. Lou Robin made sure "Little Billy Miller, as I was to become known to Johnny, June, and the Cash organization, was able to visit with Johnny at every venue.

I literally grew up around Johnny, and he watched me go from a little kid fan to a friend and businessman he liked to hang out and visit with whenever his schedule permitted. Johnny came to California quite a bit, where I eventually settled, and would often call when he was in town for more than a day. He loved to get out and walk and explore, and in the '90s we frequently visited at a business I operated in Fashion Island, a high-end shopping mall in Newport Beach.

John's revised lyric sheet for a Folger's coffee commercial.

Johnny was a collector of many things, including autographs by historical personalities, and my business in Newport specialized in celebrity autographs. During one of our conversations, it was evident to me that Johnny loved presidential history, and I set out to build him a complete set of autographs of all the United States presidents. Over the next few years, I'd surprise Johnny with the autographs, and he'd always manage to slip in a gift for me along the way. He'd been aware of the collection I'd been building on him for many years and contributed some amazing things over the years. He'd give me an expired passport, old credit cards, handwritten lyrics, stagewear, and much more, knowing that I'd treasure them and eventually build an archive suitable for public exhibit.

One the most memorable visits took place in the late '90s, when Johnny dropped by the gallery at Newport. He arrived shortly before I did, and as I entered the gallery (with my employees standing in awe of Johnny), he said, "I have something for you." He made his way to the back of the gallery and sat behind the desk, and I sat in front of him in the chairs reserved for customers. As he opened his black binder, I was amazed at what he'd done for me. "I wrote these out for you 'cause I heard you'd like to have them," he said. There, in Johnny's own hand, were the entire lyrics to "I Walk the Line." I was overwhelmed, as I had been many times, at his generosity, but this was even more special. Apparently, two years prior, Johnny had heard about a conversation I had with someone in his organization in which they asked me what I would love to have for my collection. Jokingly, I said "Johnny's handwritten lyrics to 'I Walk the Line,'" not thinking it was even a possibility. Well, Johnny tucked the comment into his mind and, at a time he chose, fulfilled my secret request!

When we were done at the gallery, Johnny wanted to see Clint Eastwood's *Pale Rider*, so we decided to walk to the theater at the mall. As we walked, people stood back and gasped: here was THE Johnny Cash,

JOHNNY CASH

Re: Guild Guitar
Model D60SBE
S.N. D600067
                    Hendersonville Tn.
Mr. Bill Miller   Feb. 23 1993

Dear Bill,
    Please accept this guitar &
mine as a personal gift and I
token of my friendship.
    I've used this guitar on every
concert for more than
10 years. It plays better than ever.
I hope you enjoy it.
        Best Wishes,
        your friend.
        Johny Cash

strolling through the mall like everyone else. We talked about a lot of things, and during the conversation, I asked him who his favorite president of all time was. Without skipping a beat, he said, "James Garfield. You know I wrote a song about him?" I nodded that I was aware, and he replied, "Let me sing it for you." Believe it or not, as we made the lengthy walk to the theater, I was treated to a private rendition of "Mr. Garfield" by its composer. I'll never forget that day as long as I live. Johnny was as relaxed and in as good spirits as I'd ever seen him.

When my youngest son was born, he was named Jordan Cash Miller. A reporter from our local newspaper, the *Press Enterprise*, called Johnny and asked him about our relationship and a recent event I'd attended at his home in Hendersonville. During the conversation with the reporter, Johnny said that he was Jordan's godfather and that he took that very seriously. He told the reporter about the meaning of being a godparent and what it has meant from a historical standpoint through the ages. What amazed me the most was that we'd never asked Johnny formally to be Jordan's godfather; Johnny had proclaimed it so, and obviously no one complained! A handwritten letter from Johnny to Jordan followed shortly, offering encouragement, prayers, and support for the newborn boy.

Through the years there were many, many visits and good quality private time between Johnny and I. He always took time, regardless of his busy schedule, to visit. We talked about life, love, politics, religion, collecting, family, and many other things friends talk about. Sometimes the subjects could get fairly deep and personal; other times, we'd simply talk about nothing in particular. Through it all, I never doubted that he was a true friend. He was the most thoughtful man I've ever known.

In late 2002, a few years after Johnny had stopped touring, I was approached by the Richard Nixon Presidential Library about loaning some of my collection for a seventieth birthday tribute to Johnny they wanted to mount. I was thrilled with the concept, since the collection was doing little good for anyone but me if the public didn't see it, and I agreed. When the curator asked if we could feature one of Johnny's recent awards in the exhibit, I called Kelly Hancock and asked if she could relay the request to Johnny. I suggested that perhaps his Kennedy Center Honor might be appropriate, considering that this was a presidential library, and Kelly agreed to ask Johnny for me. True to form, and ever mindful that I had built a truly historically significant collection on him, Johnny agreed to the loan. And when Kelly called to confirm, she had another surprise, direct from the man himself. "In addition to the Kennedy Honor, John wants to send the National Medal of Arts from President Bush for your exhibit, too." It's not hard to see why Johnny Cash is my hero and mentor.

The last time I saw Johnny was in August of 2003, less than three weeks before he passed away. He appeared to be in good health during our visit and looked better physically than I'd seen him look in a long time. As we were preparing to leave, Johnny handed my wife, Shannon, and I a gift bag. As I looked inside and removed the contents, I was once again amazed at the dear man's thoughtfulness and generosity. Inside was a beautiful stained-glass window depicting he, June, and John Carter. It was the same piece I'd seen hanging inside his kitchen window during many visits I'd made to Hendersonville. It had been in the home for nearly thirty years. "Hang this in your window and let the light shine through it, " Johnny said. Shannon preceded me by a few seconds in leaving Johnny's room, and as I was walking out, I turned back, walked to John and said, "Thanks for everything, John. It's always an honor. I love you." John replied, "Love you, too," and I turned and walked out.

Little could I have ever imagined that this would be my final visit with the man who had literally been a part of me for every single day for the past thirty-four years.

I love you and miss you dearly, John.

AL QUALLS

Fort Walton Beach, Florida

Shoe Size 13

as an avid gun collector, a mutual friend of both John and I, Lash LaRue, was always helping find additions for my collection. He knew John wanted to dispose of a large portion of his collection and suggested we get together.

To my surprise, I received a phone call from Johnny Cash and was invited to Nashville for a visit. John was a very generous man. I bought all of his surplus guns except the one I wanted most, and he really kept me going on it until we finished the deal. He laughed and said, "The reason I wouldn't sell this one to you is because I wanted to give it to you since you liked it so much."

After that day, another dollar never changed hands between us; however, many gifts did. Through our mutual love of western movies and collecting cowboy guns, our lifelong friendship was established.

During this time, there have been many Johnny Cash stories and experiences, which are special to my family and I, as we were fortunate to get to know the man John Cash as a friend up close and not seen from a distance as a superstar. There are many stories I would like to share; however, following are my two favorites.

Sons and dads (from left): John Carter and John Cash, Donny and Al Qualls.

Once, at a Banana Republic store, I found a very comfortable lightweight safari jacket, and since John and I wear the same size, I also bought one for him and mailed it to him. The man who had everything fell in love with that jacket, and he started sewing different patches and insignia on it from his travels. Johnny wore it on a daily basis.

One of my closest friends and a staunch Johnny Cash fan, Bob Frix, had recently received his second general's star in the U.S. Army. Bob sent Johnny one of his first stars, which was given to him by a friend, a brigadier general of the unit of young soldiers from Fort Campbell, Kentucky, who were killed in the late '80s airplane crash at Gander, Newfoundland. John was in awe of the gift and wore the stars in honor of the troops.

Sometime later, at a dinner party at Bob's residence, a junior officer brought up the subject of seeing Johnny Cash on television wearing a general officer's star on his jacket. The junior officer felt it was offensive. He then turned to Bob and said, "General, doesn't it bother you, as hard as you worked for your star, that someone would wear one?"

Frix turned to the guy, looked him in the eye and politely said, "I gave him the star." I thought the man was going to hide under the table; however, he gulped and remained quiet for the balance of the dinner.

On the cover of the Nitty Gritty Dirt Band's album *May the Circle Be Unbroken II*, as in many other publicity photos, you will see John wearing this jacket—and believe it or not, it's khaki not black.

Several years later, John called me, very distraught. Someone at the Denver airport had stolen that Banana Republic jacket and he asked if I could possibly find another one. That particular style of jacket had been discontinued for some time. Having only worn my jacket a few times, it was almost like new, so I took it from the closet and sent it to him as a replacement. He called back and was like a kid who just got a new bicycle for Christmas.

A phone call to Bob Frix, and another general's star was on the way.
Another old-time friend from Florida Ranger Camp days and an avid Johnny
Cash admirer, Dave Bramlett, also sent him one of his stars. Camp Rudder,
the U.S. Army Ranger Detachment, sent a Ranger tab, and once again John
had his security-blanket jacket and a starter kit of things to sew on it.

I was pleased to see him wearing it on the insert from one of his last
American Recordings CDs, and it's hard to believe a jacket with some patches
would excite him that much. He really treasured things from the military and
always loved the troops. The jacket was John's second-favorite gift.

Early 1991 was an emotional roller-coaster ride, as John had recently
lost his mother, Carrie, and my wife, Peggy, was expecting our third child.
John's birthday was February 26, right on top of my son Robert's due date,
so we were both pulling for him to be born on John's birthday.

It was the most difficult time for John I had seen. He and his mother
were extremely close, and the only way to describe him would be
devastated. In the spirit of O. Henry's "Gift of the Magi," as I
felt he needed a lift, I sent John for his fifty-ninth
birthday one of my most prized possessions,
a Colt .45 pistol used by John Wayne in
one of Wayne's western movies.

We missed the February 26 date for my
son's birthday, but at 2 a.m. on the morning of
February 27, Peggy and I made our mad dash
to the hospital. She was in labor. Our son was
not punctual, as he waited until 5:45 that afternoon to make his appearance. We were worn out.

Unknown to us, John left early on the morning
of the twenty-seventh to go on tour to Canada.
John took his bus, which he loved, and that bus was
his second home. John's sister Reba had assembled his
mail, birthday cards, and my gift for him to open on
his bus. Some seventy-five miles out of Nashville, John
opened my gift. Being familiar with the gun after seeing it
at my house, he couldn't believe his eyes.

JOHNNY CASH

Cash Home
280 Caudill Dr.
Hendersonville, TN 37075
May 15 1999

Mr. Al Qualls,
  Dear Al,
There were 100 of those belt buckles
made in bronze. Only one was made in
gold. And it's yours. It's been in my life
for 24 years. It is not a payment for anything you've given me, or done for me.
It's a gift to you as a friend.
Wear it in good health. Your
friend,
                    Johny Cash

RE: 99 bronze belt buckles and
    one gold.

Recipes and Memories
from
Mama Cash's
Kitchen

Over 30 New Recipes!
2nd Edition

John sports the jacket
Al gave him on the
cover of Mama Cash's
cookbook.

He was so excited that he had the driver turn the bus around and head back to Nashville to put the pistol in his safe, as he was afraid the Canadian border officials might take it from him.

He then called my office to thank me and was told I was at the hospital with Peggy awaiting Robert's arrival. Unknown to us, during this day John would call the hospital to check on how things were going, and true to John's character, he took the time to chat with whoever answered the phone.

Needless to say, the hospital switchboard and staff were all thrilled that it was really the Man In Black calling on the phone. The competition was keen for who would get to answer the next call. The next day a beautiful flower arrangement arrived for us from John and June, and the hospital was abuzz.

Our family has many Johnny Cash memories like the framed "Happy Birthday Donny Qualls" message when John wished our oldest son a happy birthday live on the cable television show *Nashville Now*. My daughter Polly's picture is on the "celebrity wall" as a four-year-old, only waist high, holding John by the leg at Captain Anderson's Restaurant in Panama City, Florida.

Today, I still feel John's presence and spirit, like each year at the Golden Boot Awards when I wear the beautiful leather coat by Manuel that John wore on the 1987 Johnny Cash Is Coming to Town concert tour. That coat was a Christmas gift from him. Of the many gifts we exchanged, I have no doubt that John Wayne's Colt pistol was his favorite. I never saw him become excited over anything else as much, and I am glad it was part of helping him to heal from the loss of his mother. He joked with me once that times were bad and we were having to give each other second-hand presents.

John was one of a kind, and I feel fortunate to have been his friend and shared our time, common interests, and friendship. It was one of my greatest experiences.

LOU ROBIN

Westlake Village, California
Shoe Size 9 MEDIUM

*M*Y COMPANY, ARTIST CONSULTANTS Productions in Los Angeles, worked with Johnny Cash, first as his exclusive concert promoters from February 1969 until the summer of 1972. At that point, Johnny's manager, Saul Holiff, left the group by mutual agreement.

Up to and at that time, my partner, Allen Tinkley, and myself had been doing the concert promoting of the Johnny Cash shows, Simon and Garfunkel, Bill Cosby, the Tijuana Brass, and several rock groups worldwide. Even so, we chose to take on Johnny and June's management, with an eye to expanding our scope of activity in the music business.

Johnny and June accepted our proposal, and Artist Consultants represented them until their deaths in 2003. Even now, I continue on in a similar capacity for their estates, helping to watch over their business interests and creating new levels of appreciation of their lives and their music with guidance from John and June's children and the trustee of their estates.

Johnny was loved and respected worldwide by everyone, from royalty to the hard-working laborer. It is fascinating to see how he could transcend the language barrier when necessary, where his familiar music was the common meeting ground between him and his audience.

151

In the early years working with the Johnny Cash Show, I spent about 120 days a year on the road with the Cashes. We played great places, unusual places, as well as exotic places, and sometimes just places that would fill a hole in our tour schedule. English writer Peter Lewry's 2002 book *I've Been Everywhere* chronicles all these tours and places in great detail. I was honored to have written the foreword for that release.

Exotic places, like Thailand, Singapore, Hong Kong, Hawaii, and Montego Bay, Jamaica. Great places, such as the British Isles, Germany, Scandinavia, Czechoslovakia, Australia, and New Zealand. And many unusual places for the Cash concert tour, like Hungary, Poland, Finland, Belgium, Guantanamo Bay, Cuba, and the former East Germany.

Many places and many memories, some more prevalent than others. On the way back to Dublin, Ireland, from a mid-1980s concert in Northern Ireland, some of us were asleep in the chauffeured sedan that was being driven by someone that "knew all the roads." Apparently, he took a wrong turn at an unlighted crossroads. We entered a small town a few minutes later, and as we came around a corner going at a pretty high rate of speed, we came upon several British machine-gun emplacements and floodlights that made 1:30 in the morning look like high noon.

We stopped cold in our tracks in the middle of what was probably the line of fire. Silence. Except for the sound of our hearts pounding! Slowly, the driver eased back around the corner where we changed our direction and retraced our steps to the correct turn in the road. We were really lucky that the soldiers didn't start shooting. Maybe they were asleep, too. That town turned out to be the scene of many bloody clashes in the ongoing violence in Ireland.

One night in the late '80s, we played to 5,000 people at a converted warehouse about 100 miles north of Helsinki, Finland, that doubled as a sports arena. The only problem was that the stage was on a balcony—twenty feet above the crowd! That high stage turned out to be a safe place above the revelers, including about 300 who had come up to the concert on a special train from Helsinki that had unloaded these folks at a siding next to the arena. I often wondered how many inebriated fans didn't find their way back to the train after the show.

Another night, in New Brunswick Province, Canada, England's Prince Charles came to the Cash concert, with many of his naval comrades with whom he was in training at the time. He knew everyone's place or order of performance in the Johnny Cash Show as soon as they were introduced to him, and he also remembered their names as well, all before he had even seen the show. Very impressive!

Johnny met Rick Rubin, owner of American Recordings and a renowned rap producer, one night in 1992 after a show in Santa Ana, California.

Johnny was unhappy recording with Polygram Records, as the original reason for his signing with them was that the president and chief of promotion were friends of his, and they had moved to Polygram over from Columbia Records. But now they had subsequently left Polygram.

I met Rick backstage and took him into Johnny's dressing room, where they stared at one another, assessing what they saw, for a full two minutes. They began to find out that they had similar thoughts about Johnny's musical goals and approaches to recording. Thus began the final high point of Johnny's career, that lasted until his death. Johnny and Rick decided that Johnny would record songs that he wanted to do and also record those songs that Rick suggested to Cash via cassette exchange.

They would meet at Rick's home studio in Los Angeles and listen and record even more songs. After maybe forty to fifty songs in various stages of completion were considered, they would finally get the selections for an album down to twenty-five. From there, it would become very difficult.

They usually ended up with fourteen to sixteen songs for the album that, hopefully, would have a cross-section of appeal. Many of the songs that didn't initially make each album ended up in the label Lost Highway Records' *Johnny Cash: Unearthed* boxed five-disc set, released in late 2003. The title of this boxed set was chosen by Johnny just two months before his death.

Johnny and June Cash were wonderful people to work for. They were considerate, respectful, and generous to all those individuals who worked for them. That is why so many spent decades with the Cash family, and for some, generations in their employ. Sure, there were some bumps in the road as the years passed by, but the loyalty of most of the "road gang" and the Nashville House of Cash office staff was in appreciation of, and out of love and respect for, Johnny and June. It is unfortunate that as this is written, some former employees have chosen to try to destroy the Cash image by rumor and innuendo for financial gain.

Those many who loved Johnny and June's music and the image that they portrayed will help to keep the true memories alive. It is a lonely feeling now for me, because I can't pick up a phone and ask Johnny or June what they think of this project or that idea. I would always get an objective answer, no matter how they were feeling at that moment.

DAVE ROE

Nashville, Tennessee
Shoe Size 10¹/₂

I REMEMBER TELLING ONE my best friends in my hometown in Hawaii, where I grew up, that I had just gotten the gig playing bass for Johnny Cash. I had lived in Nashville for twelve years, making a great living playing my bass guitar and getting to travel and record with about a half-dozen other major country artists. I was feeling very lucky and proud, I might add. It shocked me to hear him say, "Cool, you finally did something with your music."

I instantly realized, he was as right as he could be.

My friend Hugh Waddell, who compiled this book, was at that time working as Johnny's publicist and personal aide. When the bass slot with John came open in 1990, I went and auditioned at his House of Cash offices, one-on-one with Johnny. I've never been more nervous for an audition, which are all sort of nerve-racking anyway.

I didn't get the job at that time, as Johnny had decided to revert back to his more traditional sound and use an upright bass (acoustic bass fiddle) instead of electric bass guitar, which was all I played at the time. It was a very pleasant visit, and I remember thinking how cool it was just to hang out with him for a minute, anyway.

155

A couple of years later, when the bass guitar position with Johnny Cash opened up again, Hugh called me and said that he had told Johnny that I had started playing the upright and had become a really great rockabilly slap-style bass player. You see, playing slap upright bass is much more than being able to just play one.

The style of bass Johnny's music truly demanded was a variation on an old hillbilly and big-band style, where the bassist combined playing his bass notes with a percussive beating on the bass itself. You played this form, or technique, along with pulling the strings and letting them snap back on the finger-board, all in rhythm.

Dave onstage with Bob Wootton and John.

All of Cash's and Elvis Presley's early records employed this style, as the bands then rarely had drummers. This made the task quite daunting, as well as puzzling. Hugh wanted so much for me to get the job with Johnny Cash that he failed to tell Cash that it had been many years since I had even played the upright bass. He had convinced John that I was who needed to be hired to play bass, and Cash listened to him. Hugh knew I'd get the job, then go buy an upright bass, then get the technique down. He was right, as that's what eventually happened.

But, being completely ignorant of all this at the very beginning, I arrogantly accepted the job. Johnny rarely rehearsed, so my job was to show up with a bass (which I had to borrow) on such and such a date in Charleston, West Virginia. So off I went, without a prior rehearsal or a real clue as to what I was in for, playing the rockabilly style John had helped perfect at Sun Records in the mid-'50s.

Johnny and the rest of the folks on the show had no idea how awful it was all about to be. After the show, which was the worst I ever played in my entire career, Johnny called me back into his dressing room. Knowing that I was about to be sent back to the hotel, with hopefully full severance pay, I listened as he asked the loaded question.

"You don't really play upright bass, do you, son?" "No sir," I humbly replied, "not really." "And the slap bass thing I want is really out of the question, then, isn't it?"

"I couldn't if I tried, sir," I said, probably very meekly. "Then why," he asked, "did you come out here?" "Because it was worth a shot, I had fun, and I got to play a concert with Johnny Cash."

He flashed me a puzzled look, followed by a warm grin. "Would you like to have this gig?" he asked. I told him that I would love it. At this point, I was a little in shock, since I was expecting the opposite of what appeared to be unfolding. He then told me, "I really want to have the old slap bass style back in my music. If you want to give it a try, I'll give you six months, and I need at that time to be able to look around and see that you're the right guy for the job. Is that OK?"

I can tell you now, in the music business—whether New York, Los Angeles, or Nashville—musicians just hardly ever get those kind of breaks. In Nashville alone, there are so many great musicians, slap bassists included, that no artist ever has to be without who they need. There are musicians waiting and looking for work that can play anything. Cash offered me a chance to rise to this musical occasion, to prove my abilities and I will be forever grateful.

I guess I'm different than most of the folks who worked with Johnny Cash in that I can't tell you that I was close to him. Although I played bass for the Johnny Cash Show concert tour for the better part of eight or nine years, and later on took part in his final sessions, I could never tell anyone that I was by any means on his short list of friends and acquaintances. I was, however, deeply and forever changed by having known him.

According to my probably inept calculations, somewhere around 275 to 436 other people were blessed enough to have been directly encouraged, sheltered by, nurtured, saved, or otherwise mentored into making something of themselves beyond what they ever possibly imagined by either Johnny, June Carter, or a combination of both.

I don't want to imply that my relationship with the Man In Black was by any means detached or impersonal. I don't think that you could be around his special kind of energy and not be affected in the most intimate of ways. My friendship with him had its own kind of seriously private dynamic in that I could never get past the formality of personality that being in the presence of such genius presented.

Johnny Cash did so many amazing things for me, starting with hiring me to play with him when I was so clearly the wrong choice. He gave me a couple of over-the-top gifts, such as a very expensive electric bass guitar.

On a tour we had done in Europe, I was having to rent upright bass instruments from wherever I could. For a BBC show in England, the bass was so rough you could have shot arrows from the strings. Another time, in Vienna, Austria, we rented a late-1700s instrument that was phenomenal. This instrument had been used exclusively for classical music.

When the Johnny Cash Show opened up and I started that boom-chicka-boom rhythm, a man in the fourth row stood up all aghast. It was his instrument, and he was in shock to hear rockabilly music coming from its aged frame. During the intermission, I reassured him that his instrument was being played properly and was well taken care of during the concert.

Anyway, John and June and I were in New York City, and I was window-shopping on Forty-eighth Street at Manny's Music. In the window was this prototype Ampeg Baby Bass, an electronic marvel in sound and size. John and June walked up, and John asked me, "Would that be a good bass for you on the road?" I told him yes, and I walked on thinking nothing of it.

When I got back to my hotel room later that day, there was that bass laying on the bed! John had gone in and bought it for me. It was a very pricey guitar. The funny thing was that on the next European tour, I had used this bass for seven or eight nights with no problems. It sounded great and was so lightweight and easy to transport. This was an electrical bass that emulates the sound of an upright; however, it was not great to look at.

During that tour, Johnny strolls over to me one evening onstage and whispers, "Can you do something with that bass so that I never have to see it again? I just can't get past the way it looks." That was the last time I used it on his tour. Johnny wanted to see an old wooden upright bass guitar, not this modern, bass-shaped, fiberglass electronic marvel.

Toward the end of his life, Johnny Cash included me in his last recorded efforts, even though that may have been the wrong option, with all the musicians at his disposal. To this day, all of that has made me feel special and very aware that he was always so keenly aware of everyone and everything in his environment.

By the year 2002, I had become Dave Roe, the guy that plays that old hillbilly bass. Most of my work now involved the upright bass, in particular the old-style rockabilly- and country-sounding bass. My life had come to a place that would not have happened without Johnny Cash.

On one particular day in 2002, I'm at Johnny's little recording studio, Cedar Hill Refuge, a log cabin in Hendersonville. We're on a break from recording and over a sandwich I get a chance to tell Johnny Cash that I really appreciated the chance he gave me those few years earlier.

Smiling, he looked at me and said, "Dave, you're welcome. I guess I just liked you, and you've done a great job for me." There I was, blessed again. Playing bass on what would end up being his last record. A man who had done what no other artist in pop history had ever done, reinventing himself at the end of his life. Leaving us more popular than ever and leaving me with the ability to keep some of him around.

I was never afforded the time or opportunity to really just hang out with Johnny Cash, like his good friends were lucky enough to do. Ours was a working relationship, which was just as bonding and just as cherished. I got to play rockabilly upright bass with Johnny Cash and, I might add, totally because of him. That does make me one of the 437 luckiest people in the world.

JOHNNY CASH

How do you like the way my pen writes?

Johnny Cash
May 20 1992

MICHELE ROLLINS

Greenville, Delaware

Shoe Size 10 *MEDIUM*

*M*Y INTRODUCTION TO JOHNNY and June Cash occurred in the spring of 1976, when Johnny's good friend John Rollins invited me to attend a Johnny Cash concert at Wolf Trap, Virginia.

I must confess a lack of familiarity with country music or an interest to become more familiar with it at that time. I was a "sophisticated New York City girl" who was not surprised that my mountain-born, north-hills-of-Georgia, soon-to-be-husband was a country music fan and, more importantly, a Johnny Cash friend. Under duress, I took my seat—and for the next two hours laughed, sang, and cheered for a music I had no idea I loved. After the show, I laughed, sang, and cheered for the two people who were so lovable.

Johnny Cash had met John Rollins in 1972, when they arrived in Jamaica and stayed at Round Hill, an elegant resort west of the airport. John and Johnny, both products of rural farm childhoods, were astounded at how much they had in common and how determined they both were to exit farm life while sending money home to improve their family's sparse

160

existence. In later years, June often said it amused her to hear John and Johnny "out poor" each other.

On subsequent visits to Jamaica, they stayed in our guest house at Copperwood on Rose Hall east of Montego Bay. When John Rollins experienced financial difficulties, as often happens several times in the life of very successful entrepreneurs, June asked Johnny, "What can we do to help this wonderful man who has never asked us for anything?"

Johnny's answer was simple: "Let's see if John Rollins will sell us the Cinnamon Hill Great House."

Every plantation had a stone great house where the owner lived, which was set far enough back from the coast so that cannonballs from Spanish pirate ships could not reach it. The Cinnamon Hill

John with Michele and John Rollins on the Cinnamon Hill Golf Course.

Great House, built in the 1700s, was originally the home of the Barretts of Wimpole Street. The Brownings lived on the plantation to the east of Cinnamon Hill, Greenwood Great House, and it is speculated that Elizabeth Barrett Browning may have written some of her best poetry on the veranda of the great house at Cinnamon Hill. The house boasts a hurricane room that I have not seen the likes of anywhere else in the world.

June and Johnny set about making Jamaica their second home. In later years, they referred to Cinnamon Hill as "a place of healing." Johnny often talked about arriving in Jamaica in the fall, pretty beat up after touring the state fair circuit in the summer, and leaving in the spring ready to tackle the performing world again.

It was at the Cinnamon Hill Great House after I had married John Rollins that June related their second introduction to me.

John Rollins had showed them a Ukrainian record album of which I was on the cover in Ukrainian dress—the first Ukrainian-American to be Miss USA. John Rollins said, "I'm going to marry that girl," and June's response was, "You must be kidding."

Knowing that reaction to my album cover, how could June and I become anything but best friends? I recall the day sometime later that she asked me, "How do you know that you are strong enough to be married to John Rollins?" I responded, "How did you know you'd be strong enough to marry Johnny Cash?" She stopped and said, "I just had to." "My sentiments exactly," I told her.

For twenty-five years, we shared New Year's Eve on the beach at Rose Hall—bamboo bonfires crackling like fireworks. They played guitar and we sang with our hearts. Later, at John Rollins's funeral in Delaware, Johnny and June sang the Rollins family through our tremendous loss. Johnny and June sat on the altar singing, and Johnny said, "June, I just can't sing," he was so distraught. June, in her wonderful gentle humor, said, "Don't worry, baby, John Rollins could *never* sing."

June snapped this photo of John at Copperwood, the Rollinses' home in Jamaica.

Johnny and June were godparents to our son, Michael, but June's heart was so large she treated all four of my children as godchildren, and one of John's earlier children as well. Their life was dedicated to the support of young people, and Ted played guitar with them, Michael played flute and sang, Monique sang with June when she was touring to promote *Press On*, and my daughter Michele frequently did their makeup when they made special appearances in Jamaica.

In fact, at the Rose Hall Great House when Johnny Cash was in concert, he referred to the lifestyle of Annee Palmer, "the White Witch," who murdered her husbands and used voodoo to control her slaves while pretending to be civilized, dancing minuets in the evenings. Johnny said

Annee would be shocked to hear his country and rockabilly music on her veranda, so he asked his godson Michael to play some of those minuets on his flute—a very proud moment for me. All of the concerts and appearances Johnny and June performed were for the benefit of the S.O.S. Village on Rose Hall.

On one of Billy Graham's frequent visits to Jamaica, John Rollins introduced Johnny and Billy to Dr. Harlan Hastings, famed surgeon and chief administrator of the Cornwall Regional Hospital. When they visited Dr. Hastings at home, he and his lovely wife, Jennifer, had nine orphans living with them at the time. John said to the Hastings, "This needs to be formalized, and you need some help." They enlisted Heinz Simonitsch, who met with the Austrian organization S.O.S. The S.O.S. Village was on its way. John Rollins donated the land, and Johnny Cash did the first concert, which raised the money for the initial house on the orphanage grounds. Johnny not only sang, he auctioned his guitar and then his shirt. The children of the S.O.S. Village were often in the Cashes' thoughts and prayers as Johnny and June continued to donate time, money, and clothing to the currently existing 100 children in ten buildings.

When word of June's death reached Jamaica, the reaction was shock as we waited to see if Johnny could recover the loss of his soulmate. Johnny threw himself into recording at a frantic pace and recorded over fifty songs after June's death, including the song he sang with his daughter Rosanne on her new album, "September When It Comes." When September came, Johnny joined June. The prime minister conferred with me as to how best to salute these world-famous "Jamericans." The prime minister had already canceled one celebration for Johnny and June in January 2003, when he was scheduled to present them with the Order of

John Rollins and John Cash relax on the porch of the Lewes, Delaware, beach home home of Randall and Peggy Rollins.

John and June with the Rollins family. Top, from left: John Rollins, wife Michele, daughter Michele, son Marc, daughter Monique. Bottom: Michael Rollins, godson of June and Johnny Cash; June and John; and Tiffany Anastasia Lowe, June's granddaughter and daughter of singer Carlene Carter.

Jamaica, the highest honor that could be bestowed on a person in Jamaica. They had to leave for health reasons. The prime minister decided that he wanted to bestow that honor posthumously at Air Jamaica's Jazz & Blues Festival, where the Cash family and friends had agreed to do a musical tribute to Johnny and June.

On January 23, 2004, on the grounds of the Cinnamon Hill Great House, 12,000 people stood and cheered and sang with Larry Gatlin as he sang the song he wrote for Johnny the night he heard Johnny had died, "A Man Can't Live With a Broken Heart Too Long," and Jimmy Tittle sang "Jackson" with June's fabulously talented daughter Carlene. John Carter and Laura sang medleys of Johnny's songs, and the tribute opened with a video, *Hi, I'm Johnny Cash* and Johnny's recording of "Annee Palmer, The White Witch of Rose Hall," that neighboring great house where things just weren't right. He first recorded it on a 45 record, and we sold it at the Rose Hall Great House, all of the proceeds going to the S.O.S. Village.

When the 45 record went out of style, I became worried that we would lose the benefit of Johnny's recording of "Annee Palmer." I asked him to record it one more time when he was performing at the University of Delaware. He had become popular with college-age students once again. I gently requested that he sing the "Annee Palmer" song when he rehearsed that afternoon. In a very uncharacteristic dramatic pause, he looked down at me and said ominously, softly, "Michele, I don't rehearse." I remembered thinking "Oh, my word, ten years of friendship down the drain." When he laughed and repeated "Michele, I don't rehearse, but why don't you video-tape the show and I'll sing it in the show," it was a double thrill for me since it meant videotaping Michael Rollins as he played his flute and sang backup with June.

The S.O.S. Village children were never far from their minds, and when Johnny died, the family requested that donations, in lieu of flowers, be sent to the S.O.S. Village.

On the night of the tribute when I went backstage, my son Marc called to my attention a group of the S.O.S. Village children immaculately dressed and in attendance to salute their mentors and benefactors, Johnny and June. Why not? I remembered all of them sitting quietly on the veranda of the Rose Hall Great House above the stage where Johnny and June performed in prior years. In fact, they had attended every concert the Cashes had performed. Why would they not appear on the night of their tribute?

Marc gave me the look that said "Make it happen!" and after the prime minis-ter presented the award to John Carter Cash, the only son and only child of Johnny and June, and Minister Asamba presented all five of the Cash and Carter offspring with a portrait of the Cinnamon Hill Great House, and after the musical tribute by the family and friends of the Cashes, I went onstage to thank everyone who

Michael Rollins and June sing backup for John on the steps of the Rose Hall Great House.

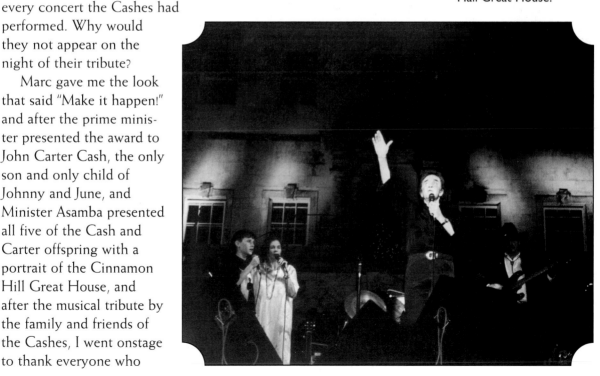

John Rollins and John
plotting and planning—
"Best Friends."

had participated. I had the children en masse follow me onstage.

The Cashes could have escaped to any destination in the world, and they chose lush, tropical, beautiful Jamaica, and I had to introduce the audience to the reasons for Johnny and June's love for Jamaica: "It was the people of Jamaica, and I have some of these young people with me tonight," I said, "the children of the S.O.S. Village."

At that moment, the children were cued to smile broadly and wave to the audience. Their beautiful faces were the hit of the evening, and we had indeed paid tribute to Jamaica's own Johnny and June Cash.

Following the family tribute, Kenny Rogers dazzled the audience as he performed his many hits, including several of Johnny's songs in his honor.

Johnny and June were world-renowned music legends, but the Johnny and June of Cinnamon Hill were warm, wonderful, fabulous friends, whether we were eating two pounds of bacon at breakfast in earlier years or cheddar cubes dipped in raw sugar at tea time—"a Southern dish," June called it—right!

The Cashes said they came to Jamaica to heal, but in fact they came to heal us. They healed everyone around them with huge doses of unconditional love. When I ride my golf cart, as we did so often, I will always feel their presence in my heart and around the Great House of Cinnamon Hill. Johnny and June could never be just a memory.

TED ROLLINS

Pompano Beach, Florida

Shoe Size 12 MEDIUM

*C*ALL ME JOHN. Mr. Cash lives up the hill in the other house, and he's my daddy." Then in the blink of an eye, he threw down the throttle on the boat and we were gliding across Old Hickory Lake like the wind. It's pretty amazing to be a boy of ten and have a forty-year-old to hang out with, and that's the way it was for me for the next thirty-one years of my life. I had a truer friend than you can ever imagine—one that I could tell anything to and not be judged. One who would laugh with me at things most people couldn't even get their head around. And, someone who would lead me in my spiritual growth as I came along in life. My eulogy (one of many) at his funeral really summed it up for me:

> Words cannot describe what a wonderful man John R. Cash was. He was a brother in arms that stood tall by your side through thick and thin. He was a partner in crime when you could no longer hold back the urge to raise a little cane (I really wanted to use the word hell here because that is really what it was, but we were in church). He stood up for what was right no matter what the cost. He was a wise

counselor and a great storyteller. He taught you to appreciate all things and had an uncanny ability to show it you through his eyes. He was a warm and loving father, grandfather, and husband who was just a kid at heart. And he was the truest Christian and disciple of Christ I have ever known. He loved unconditionally. He lived unconditionally. And not only did he touch our souls—he lit them on *fire*.

Well, he really did light my soul on fire. I came to know John when my parents were divorced about three years after we first met. He had a gig up by our home in Delaware, and I decided that I would help with whatever I could while he was up in our area. So, I began helping them each day carry all their bags and things from where they were staying to the theater where they performed each night. Kind of a self-appointed roadie. Well, John and June observed this every day for almost a week, and when it was time for them to travel to the next town, John said, "Um, Ted—son—why don't you just come along with us for the rest of the summer and help out on the road?" In a euphoric haze, I am sure that I managed to get the words "Yes, sir" out, but all I can remember is packing my clothes and heading to the next stop on the tour, Wolf Trap, Virginia.

Days blurred and before I knew it, I was on a plane back to school for the fall. I repeated this year after year, and year after year I started to perform a little bit more. It gets in your blood, the road. I have been places I never would have imagined with John. We have had many laughs. John was such a wonderful man, and as Kris Kristofferson put it, he was like "Abraham Lincoln with a wild side." I would like to share with you several of the wild-side stories as well as a couple of the Abraham Lincoln stories.

We were on the road in Iowa, I believe Des Moines, and I was just a kid of sixteen at the time. John had asked me to take the rental car and go to the store and pick up some things, and told me that when I got back to wait in the car and that he would be down and I could drive him over to the venue. Well, I went to the store and returned and sat there waiting for a while (which was hard for me to do at sixteen) and happened to notice this pesky little stone chip in the windshield. To pass the time, I decided, in my full-on youthful exuberance, to take my hand and see if I could beat on the stone chip until the window cracked a little. I cannot even imagine what I was thinking, other than it might be entertaining.

I beat the window a few times with my fist, and sure enough, the windshield began to crack. About that time, John came down and got in the passenger side of the car. He said to me "Uh, Ted, who made this crack in the windshield?" And I was sitting there thinking, *Man, I hope he doesn't get mad and fire me.* I managed to eke out the words "Uh, John, it was me," and waited to take my medicine. Then I watched with a thrill as he said, "Well, you didn't do a very good job," and took his hand and beat on that windshield until the crack ran clear across the glass. It was at that point I realized I had a soulmate/partner in crime and a true friend.

These types of things happened regularly with us, especially when we would sneak off by ourselves. John taught me every day about the freedom of the road and how you could learn something from everyone. Oh, and the pleasures that come with a little rowdy activity now and again.

Another time we went to Jamaica to stay at Cinnamon Hill, his restored great house. We decided to take the rental car out for a spin and got into a little bit of trouble. By this time I had spent several years on and off with John and had started to get the groove. So, one day we were driving down the road itching to get into something, and I saw this Jamaican roadblock and said to John, "It sure would be bad if we were to just swerve a little and hit that roadblock with this rental car, J. R." He said, "You know, Ted, that roadblock is really calling out to me." With that, we both buckled up our seatbelts and decided that it would be best to hit the roadblock.

Well, when we hit that roadblock, one of the boards came in the window and hit John in the nose and he stopped the car. His nose was bleeding a river of blood, and he turned to me real calm and said, "Looks like I won't be scuba diving tomorrow. Maybe we ought to get back home and put a bandage on my nose and let June look at it." With that, we headed home, and June and I helped John straighten his nose back out and put a

bandage on it. He said he was glad that it broke because it had broken before and did not heal straight and that this would give him the chance to put it back the way he wanted. A few days later, we were on the way back to the U.S., and John had decided to tie a bandana around his face, like a train robber in an old western, to hide his nose. We traveled like that for about a week. He even performed with the bandage on his nose. He just had us color it in with makeup.

We got into more things than I have time to write, but we also had more talking times and visits where he would teach me about life. We would sit and talk about things, like my parents' divorce, when I would tell him about my troubles with that. He would offer sage advice and keep my confidence. I can recall another time, when I grew older, he decided to take me to a church that he had been attending in Tennessee. Coming from Delaware, I had never really been exposed to the evangelical-type churches of the South. John thought that it would be a good idea for me to go to church with them, so I did. At the time, June had a cousin that I was hanging around named Dickie Joyner, and Dickie was spending the night Saturday and then going to church with us the next day. Well, Dickie must have been to this church before because he spent the entire night and the next morning warning me about the church. He would say, "Ted, man, you have no idea—this is going to be a different experience!" I said, "Come on, Dickie, how bad can it be? It's just a church, and I have never had any problem going to church."

He said, "You just don't understand; but whatever you do, don't raise your hand." I thought, *You know, that is a little bit different.* "Whatever you do don't raise your hand" was never any thing that I had heard when going to church. *This might be interesting.* Dickie continued with his warnings as we rode to the church with John and June. We sat down, and John looked at me and smiled, while Dickie just sat there with a worried look on his face. The church was fairly normal-looking, like most churches, I suppose. The

service was, too, until we got to the end and the
preacher started yelling and carrying on like I had
never seen before. At that point, Dickie put his
elbow in me as if to say "See, I told you that this
was going to be different." But I was with John, so I
did not worry—and what happened next was the
most interesting thing.

The preacher started talking and telling people
to raise their hands if they wanted to be saved. He
went on and on and finally said, "You know, the
Devil is telling you not to raise your hand." And
with that, I thought to myself, *Nobody is going to tell
me not to do something—especially the Devil.* So, I raised
my hand and watched Dickie's eyes get as big as two
bowling balls. Well, the preacher said, "OK, those of you with your hands
raised, come on down front."

I got a little worried at this point, but John and June walked me down
the aisle and started with about fifteen other people to pray and put there
hands on my shoulders and head and kept asking me if I felt anything and
if I was saved. I never had been saved, I guess—until that day when all that
happened. I finally said that I felt something, and they all started to shout
(except John) and I got up and we went home.

When we got home, John sat down with me and explained what had
happened and said, "Ted, I am so proud of you for accepting Jesus into
your life." That was the seed that John planted and that has grown in me
for the last twenty-five years of my life. He then took me out in the boat
on Old Hickory Lake with June and a couple of other people and baptized
me in the water of Old Hickory at sunset. I can still remember this like it
was yesterday.

He continued to teach me throughout the years about the soul and being
a good Christian, which was a way of life more than anything. I could always
count on his wise counsel and ways when I hit a crossroads in my life.

So, not only could we raise hell together, we could also ask for forgive-
ness together. We bonded. As the years went by, I went off on various

paths, to college and to graduate school and ultimately to work in various places, but I never felt more at home than with John on the road or at home. In fact, I would occasionally go out on the road or to see John at his home when life got hectic. It would always restore my mind.

He had a unique way of looking at things. Like eating candy—he would say, "You know, if you eat it after eight o'clock at night, Ted, it doesn't count." We would sit around and make up lyrics to songs about people that we had met that day.

Carlene Carter, Jimmy Tittle, Ted Rollins, and John Carter Cash at the 2004 Johnny Cash memorial concert in Jamaica.

A few years ago, I went to visit John in Jamaica, and we started talking. Then he said, "Lets go for a golf-cart ride." We rode for a few minutes down the mountainside of Jamaica, looking at the Caribbean Sea.

Then he showed me where we could get golf balls that had been hit into the rough at the golf course. We collected a cart full of golf balls and then decided that we need to create a sport. *Create a sport.* How many people think of that on any given day, especially with a golf cart and balls? We decided that we would lay the golf balls out on the fairway (never mind that there were people playing golf) and that he would drive the cart as fast as he could and I would hang off the side and with one hand hold onto the cart and with the other grab up the golf balls we had laid out in our own version of a golf-ball slalom course. The name of this sporting event is Ball Busters. We got so good at this that afternoon that we even thought we might try to petition the Olympics to add an event. At seventy years old, he had the spirit of a sixteen-year-old.

For the record, I would like to say that there was nothing that John loved more than his children and grandchildren and great grandchildren. I cannot remember a time that we spoke that he would not refer to them:

"You know, Ted, I am so proud of Rosanne [or John Carter or Cindy or Tara or Kathy]," he would say and then would speak of the things that they were doing.

Sometimes I would come stay in the cabin he had over in White House, Tennessee. John loved this cabin and always got excited when I stayed there. He would say, "Ted, doesn't that cabin just put you at ease?" He loved to spend time there. As he grew older, it was harder and harder for him to go there. One night I was coming into the cabin for the night and he had been there to check on it. He left me a bag of parched peanuts and the note that I have attached here. He wanted to make sure that I had something to eat and had left me a sackful of peanuts that he had parched.

The last time I saw John, after June had died, he was not feeling too well. We sat there and talked, and it seemed that he had lost his spirit. This drove me crazy because most of my spirit that I had developed was planted by John. So I said, "J. R., what you need is a little sunlight." He said, "I really would like to see the sun. I have been cooped up in this place for a long time now."

The only problem was that the hospital would not let us take him outside. So we did what we needed to and broke out of the hospital. This caused quite a stir, but it was worth it. I rolled John in his wheelchair to a place in the sunshine and let him soak it up, and it was as if his batteries were being charged. He came to life, and we sat there and talked until the sun set. This is the last memory I have of my friend John: sitting, washed in the warm orange glow of the setting sun on a back portico of Baptist Hospital. This was the last time we connected and told stories and shared a laugh.

There was nothing that I would not have done for John. He was one of the greatest influences in my life. He taught me about love, friendship, family, and myself. I truly miss him and will carry a piece of him with me wherever I go.

FERN SALYER

Maces Springs, Virginia

Shoe Size 8 *NARROW*

*T*HE FIRST TIME I met Johnny Cash was in the spring of 1963. He was sitting at the kitchen table at Uncle Grant's, eating fried chicken. John and June had been on tour and came by for John to visit June's Virginia homeplace and meet her people. They were also looking up information about the Wilderness Road for a song June was working on, "Road to Kaintuck."

I remember those piercing eyes that seemed to search your soul. He was very polite and mannerly, a trait of the Cashes I later learned. He was so intelligent and listened so intensely, I felt intimidated. I knew he was no ordinary man.

My husband, Walt, who was in the Air Force in the 1950s, first saw Johnny along with Elvis at the Louisiana Hayride. Johnny had just released "Hey Porter" and "Cry, Cry, Cry" at Sun Records on 45s. He said to me, "Listen to this; this man's gonna be really big." The deep, deep voice and the chick-a-boom sound was so different. I said, "It's on the wrong speed." He told Johnny later, and I never lived that down. Johnny didn't have all of those 45 originals as Walt did. He offered them to him, but Johnny said that he'd like to have them but to give them to our son.

Another time they came by excitedly carrying a 45 that hadn't been released, "Long-Legged Guitar Picking Man," and wanting us to listen. June had written or helped write it. It wouldn't play until Johnny put a nickel on the needle arm. We thought it was great.

On a Sunday afternoon around 1967, June and John came rushing in yelling, "We're starved!" June told John, "We'll go to Fern's. She always has something cooked." I had been to my mom's and hadn't cooked at all. I had to cook something fast. I hurriedly cooked sausage, fried apples, gravy, eggs, and biscuits. It seemed everywhere they stopped, no one had cooked that day. Thirty-five years later, Johnny was still talking about that food being so good. It was the worst food I ever cooked. It was awful! He was just very hungry.

John and June with Fern Salyer.

A little later, Phil, my oldest son, was looking at Johnny's belt and buckle. Johnny said, "Son, do you like that belt?" Of course Phil, who was seven, said he did. Johnny took the belt off and said, "You can have it." June said, "Johnny, ain't that your Folsom Prison belt the boys in prison made for you?" Johnny said, "Yes, but he wanted it." Of course, I didn't let Phil take it. Johnny told the boys—Phil, age seven; Joey, three; and Shane, one—that he would bring them a belt the next time he came up.

Several years later, they were on their way up, and Johnny told June he had to stop and get three belts. Here he comes up the walk carrying three long belts. He calls each kid up, measures each belt to fit, cuts it off, and makes three lifelong friends. They all are avid Johnny Cash and June Carter Cash fans and have everything they've recorded. What a nice thing it was for a man of his stature to remember a promise to kids that might be so unimportant to others.

On one of their trips to Maces Springs, Virginia, my grandson and I were waiting for their arrival to greet them. Marcus, six years old, excitedly ran up to Johnny and asked him if he had his guitar and if would he play "Don't Take Your Guns to Town." Johnny said, "Yes. Marcus, do you have a guitar?" Marcus said, "No, why don't you get me one?" John said, "I will."

A trip to Maces Springs meant a trip to Walter Mead's Antiques in Nickelsville. Here comes Johnny out of Mead's carrying a guitar. He said, "I finally found one with a neck small enough for Marcus." I told him Marcus would have been happy with a toy. He said, "Give him a toy and he'll treat it like a toy!" Another kept promise!

Then there were the New York trips. June needed to go for dental work. John didn't want her to go alone. Mom was ill; I had a cold and felt the timing was wrong. June said, "I'll have John talk to you." I went to New York! The memories of being in New York with June are precious. I believe John did it for me as well as for June. He'd always say, "Thank you for taking care of my baby." I felt honored that he trusted me to take care of the most treasured thing in his life.

John and June loved to perform at the Carter Family Fold; an old-time music facility established in 1976 in honor of the Carter Family by Janette and Joe Carter, children of A. P. and Sarah. John was always very supportive of the Fold and gave many concerts there. When his health forced him from the road, his only live performances were at the Fold. The people here loved him so much that if all he did were walk on the stage, he'd get a standing ovation and make the audience's day. They loved the man as well as the entertainer. He would always say, "It's good to be home."

One late afternoon while at the Virginia home, June and I walked around the hill at the foot of the mountain to Grandma's house, a trail June and I did many times as children. We stopped and looked at the tall trees we had played under years ago. It was one of those "do you remember" walks. We were so engrossed with our memory walk that we didn't notice dark was catching up. Johnny wasn't able to go, but he became worried about us. He had gone a little way and was waiting for us.

John needed to return home for an appointment, and June wanted to stay longer. John asked me if I would bring her home a few days later. Johnny went home with the help, and I stayed with June and took her home a few days later. We stopped at the Haggle shops, of course, on our way. John called often to see if we were OK and warn us about a severe storm heading our way. When we got to Gallatin, Tennessee, we could see these dark clouds hovering over us. John called again. June said, "John, we're in the storm. Fern is feeling for the road. We can't see, and I'm praying." When we arrived at the house, John was waiting outside with two large umbrellas. He also had supper for us. We had three wonderful days preparing for John Carter and Laura's tea prior to their wedding.

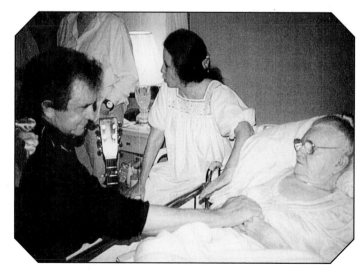

John and June visit June's aunt Ora Carter, offering comfort and a few songs to lift her spirits.

I can't end this chapter without sharing June's special birthday party with you. She really wanted all of their children and grandchildren to come for a week. John and I worked very hard for this. Their houses were full, tents and campers all over. On the Friday before her birthday on Sunday, he had a special night to honor all of their grandchildren and other special ones, including mine. We had a luncheon at the Mount Vernon United Methodist Church shelter on June's birthday, June 23. This church was very special to June and John. It was a State Historical Landmark because the Carters attended there. June said, "This is the best birthday I have ever had."

She had all of her family and relatives with her at home. John made this one of the most special days in her

John's final live perform-
ance, June 21, 2003, at
Carter Fold with son
John Carter.

entire life. She came back the next year on her birthday, too. It was great,
but she didn't have all of her family here. She called me just before her
heart surgery and said, "I'll see you in June on my birthday, and all of my
birthdays from now on will be in Virginia. John told me so." She didn't
make her birthday in Virginia in 2003. God gave her the best birthday gift
of all—He took her to her heavenly home. Johnny came though, just like
he said. He came with June's spirit and a suitcase full of memories, with the
promise to her, "I'll see you soon!"

All of these things I have shared with you are things in my life that
have made me so fond of this generous and caring man who was so much
greater because of his faith in God. I feel so honored to share some of my
most precious memories of John R. Cash. Yes, I still miss someone.

TARA CASH SCHWOEBEL

Portland, Oregon

Shoe Size 10

The Lessons I Learned from My Father

*Ice cream tastes so much better after being churned
on the front porch of an old home in the country,
surrounded by a lot of loved ones.*

*It is far better to pile into a Jeep with ten others,
singing "Children Go Where I Send Thee,"
than it is to watch television.*

*You will never find arrowheads in an old creek bed
if you don't spend a lot of quiet time looking for them.*

*Watermelon tastes better
with salt on it.*

*Mistletoe is abundant in the woods,
and it's free, if you have a shotgun.*

*Silence and humming can say volumes more
than words.*

Always throw the small perch back.

It's always best to end a fine day
with a bowl of ice cream.

Always talk to your worm
when baiting a hook with it.

Whenever passing cows, always greet them.

Stick to the rules, then break them.

If something is stolen from you, let it go,
then buy forty of them to replace it,
and put them everywhere.

Children should skinny dip and catch fireflies.

Sometimes your closet can be
the coziest place in the world.

There really is such a thing as comfort foods,
and you should have them every day.

Chili tastes better when cooked
at sixty miles per hour.

Expect to be respected.

Always kiss your babies on the lips.

If you see clean, clear water trickling out of
a mountain, always stop and take a drink.

When you order soft serve ice cream at a drive-thru,
you must eat it in under three minutes.

Wearing black really does make you look thinner.

If you don't like something on your body,
take out your pocket knife and change it.

You're never too old to be cool.

MAURY SCOBEE

Montreat, North Carolina

Shoe Size 10¹/₂ D

*T*HIS IS THE FIRST time I have ever been asked to write my thoughts about any friend of mine! I was shocked, yet thrilled, when Hugh Waddell called to ask me to be a part of this collection of fond memories of this giant of a man Johnny Cash!

A verse in the Bible says that, as Christians, our steps are ordered by the Lord (Psalm 37:23). Throughout my life thus far, I have seen this happen many times over, and that's really, I believe, how I had the wonderful opportunity to meet June and Johnny Cash.

I grew up in East Texas, an oil town in the piney woods of Texas called Longview. We moved away in the late 1950s when my dad got a job in Kansas. His other job moves took us to Missouri and Mississippi, but a few years after that, I found myself back in Texas again. It was now the late 1960s there in Longview, and I was going to LeTourneau College, which specialized in business, engineering, welding, and aviation. I was studying engineering, and after a couple years of school, I bumped into Franklin Graham, son of evangelist Billy Graham, at the college post office. We became friends.

Maury Scobee with
Ruth and Billy Graham.

There's another one of those examples of my steps being ordered by the Lord, I think! Somehow, a couple years later, Franklin felt I might be the person to consider moving to North Carolina to help his mother and father. Not being ready to commit myself to accept some jobs when they were being offered after college, I turned down lots of great work experiences because the people, when they interviewed me, talked of where I would be in five years or ten years. That was it for me, since I could never imagine working for anyone that long, and I would graciously turn down their offer.

When the Grahams called me to prayerfully consider coming to help them, they thought that we should look at only six months, in case after that length of time they might not like me or I might not really like working for them. So, sure enough, it was the right terminology in my book, and I accepted their request to come and help them and moved to western North Carolina in the spring of 1977. After a month, Reverend Graham held one of his Crusades in the new civic center in Asheville, North Carolina, seventeen miles from his Montreat home.

All sorts of Christian musicians over the years were invited to come and sing on the same platform where Billy Graham preached at these Crusades, and guess who were the first such artists I met? June and Johnny Cash! Little did I know that our paths would cross many, many times in various situations over the years and bring us together to become friends. By the way, my six months has now stretched out to over twenty-seven years, and June and Johnny always appreciated the fact that I really put my own life on hold to serve the Lord by serving the Grahams all these years.

Mahalia Jackson, an old black gospel singer, once had a hit song called "I'm Gonna Live the Life I Sing About." Many times we hear about or read about today's singers who happen to be Christians, and how they live the life they sing about. I observed how Johnny and June lived out their Christian faith and lives!

Soon after Johnny's jawbone got broken, and his mouth was wired shut for all those months in 1988, he was sitting at home by himself, as June was off on a trip somewhere. While he was eating breakfast and reading the morning paper, he saw where Reverend Graham had had emergency surgery to remove a rib at the Mayo Clinic in Rochester, Minnesota. Johnny figured I had accompanied Reverend and Mrs. Graham to the Clinic and called a few hotels and sure enough tracked me down! He told me he wanted to come up and visit Reverend Graham for a few minutes and pray for him, to assure him of how concerned he was for Reverend Graham, yet how much he loved and admired him too!

He asked me to reserve him a hotel room and said he would call me again when he arrived and got checked in. Later he told me that he had called the airline himself, booked a flight himself, and he was ready to jump on the commercial flight and come see the Grahams. Here was a man who was really suffering from the pain of dealing with the recovery and healing of his broken jaw, yet he was willing to travel alone (and being as well known as he was, it wouldn't be easy) to come pray for the Grahams! That really impressed me but also showed me that there was more to his faith and life than most people might think. It's one thing to sing about doing God's will, and it's quite another thing to actually live the life you are singing about!

Another similar situation happened with June. She happened to be home by herself (Johnny was traveling on the road someplace) and read about Mrs. Graham being in the

Sunday, October 30, 1994 4:00pm

Calendar-wise, this is the last day of the Crusade. It is not, however, the end, but rather the beginning. Let us leave as an army of compassionate people. Let us proclaim Christ and His love as the answer to the deepest human need. Let us go back to our homes with a new dedication, with a new discipline, to pray and to live Christ.

Johnny and June Cash

Sook Lee

Johnny and June are known and loved by audiences throughout the world. They demonstrate a superb ability to communicate with people of all ages and backgrounds. They have participated in numerous Crusades over the years.

Johnny has placed 26 albums on the Pop Charts since 1955 and has been honored with 23 B.M.I. Songwriting Awards. To many people, Johnny Cash symbolizes America. His hit "Ragged Old Flag" has been one of the most requested from his fans.

Soprano Sung Sook Lee is an extraordinarily talented artist whose impeccable performances in opera, with symphony orchestras, and in recitals, have ranked her as one of the world's finest singers.

After completing her formal training at the Juilliard School on full scholarship, she was immediately catapulted into a brilliant international career.

In 1985, Sung Sook felt led to give up her opera career and has been involved in a concert ministry, glorifying God through the singing of great sacred literature and hymns. She makes her home in Atlanta, Georgia.

hospital with meningitis. She immediately came by herself to the hospital in Asheville without calling anyone and sat in the lobby praying for Ruth, hoping she could get hold of one of Reverend Graham's staff or family members to find out Ruth's room number so she could go in and hug her and pray for her! The hospital employee who was working the welcome desk that day recognized June Carter Cash and got word through the hospital security to Mrs. Graham's hospital room, and someone—I've forgotten who—went right to the hospital lobby and found June on her knees praying.

On many occasions, I drove Mr. and Mrs. Cash to and from the airport when they came to visit the Grahams or on their many visits to Reverend Graham's Crusades. Riding in a car has always been something I have

---

Greetings—
June
Popcorn

For 25 years I've been a professional Entertainer. My personal life and my personal problems have been widely publicized. There have been things said about me that made people ask "Is Johnny Cash really a Christian?"

I take comfort in the writings of Paul who said, "What I will to do, that I do not practice." "But what I hate, I do." And he said, "It is no longer I who do it but the sin that dwells in me." "But who," he asks "will deliver me from this body of death? And he answers for himself and for me, "Jesus Christ our Lord."

I am living through the grace of my Lord Jesus Christ. I believe in Him. He is Lord. I Love Him. Still, believing is not enough. James said "Faith without works is dead. Even the demons believe"

I spend a lot of my time working with drug addicts and alcoholics! Only someone who has had such a problem can have complete love, compassion and understanding for such people. I love drug addicts and alcoholics and I think God is trying to use me to help them.

When Jesus said He was sent to heal the broken hearted and preach deliverance to the captives I believe these are some of the people he was talking about.

If some lost, lonely person somewhere out there on a dirty bed in a dark room can see the light of Jesus Christ in me, that is my reward. My faith is alive and working.—And I'm not just eating Billy Graham's popcorn.

But to get to be here tonight is not just the popcorn, but the icing on the Christian Cake. I love to hear Billy preach and I love this Choir.——— I want to do an old country gospel song called Family Bible, and before I do I want to tell you that I've just recorded the whole new testament. This did more for me spiritually than anything in years. I've always loved the word, but to read the entire new testament aloud showed me a new dimension in the Word. The spoken word. What power there is in the word. What beauty and depth. For an example, here is some of my private scripture. Mark 8:27—end

Family Bible

loved doing over the years since it's so relaxed and the conversation is good. So, I always cherished those times that I drove John and June and some of their family or staff anywhere. They were always so gracious and kind and loving and fun, and always had interesting things to talk about.

Most times when the Cash party were to arrive in a Crusade city, we came to the airport in one or two or more vehicles since they would invite friends or family at the last minute to join them on the trip to the Billy Graham Crusade. It was always great to meet the various ones John and June would bring along.

We were in Portland, Oregon, I believe, and John and June had come a day early and stayed a day later just to be with the Grahams a little longer. I had planned to take them to the airport, and it seems to my memory that they only had one other person with them on this trip, and it may have been Hugh Waddell. At the last minute, Reverend Graham said he would like to ride to the airport with us. I left the car on the curb at the front of the airport, hoping I wouldn't get a ticket or be towed while we went inside. Reverend Graham and June wandered down to the waiting area, while I helped John and Hugh get checked in.

We walked in there to join them, and I was checking out the crowd in a careful way looking out for not only Reverend Graham but for John and June as well. There was an excited "teens to twenties" girl walking toward Johnny, so thrilled to have recognized him and yet so overcome by the whole scene that she blurted out, "Mr. Autograph, can I have your Cash?"

Of course, we all joined in the laughter after what was said. I had actually reminded Reverend Graham about this incident for the comments he made for John's funeral, and since he didn't quote it, I wanted to include this story here. I called Lou Robin, John's longtime manager, to ask him if he'd ever heard of this happening before, and he laughed and said no. Then I e-mailed the story to John's daughter Rosanne, and she loved the story and also said she'd never heard of it happening before. I was afraid it might have happened a number of times. In March of 1993, John and June were having a party to celebrate their twenty-fifth wedding anniversary. The Grahams had been invited, and I am blessed to say that I was invited, too. Reverend Graham was out of town, but I flew over with Mrs. Graham, since we had a convenient nonstop American Airlines flight from Asheville to Nashville. The Cashes wanted Ruth to stay right at the big house with them, and I had planned to drop Mrs. Graham off and go down the street to a motel close by. As we honked at the gate to their house and drove in the driveway, we had to dodge people who were bringing in unbelievable arrangements of flowers.

The card June had in her hand was a congratulations from Elizabeth Taylor! After we hugged June and unloaded Mrs. Graham's things, June said for me to go across the driveway and stay in the small guesthouse that they called "the Wardrobe." Johnny walked in the foyer to greet Ruth and me as June explained that, basically, it was a walk-in closet with a bed in the middle where most all of the outfits that she and Johnny had worn over the years onstage were safely stored. John said it was fine for me in the middle of the night, if I couldn't sleep for some reason, to flip through the various outfits and boots and try on something to parade around in before going back to bed. Wow, what an honor and an experience!

At the sit-down dinner for several hundred friends, I relaxed and enjoyed the occasion for a little while, then decided to hang out in the kitchen area and visit with the household staff that had helped John and June for years, just in case I could maybe help them out. I had met a couple of them on a previous trip when I popped in to say hello to John and June. The staff were all absolutely wonderful, and I began to love them even more that evening, not only for how much fun they were to visit with but also in appreciation that they had dedicated themselves to help John and June over many years.

Most people are familiar with Johnny's autobiography, *Man In Black*, which was a bestseller, but he also researched and did a marvelous biography of Paul the Apostle, called *Man In White*.

He and June were on tour while he was writing a lot of that book. They noticed that two of their concert cities were near where the Grahams lived, and as good friends do, they called to see if they could come stay with the Grahams, even an extra night, since they had a night off from touring. Of course, the Grahams said definitely! The only hitch was that the Grahams would be out of town, but John and June were still welcome to use the house. I drove down to the Greenville, South Carolina, concert with Reverend Graham's secretary and brought them straight back to the Grahams' house in Montreat, where they rested most all the next day, just the two of them at the house. (Three of us were down the hall, staying out of their way, in case they needed anything, though.) When they performed their concert in Asheville the next night, they gave our entire office tickets and backstage passes so they would able to meet them all. It was so special!

After the three nights' stay, we were driving from the Grahams' house to the hotel to join the concert tour bus for them to continue their tour. Johnny mentioned to me that there had been two or three difficult chapters for him to write and finish, and he had been concerned about that.

John and June with Reverend Billy and Ruth Graham.

However, during these few days while they were at the Grahams' house by themselves, and with Johnny sitting at Reverend Graham's desk, Johnny completed those last chapters and was thrilled beyond words.

While John was seriously working on his book, June was going throughout the house being her normal fun self. I am sure that the yellow Post-It notes had just come out, and every single day June wrote and stuck a note somewhere in the house for Mrs. Graham to find. She stuck those notes all over the house where they were visible and not visible. Mrs. Graham found those notes for weeks afterwards!

After the book came out, I am sure Johnny must have done quite a number of book signings at both Christian and secular bookstores. He joined Reverend Graham for the Crusade in Columbia, South Carolina, in 1987, I believe, and stayed over the next day to spend several hours at a local Christian bookstore. I thought that would be interesting for some of the Grahams' grandchildren who were there visiting the Crusade, so I took them to the bookstore. When we arrived, the bookstore was completely surrounded with people—literally lined up against the walls of the store, all the way around, waiting in line to meet Johnny Cash and get their book signed! I know Hugh will remember that occasion. We looked around for a back door and came inside with the grandkids to stand around and watch him visit patiently with each person or group of persons. He was so nice to each one.

On an occasion when the Country Music Hall of Fame was honoring Johnny with an official exhibit, he called to invite us all to come over. I said the Grahams were out of town, but he urged me to come on anyway, which I did. It was a special event, rubbing elbows with all sorts of people from Nashville. After the program, and as Johnny and June made their way through the crowd to a reception, they spotted me and came out of their way to hug me and greet me! Moments later, the HBO English comedienne Tracey Ullman came up to me and asked if I could take her to meet the legendary Cash couple, which I did. As they chatted a few moments, Tracey handed me a cheap Polaroid camera and posed with Johnny and June. I sure hope that picture thrives with the vivid colors of their first meeting! I don't know if she ever was with them again.

In closing, I don't remember exactly when this happened, but at some point a few years ago, I was brave enough to ask Johnny what cologne he was wearing. Of course, he was happy to tell me it was called One Man Show. It took me a while to find my own bottle, which I still have. I thought, *How fitting and ironic that this giant of a music icon would wear a cologne that typifies his life, One Man Show.* That bottle of One Man Show still smells great today, and I recently thought that, like that fine cologne, the fragrance of Johnny's life is also preserved and still lingers.

Most importantly, though, I have said a prayer of thanksgiving to the Lord that He positioned me to have crossed paths with Johnny Cash, and I am blessed to say that he was my friend and I was his friend.

ANTO SEPETJIAN

Beverly Hills, California

Shoe Size 8

*T*HE FIRST TIME I met Johnny Cash was around 1988, when we bought Nat Wise's business and client list. Johnny came in like anyone else and introduced himself to me and my family. It took me some time to think about Mr. Cash and to remember his first presence in the store when I took it over. Nat had called us a year earlier, when he wanted to retire. He told us, "I think you're the only ones to do the type of work I do, with quality and to the customer's satisfaction." I had my own shop in Beverly Hills, but to acquire Nat Wise's name and reputation along with his shop, well, my two sons, Ken and Jack, and me were glad to accept.

On Johnny's first visit after we took over the business, my daughter was there, and she told Mr. Cash that she was at a Billy Graham Crusade in July of 1985, where he had appeared giving his testimony and he and June also sang. He took my daughter aside and spoke to her for a while about how important God is and how honored he felt being there. She was speechless that a man of great fame and status could speak to her like that—to be so real and personal and down to earth.

We have encountered and worked with many celebrities. We changed the name of the business to Anto Distinguished Shirtmakers and continued

the Nat Wise brand. When we looked over Nat's client list, it was a who's who of great men of entertainment. From the late Frank Sinatra, and Sammy Davis Jr. to Jerry Lewis, Jay Leno, Arnold Schwarzenegger, President Ronald Reagan, Eddie Murphy, Christopher Walken, Al Pacino, and Tommy Lee Jones. And Johnny Cash. There is only one of him. His voice was so different and so recognized and loved. We made his shirts, but we were still fans!

Johnny had started coming to be fitted for shirts from Nat in the late 1960s. Nat passed away about ten years ago; however, from the first shirt Nat made him to now, we probably made hundreds of shirts for Johnny. We didn't make jackets, vests, or slacks for him, just shirts. And no, he didn't just get black shirts, as you might think. As he usually wore his many dynamic styles of black coats onstage, most people didn't really pay attention or notice what color Johnny's shirts were under the coat. He would order red, blue, and burgundy shirts with those pleated fronts.

He liked silk shirts of purple, black, lavender, and light blues, and would order twelve shirts just alike. Mr. Cash was a regular client, and he'd call or have his sister Reba or someone call and give his order, or when he was in town he would stop by to see us. We'd ship whatever he ordered to his House of Cash most of the time.

In the early 1990s, he wanted a different look. We changed the style of the pleated-front shirt, which he always had since the early 1980s, to more of a casual look, with two pockets and a fuller-looking shirt. He always wanted the double cuff for use with cuff links, and Johnny liked extra room in his sleeves for movement when playing guitar. His favorite fabric was the four-ply silk, and that was what he ordered most in his black silk shirts. In this new pattern, he also ordered white, maroon, lavender, royal blue, and purple shirts.

We didn't have to take new measurements for John's sleeves or neck, as they stayed pretty much the same for years. We were so proud to know that Johnny Cash wanted and wore our shirts. He wore them well. I think he liked giving them away to friends and fans, just to get to wear a new one. Celebrities even to this day like wearing brand-new silk shirts fresh out of the wrapping from us. "Comfort," I would tell Johnny, "it's like a good shoe. Once you find the right fit, you want nothing else."

We reserved special labels for our real exclusive or preferred customers. I remember that after 1994, I made a special label that said, "Made Exclusively for Johnny Cash". This was something that only a few clients would get, and Johnny told me he appreciated it very much. For us, he was a true friend and a loyal customer.

It's hard to find people like Johnny Cash anymore. They are a rare breed. Today's celebrities and stars lack the dignity the old guys had a few decades ago. These newcomers, well, they are day and night, being so different. It is hard to really get close like we did with Mr. Cash. We don't get attached to them like Johnny and the old school.

It sure was a privilege to have a client like him. We were proud to know that he wore our shirts and not just onstage. He was a handsome man of honor and dignity, and Mr. Cash is missed so much by me and my family. His music and his spirit will live on. As our small tribute to Johnny, his picture is forever placed on our shop's Wall of Fame, and it will never ever be removed. Like his memory from our hearts.

Assorted doodles by John, including a "self-portrait" (top left) sketched on the blackboard in the men's basketball locker room at Duke University while he was in Durham, North Carolina, performing with the Durham Symphony, December 5, 1987.

Rev. JACK SHAW

Johnstown, Pennsylvania
Shoe Size 11–11 1/2 D

FOLLOWING AN APPOINTMENT IN Cincinnati, I took the interstate toward Nashville. I kept reminding myself that I should call my friend in Nashville and let him know that I was coming. Somehow I just kept putting it off. When I finally called, about a hundred miles out of the city, I heard him say, "I wish you had called me earlier. I have to go to Texas and help fill in a date for Dolly Parton's show. I'm really sorry, Jack."

There I stood, shivering in a cold rain along I-65, a hundred miles from Nashville, and over five hundred miles from home . . . in the middle of nowhere. What would I do? There seemed to be no reason now to keep going, and it was too far from home to want to turn around. Ultimately, though, I guess I knew I wasn't going to be able to get rid of the quiet voice within me telling me to "go on down to Nashville," nor did I want to. I was beginning to realize then—and believe even more so now—that, as Jesus was led by an unseen presence while He walked this earth; likewise, we are, as we walk through this life with Him. (John 5:19-21.)

The next morning, after I left the North Nashville Holiday Inn, I took the Hendersonville exit off of I-65 and headed up the main drag to visit

another old acquaintance. Somehow, daydreaming probably, I missed the turn. I drove right past the turnoff to his home. I thought, *How did I do that? How could I do that? I've turned off onto that road at least a hundred times, and there I went and missed it.* As I mused about what to do, I decided that I would look for a place on the other side of the road to turn around. That way I wouldn't have to cross traffic when I pulled back onto the highway. Seeing an appropriate spot, I swung my car across traffic into a parking lot and right up in front of a huge sign. I instinctively looked out of the front windshield up at the sign and read, "Johnny Cash Museum." I looked down to another area of the sign and read, "Open: 9:00 a.m." I looked at my watch . . . it read 9:05! I thought, *I'm not in any hurry to get to my friend's house, maybe I'll just park and go in.*

I went inside, bought a ticket, and toured Johnny's museum. Once inside, I began looking around at all the relics, keepsakes, etc., and noticed a number of items dated 1932. There was even a 1932 Chrysler automobile. Upon closer examination, I discovered that these 1932 items were mostly presents given to Johnny somewhere back down the road for one of his birthdays. Johnny was born on February 26, 1932.

As I was leaving, I struck up a conversation with a nice, elderly lady who was stationed behind the counter amidst all the souvenirs. "Enjoyed the museum," I said to her. "I have an old arch-top Martin guitar that was made in 1932, the year Johnny was born." She replied, "Well, why don't you go to the studio where he's recording and tell him about it?" I replied "Yeah, like they would let me in." She quickly and firmly responded, "You tell them his mother sent you!" I was shocked—it was Johnny's mother I'd been talking to! And I could tell that she wasn't kidding.

My quick Johnny Cash studio meeting ended in a five-hour stay at "Cowboy" Jack Clement's recording studio that March in 1981. Inwardly, I kept thanking God for these strange circumstances that I was certain only He could have arranged. John and I were instant friends, and through the similarity of our life experiences and our mutual faith in God, that bond of friendship would grow stronger and stronger over the following years.

Noticing John's travel itenerary at Jack's studio that March day, I saw that his tour was coming soon to Pittsburgh, much closer to home for me. So, backstage at John's show in Pittsburgh, I showed him the guitar. He was so mesmerized by this mint-condition 1932 Martin f-hole arch-top. He asked how much I'd take for it. "I would never sell it. It would be like selling one of my very own kids. But I would give it to you," I answered.

"Why," he asked, "would you do that?"

I replied, "As a token of friendship, if you'll accept it. I've been a fan for years, and I've always admired what you've allowed God to do in your life."

This began a long relationship with John on the road. I traveled to many places and on numerous tours at John's invitation. I will never forget the night during a brief intermission backstage at a college venue in central Pennsylvania when he invited me to minister to those in attendance. I was privileged to counsel and pray with and see God touch several "searching" individuals who came forward that night. Near the end of the show, John announced, "A minister of the Gospel is with us and is standing near the front, at the side of the stage, and is available to talk with anyone who might have a need," just before he and June did their closing gospel numbers.

That was the beginning of a seemingly endless array of Johnny Cash Show dates that streamed by for years. Concert bookings that took us all over the world, into Canada, back and forth across the United States, through Australia, New Zealand, England, France, Germany, the Netherlands, Switzerland, and on and on, in a variety of venues that ranged from the darkest, purple-spiked-hair dens of Europe to New York's Carnegie Hall. John and June would perform, and I'd have the wonderful privilege of ministering at the close of the show. Also, we prayed before each show, as early on we had added a brief Bible study and prayer time, usually held in the dressing room or on the bus, just before each show began.

John referred to this new spiritual element of the Johnny Cash Show in a letter he wrote and gave to me in Australia, portions of which follow.

> Jack Shaw's ministry in tandem with the Johnny Cash Show may be a first in the entertainment business. The idea came to June and me on a tour last summer.
>
> Before each concert we form a prayer circle in the dressing room with our family and any other members of the group who wish to join in. Jack leads a five-minute service of scripture reading, sharing, and prayer. The service is uplifting and has put a positive power edge on our performances.
>
> Recently, we took what I felt was a bold step, in that toward the end of the concert I introduce Jack (who is positioned near the stage in the audience) and mention that he will be there after the concert to offer free counseling and advice on moral and spiritual matters. I tell them that he is a minister of the Gospel and will talk to them about their personal problems, drug and alcohol addiction, or simply about the Bible and what God has to say to them. As well as daily ministering to the needs of my eighteen-member group, many people have come down to talk to Jack after the concert every night.
>
> Lives are changed, souls are saved, spirits are lifted, and light is brought into the darkness of many hearts.
>
> We are being led by inspiration, and I believe that God is guiding Jack in this great work he is now doing . . . and the fruit of the harvest from the seeds sown along the way will be bountiful.
>
> Johnny Cash
> Perth, Australia

Although the "ministry-with-the-show" idea was generally well received, that was not always the case. I recall one instance when we were booked for several weeks at one location and the venue's management must have complained a bit. Somehow that got back to John, and he entered my dressing room one evening to tell me about it. I began bracing myself for something much different than what I heard.

"They tell me someone here is complaining about you ministering at the end of my show. Jack, what you're doing is a real and very important part of the Johnny Cash Show. Maybe what they're really saying is, they don't like my show. If I hear any more about it, maybe we'll just pack up and take the show somewhere else." I just sat in awe and silence as I watched him get up and quietly head back out the door. To my knowledge, the subject was never mentioned to him at that venue again.

I brought a newly introduced Franklin Electronic Bible with me to the show in Buffalo, New York. While showing it to John and talking about the exciting new technology it represented, and going through some of its many functions, his eyes were just glued to it. Soon I heard him say, "Can I look at it for a minute, Jack?"

"Of course." I said while handing it to him. He was just amazed at this new technology that made the Bible so easy to use in finding obscure books or familiar verses, punching in a word or a phrase or just a part of a verse . . . and having it located and displayed on the screen instantly.

John looked at me and asked, "Where can I get one of these, Jack?"

I told him, "I'll send you one 'overnight' as soon as I get back home."

At the next show date (and I should be ashamed to say that I don't remember where it was, but it was somewhere out there) John had his Franklin Bible with him, and he was glowing. He told me that he had bought every one that the local Nashville distributors had and that he was passing them around to his family members and close friends. He even told me he'd given one to a gentleman who sat near him on a plane after he noticed John working with it and became interested in it. I was with him at Nashville's Baptist Hospital when he mentioned the Franklin Electronic Bible to the doctor who was examining him. And after the doc became curiously interested in it, John told him he would have one sent to him. "Write down

A Jack's-eye view of the Johnny Cash Show from the stage wings.

his name and address, Jack," he said. "And make sure the office gets it, so I can send the doctor here one of these."

John was giving away so many of these Bibles that he began buying them by the case directly from the manufacturer. And then, you guessed it,

that really got their attention. Soon Franklin signed Johnny Cash as their official Electronic Bible representative. John and I were together at many of the religious booksellers conventions after that, as he was now representing Franklin at their booths. I was with John and June in New Jersey during the filming of the commercials and the photo shoot, the results of which you've no doubt seen on television and on poster displays in Radio Shack and elsewhere, featuring John holding a Franklin Electronic Bible. Those images were used in almost all of their promotional material.

As our bond of friendship increased, backstage one evening John asked me to call him every day. "Every day?" I asked.

"Call me every day, Jack. Every day."

So I did, without missing more than a handful over the many miles and years that followed. We'd just talk about the stuff that good friends and fellow believers talk about—personal challenges, blessings, ideas, humor, etc. But always, somewhere in our conversation, one of us would find a way to encourage the other with a newly discovered scripture and its meaning, or a new exciting revelation of an old familiar verse, or what Heaven would be like, or something from one of the many wonderful stories found in the Bible. Those conversations will forever be some of my life's most treasured and precious moments.

John had a great sense of humor. I remember entering his dressing room one night, just before Bible study and prayer, to find him with his face up against the mirror about as close as he could get, pushing his nose together with a finger on each side of it. As he looked at me over his shoulder in the mirror's reflection, I heard him ask, "Jack, will I still have this nose when I get to Heaven?"

I wasn't quite sure how to respond to that, so I just smiled and said, "Sure you will, John, except then it'll be glorified." He just turned and gave me a "Johnny Cash" grin.

We were in Adelaide, Australia, on John's birthday, and June and the girls planned a surprise party for him. We all had a ball, especially John. I watched him take one of the helium-filled balloons and bite a small hole in the end while holding it tightly with his fingers. He then released some of the contents while holding it to his mouth and inhaling. We were all silent as he pulled the balloon down from his mouth, looked at us, and, with a "Donald Duck" voice, said, "Hello, I'm Johnny Cash." An immediate uproar of laughter emitted from everyone there. It was hilarious.

I remember another time when John and I were together somewhere and I had to sneeze. John immediately and appropriately said, "God bless you." Then he went on to say, "One time I was talking to God, Jack, and He sneezed, and I didn't know what to say." I just looked at him and started laughing.

There were the desperate and trying times, too. We were on the road, in Branson, when his brother Roy died. He phoned me very early that morning to tell me that he'd just received a call informing him of Roy's passing. I told him that I would be right there. We spent the day together. I drove him to Springfield to an appointment he had with an eye doctor. Neither of us talked very much on the way up or back, but there was a strong comforting presence of God's Holy Spirit in that car, which I'm sure each of us felt and were thankful for.

John was a strong shoulder and was there for me, too, when my beautiful and bright twenty-four-year-old daughter, Sarah Grace (the youngest of the five children God blessed my wife, Grace, and I with) suffered a tragic, untimely death. His support and encouragement was a precious Godsend and deeply appreciated. I still feel it.

I recall one afternoon, riding through the back roads of Arkansas in John's Range Rover, we discussed, as we had rarely done before, how each of us had lost an older brother through horrible accidents when we were younger. As we drove along through the countryside, we shared, very sensitively, some of the intimate details and sad events that evolved on those two dreadful days. The rare similarity of each of us suffering such a loss somehow added a unique and even deeper bond to our friendship.

I deeply respected and admired John for his quiet faith and the bold stand he took in offering the light of the gospel to the needy multitudes that were drawn to his concerts all over the world in such a unique way. I am also very thankful to have been a part of so many, many hurting lives being touched by God . . . and changed forever. As John alluded to in the closing comments of his letter (mentioned above), the fruits of the harvest have been, and will continue to be . . . bountiful.

And I heard the voice from heaven saying, Write, Blessed are the dead who die in the Lord from henceforth: yea, saith the Spirit, that they may rest from their labors; and their works do follow them. (Rev 14:13 KJV)

There is so much more I could say regarding the treasured relationship and fellowship that God allowed John and I to share, and just how very much I loved and respected him . . . and dearly miss him.

While waiting out a flight delay at La Guardia's USAir Club the day after the *All Star Tribute to Johnny Cash* television taping in New York City, I composed a letter to John. I faxed it to his New York hotel. The next day, he and June flew back home, and I called the house for him. June answered and told me that they were both a bit road-weary and lying on their bed resting. "Could you call back just a little later?" she asked.

I said, "Sure, June, but before I go, could you ask John if he got the letter I faxed to him at the hotel?" She asked him and I heard that familiar voice tell her, "Why, yes, I did . . and I think that's the nicest letter I ever got."

Whether it was the nicest letter is not important to me. He said it that evening in his own gracious way! Please allow me to share the letter that I wrote to him.

Dear John:
My flight was canceled this morning so I thought I'd drop you a note and thank you for a very wonderful and memorable evening. The tribute was beautiful, very much deserved and certainly well earned.

Oliver Wendell Holmes once said, "The average man goes to his grave with his music still in him." Thank God this has not been the case with you. You've given greatly of the gift God has given you. All who have been privileged to know you can testify to that, John, as our lives have been immeasurably enriched through the touch of your life. No doubt this can also be echoed by the many countless, nameless ones who have so richly received from you without ever having the great privilege of knowing you in a personal way.

John, I know first hand that your road has not been an easy one. There's been challenge after challenge . . . some giving way to victory, and others . . . something less. But then this is often the path of destiny for those who carry God's treasured gifts in earthen vessels (II Cor 4:7–8). It just could be, though, that this is the necessary stuff that talents are nurtured in and creativity is born of. Strange as it does seem, Scripture says . . . the very tests, trials, and tribulations we suffer result in working life (!) in those around us (II Cor 4:12).

Thank you, John, for giving of your gift and your life to so many. (Thank you also, June, for holding up "Moses' hands" (Ez 17:12). I know this hasn't been an easy task . . . especially when your "Moses" has been Johnny Cash. But I also know Johnny will be the first to recognize he could not have come to this place in his journey without God having sent you.)

Thank you especially, John, that you have not been one of the average persons Oliver Wendell Holmes spoke of. Thank you that the gift God put within you will NEVER be buried . . . for you have continually poured it out to others . . . in spite of, maybe even because of, the many obstacles.

Thank you not only for the fruits of the road traveled thus far, but also for the promise of what's ahead. As I've told you many times before, I believe the best is yet to come. God does save the best wine for last, you know.

God richly bless you, John, and all your loved ones and the road ahead. I'm very proud of you . . . and very thankful to be your friend. "Grace be unto you, and peace, from God our Father, and from the Lord Jesus Christ. I thank my God upon every remembrance of you." (Phil 1:23)

Jack Shaw
USAir Club
LaGuardia
April 7, 1999

Mahalia Jackson
1. Didn't it Rain
2. My God is Real
3. Walk all over Gods Heaven
4. Take My Hand Precious Lord
5. Joshua Fit the Battle of Jericho
6. His eye is on the Sparrow
7. God Put a rainbow in the Clouds
8. He's Got the Whole World in His Hands.

Elvis
1. He Touched Me
2. Bosom of Abraham
3. Swing Low Sweet Chariot
4. Peace in the Valley

Also Need
1. How Great Thou Art
2. Why Me Lord
3. In the Garden — Kris
4. Whispering Hope — Various artists
5. It is No Secret
6. Down by the Riverside — Elvis? Mahalia?
7. Ezekiel Saw the Wheel

John and June with Eric Clapton (top right); the original draft of "The Holografik Danser," a science-fiction short story penned by John in 1964 (below); popular patches sold at the House of Cash (below right).

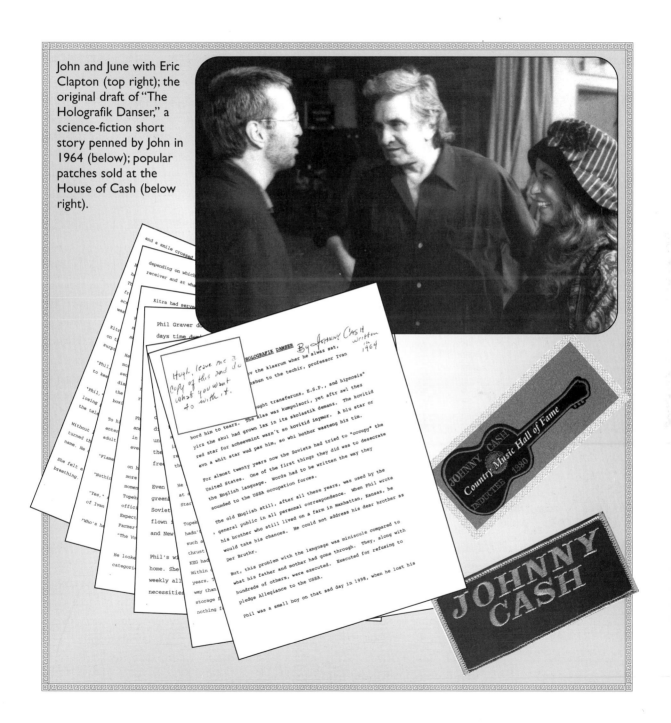

Hugh, leave me a copy of this and do what you want to with it.

HOLOGRAFIK DANSER By Johnny Cash written in 1964

... the klasrum wher he alwaz sat, ... shun tu the techir, professor Ivan

... ught transferuns, E.S.P., and hipnosis" bord him to tearz. The klas was kumpulsori, yet aftr awl thez yirs the skul had grown lax in its skolastik demans. The kovitid red star for acheevmint wazn't so kovitid inymor. A blu star or evn a whit star wud pas him, so whi bothur wasteng hiz tim.

For almost twenty years now the Soviets had tried to "occupy" the United States. One of the first things they did was to desecrate the English language. Words had to be written the way they sounded to the USSA occupation forces.

The old English still, after all these years, was used by the general public in all personal correspondence. When Phil wrote his brother who still lived on a farm in Manhattan, Kansas, he would take his chances. He could not address his dear brother as Der Bruthr.

But, this problem with the language was miniscule compared to what his father and mother had gone through. They, along with hundreds of others, were executed. Executed for refusing to pledge Allegiance to the USSA.

Phil was a small boy on that sad day in 1998, when he lost his ...

JOHNNY   CASH
Country Music Hall of Fame
INDUCTEE   1980

JOHNNY CASH

JOHN L. SMITH

Fort Wayne, Indiana

Shoe Size 9–9¹/₂

FIRST AND FOREMOST, I am a Johnny Cash fan! I am a fan of the man and his music. I've even been called a "Johnny Cash nerd." I am also a discographer. I began keeping track of John's recording career in the early 1960s for my own use. Then later I would make copies of my files, bind them in black, naturally, and give them to John each time we would get together. It was actually at his urging that I had them published. Over the years I have had four books published on the recording career of Johnny Cash, contributed a section for his autobiography, and have written several articles. I thusly became known by John and others, as his "official" discographer.

Not a day goes by that I don't walk into the den, see the multitude of photographs hanging on the walls, some signed with little messages, that I don't think of how fortunate I have been. I knew Johnny Cash. Not as long or as personal as some. But I knew Johnny Cash. I have gifts he gave me: a Martin guitar, a turn-of-the-century commemorative Wells Fargo belt buckle from Tiffany's, a shirt, and a belt he made for me, the buckle of which is a coffin handle from a Spanish galleon sunk off the coast of

Jamaica eons ago. How he got it would probably be an interesting story, too. But these are gifts, tangible things. Treasured mementos, yes, but it will be the memories that I will always hold so precious.

My friendship with John probably had as much to do with our mutual interest in Native Americans as it did with my interest in his music. I first met him on Sunday, April 23, 1967. And it was during that first visit that I presented him with a number of items from the Plains Indians. I first heard Johnny Cash on KRNT radio in Des Moines, Iowa, when I was a junior in high school. After that, I would make frequent visits to my local record store in search of those very familiar yellow labels. My collection grew as did my admiration for the man. Then, thanks to promoter and disc jockey Smokey Smith (no relation), I got to meet him.

I have related many times of how our first meeting took place. I remember it as though it was yesterday. As I walked into the dressing room, Marshall Grant and Luther Perkins excused themselves and left to sell pictures to the audience. I was suddenly left alone with Johnny Cash. He was shining his black shoes with pages from the local newspaper. Strangely, I had no butterflies, no unnerving feelings at all. From the very first, and as he did every time we were together, he made me feel as if we had known each other forever.

During our visit that afternoon we talked of many things. His great interest at the time were the events surrounding the December 1890 battle at Wounded Knee, South Dakota. He asked if I had any pictures of the event, and I told him I did and would certainly have copies made for him. In exchange for pictures, he told me he would give me one of his guitars. Idle talk, I thought at the time. When he was called to the stage, he asked me if I would mind presenting him with the items during the show. He would lead into it by singing "As Long as the Grass Shall Grow," and then I would come on and explain about the gifts and then present them to him. It was one of those moments that will remain forever as a memory.

Following the show, as the band was loading the equipment in the car, John asked, almost sheepishly, if I thought it would be all right if he accompanied me on a visit to South Dakota and the Wounded Knee area sometime. I, of course, was elated. But there was also that part of me that thought it was a nice gesture but it would never actually happen.

The following week, I received a three-page handwritten letter from John postmarked from Pittsburgh. It said basically the same thing as we had talked of earlier. And he expressed, again, his desire to visit the Wounded Knee area. It did happen, in December 1968. A film crew under the direction of producer Arthur Baron was putting together a documentary on John for the Public Television Network, and they wanted to film him at Wounded Knee. An added event would be a benefit show for the people on the Rosebud Reservation.

I arrived to picked up John and June from the Rapid City airport the afternoon of the concert. While waiting for their plane, I noticed a number of television and newspaper reporters waiting for the same plane. I thought it strange that so many knew of the their arrival. When the plane arrived, John and June walked almost unnoticed through the crowd of newspeople, and it became obvious they were waiting for someone else. So John, June, and I stood off to the side and waited to see what was happening.

Then, suddenly, Henry Fonda appeared and, unknown to John and June, he had been on the same plane. Fonda was there to narrate a film on the carving of the statue of Crazy Horse in the Black Hills. A few years before, Fonda had a television series, *The Deputy*, and John had appeared on at least one episode. When John got off the plane, he was carrying his usual black bag, but when he saw Fonda, he quickly walked directly toward him and set the bag down in the middle of the airport. June asked me if I would please go retrieve the bag, as it contained all of their gate receipts from the last several shows they had done across Canada! It was a heavy bag.

I have talked in detail elsewhere of the events of those two days in December 1968. I remember on the two-hour drive the next day from St. Francis to Wounded Knee, John had acquired a "Billy Jack" type hat that made him appear even taller. At some point, we all stopped for a bathroom break. The very rural rest area consisted of a two-hole building with no roof. John went in and suddenly stuck his head out of the top, hat and all, and waved to us. After that, he would kid me about the "little outhouse on the prairie."

We arrived at the small community of Wounded Knee on the Pine Ridge Reservation and were ushered into the historic combination post office, trading post, and general store. Word of his coming had, of course, preceded him, so there was a rather large crowd, with all of us huddled shoulder to shoulder. None of those present had been to the concert the night before, and John said if he only had a guitar he would certainly put on a show right there, spoken more as an afterthought, I think, than reality. But from some darkened corner of that small trading post someone produced an old black guitar. True to his word, Johnny Cash and June Carter stood in the crowd and sang several songs to the delight of the rural audience. This segment was filmed by Mr. Baron's crew, but unfortunately, this portion of the documentary ended up on the cutting-room floor.

After the tour of the battlefield, we were treated to a meal at one of the local ranches. Before we left, John, wearing his Billy Jack hat, rode around the front yard on the family's favorite pony. Another Kodak moment.

A side note: The photographer for Arthur Baron's crew was Ron Elfstrum. He would be cast as Jesus Christ in John's film *The Gospel Road*.

The most remarkable thing about the whole two days was the drive back to the airport after the Wounded Knee tour. I purposely took an old road that locals had pointed out to me many times as the route Big Foot, the Miniconju chief killed at Wounded Knee, and his small band of followers had taken on their way to Pine Ridge. June almost immediately fell asleep in the back seat. With the local history lesson still fresh in his mind, I knew John's thoughts were racing. We drove in silence for a time, and then he suddenly began asking more questions about the events on that day in 1890. I would relate what I knew, and he would scribble words on a folded piece of paper produced from somewhere. When finished, he would fold it back up and place it in his pocket. More silent miles, then more questions, more writing. I was amazed at the questions and the detail he wanted to learn.

This pattern continued for the two hours it took us to reach the airport at Rapid City. June was now awake, and before we said our goodbyes and left the car, John said he had written a song and wanted to sing it for us. The song was, of course, "Big Foot." John recorded the song at the House of Cash studios on June 5, 1972. A few days later, he performed in Des Moines and proudly told me he was going to include the song in a forthcoming album entitled *America*.

July 1968, Rapid City, South Dakota. We sat on folding chairs in the small Masonic Temple building. It was a full house in the middle of tourist season, and the show was proceeding nicely when there came a loud shouting from the back of the hall. John noticed it, too, but kept right on playing. The shouting continued, and then we saw a man, an Indian, obviously under the influence of bottled spirits, walking down the center aisle yelling incoherently at the man on the stage. The closer to the stage the man approached, the more nervous the atmosphere.

I watched both John and the man. Finally, John stopped whatever song he was singing at the time and began the chorus to "As Long as the Grass Shall Grow." The man immediately stopped still in his tracks and almost came to attention. Once the song was finished, he turned and silently left the building. We found out later he was taken into custody, and I remember John saying if he had known the man was going to be arrested, he would have at least bailed him out.

August 1969, Ryman Auditorium, Nashville, Tennessee. I sat in the heat of that famous old building, on extremely hard wooden seats, actually pews, and watched John rehearse for his ABC-TV show later that evening. The guests on this particular evening were Pat Boone and Diana Trask. Next to me was Barbara John, John's manager at the time. John had invited me down and made it a point to emphasize the importance of the discographical material I kept him supplied with. He was using it to pick the songs for the various shows. As John wrote in volume one of my *Johnny Cash Discography* series, "the mind slips, but your words are always there."

Barbara was very excited about a new song John had performed earlier in the year during his San Quentin show and thought it just might receive some air play on the country stations in spite of its title. "So what is it?" I asked. She smiled and said, "Well, it's called 'A Boy Named Sue.' Do you think country radio is ready for that?"

February 23, 1993. Des Moines, Iowa. Both of my parents passed away within weeks of each other. I had been in contact with Marty Stuart and Waylon during that time, and they must have passed the word on to John about their passing. I received a handwritten letter of sympathy from him. All the years we had been friends, he still talked about those trips to South Dakota. He wanted so much to get back there, as he indicated in the letter: "I still hope that soon we can ramble those reservations together."

April 24, 1993. Farm Aid, Ames, Iowa. We rode with Waylon on the bus to Ames. The Highwaymen were performing one or two songs, one of their last shows together. Although John was staying at the same hotel, he opted to drive separately. Once we arrived at the stadium, we all went out to walk around and to see who was there and do a little visiting. I needed to return to the bus at some point, and the minute I stepped aboard, I came face to face with John. No one else on the bus but the two of us. He was standing there, wearing his Ben Franklin-type reading glasses and with his palm outstretched and holding a number of different pills. Apparently, he felt he had to explain the situation to me.

"John L.," he said rather quietly, "these are my 'no-fun pills.'" I took

that to mean this was medication prescribed by his doctor and not those other kind of feel-good items. I just stood there, shrugged my shoulders as if to convey that it was none of my business. Then he continued, "John L., I'm supposed to take these at two o'clock." I looked at my watch and told him it was pretty close to that time now. He looked at me, drew himself up, fussed with his collar, as I'd seen him do so many times, smiled wickedly, winked, and asked, "A.m. or p.m.?"

It was after the Highwaymen performance at Farm Aid that John asked me to meet him at his trailer dressing room. I knew Waylon was anxious to leave, but he graciously allowed me the time to seek John out. As I entered his dressing room, daughter Cindy was there and quietly stepped outside. On one of the first Highwaymen tours, John had stopped at an antique store somewhere in Michigan and purchased a very old Native American beaded neck piece that he would wear during many of the concerts. He and I used to wonder about its origin, tribal identity, and its purpose. On that evening, after his Farm Aid appearance with the Highwaymen, John gave it to me.

I have written elsewhere how we just stood there and looked at each other, neither knowing exactly what to say. Finally, we embraced, and I noticed that I was not the only one that needed to wipe away a tear or two. Once I had time to sit down and really examine the item, I noticed that this extremely valuable piece of history now included several silver conchos that had not been there before. The next time I saw Marty

Stuart, I mentioned this and expressed the fact that John had done this to such an old and valuable piece. Marty just smiled and said, "John L., he just finished it!"

During our times together, I have seen several different sides of Johnny Cash. He was like a chameleon; he could be anything you wanted him to be at any given moment. But to me and my family, he was always the most gracious man I have ever known. He remembered the day our youngest daughter was to be born and wrote a short note "reminding us." On another occasion, unbeknownst to me, my daughter had written him and explained that she had received a good report card and included a signed picture of herself. I have no idea what her letter said, but I still have the letter he wrote in return. And he also included a picture, signed.

I have written four books on the music of Johnny Cash. During all the years of preparation and the incessant questions, he never once failed to see to it that I received everything I needed to complete the task. He referred to the Smiths on more than one occasion as "extended family," and that was special. He asked me to write the liner notes for his *Just As I Am* CD. He asked me to contribute a listing of his releases for his autobiography. He once kept a governor's wife waiting while he opened a birthday present we brought for him. He wrote an introduction for the first volume in the discography series and then a few years later penned a beautiful tribute as a foreword to my recording history on Waylon Jennings. A vintage copy of his very first Sun album came one day out of the blue, with a very personal message written across it and signed, "Your fan, Johnny Cash." It don't get much better than that, Hoss.

April 22, 1994. Columbia, Missouri. It was a hangout for the local University of Missouri crowd. Small in comparison to some of the bigger venues he had played. The crowd consisted mostly of college students, at least on the main floor. There was a small balcony occupied by the "older" generation. It was as if the room was truly segregated by age. But it was totally amazing to watch this college crowd, some wearing Sun T-shirts, some passing forward old Sun albums hoping for an autograph. College students in their late teens, early twenties, singing along to "Folsom Prison Blues," "I Walk the Line," "Big River." John had truly reached another level of audience, thanks, in part, to his association with Rick Rubin. But Rubin was only the catalyst for this younger group. Once Johnny Cash was "discovered" again, the crowds became ageless.

Standing under the tent at graveside in September 2003, all the years came flooding back. Branson, Missouri; the Affordable Art Tour with Waylon and Brooke Shields; Watertown, South Dakota, with Steve Goodman; La Crosse, Wisconsin; Bloomington, Minnesota; Anderson, Indiana. So many different places. So many wonderful memories. I realized this was not a time of sorrow so much as a time of resignation. And as someone in the crowd began to sing "Will the Circle Be Unbroken," and as we all joined in, it seemed so appropriate.

All the years I knew John, I never once felt uncomfortable around him. But John, if you can read this, there is one thing I never had the nerve to tell you: It wasn't the Irish that settled in Pella, Iowa, it was the Dutch!

DUSTIN TITTLE

Nashville, Tennessee
Shoe Size 12

Phoenix Rising is a short story I wrote about my grandfather, John R. Cash, for my Advance Placement English course, taken during my senior year of high school in 2002. The assignment was to choose a specific person who has had a profound impact on my life and paint a picture of him. It goes without saying that my Grandpa John affected me immeasurably.

He was my idol, my hero, my pride, and he continues to fill these roles to this very day. Through his death, I have realized even more the enormity of his presence, and the magnitude of his loss. He is irreplaceable. Not only do I mourn for my grandfather, but I mourn for the passing of the greatness that he was. Grandpa told me this was the "best thing ever written" about him. I'm sure he was biased, but I still wanted to share.

Phoenix Rising

February 21, 2002

With age, many men become merely the shadows of what they once were in their youth, choosing to capitulate to old age's rape of their mind and body. He has, time and again, risen like the Phoenix from the ashes only to appear with such strength and fortitude that a handful of adolescents would be put to shame. He is my grandfather, he is my friend, he is, like the Phoenix, a mystery to me.

My grandfather, J. R. Cash, lived through the Great Depression, World War II, the Korean War, Vietnam, Sonny and Cher, and Senator Joseph McCarthy to name a few. He has known times of deep trouble and times of great joy, the former far outweighing the latter. His face reflects all he has seen. The times of trouble are evident in the deep pores of his face—it is a rough face, one fit to light a match on.

One of the most dramatic features found on his commanding physiognomy is the deep, unique, and somewhat mystical scar on his right cheek. He would tell you that he got it battling a scalawag in a bar fight, or some other dramatic scene; in actuality, he made the mistake of letting a drunken dentist remove a cyst from his jawbone. I'd tell the bar story, too.

His eyebrows are greyed and bushy, and rest above his big, brown eyes. The Cash nose; it's large, pronounced, and round—and never fails to pass from generation to generation; he has it, his children have it, and most of his grandchildren, including myself, have it—it is the *piéce de resistance* which completes the portrait of a typical Cash.

Finally, the voice—his most unique feature. He has a deep, baritone voice which no one could mistake to be that of anyone else. I spent the night at his home four years ago and, at about five o'clock in the morning, I heard him bellow, "Dustin, time to get up, son." Needless to say, despite the consuming feeling of utter fatigue, I rose with haste—the voice demands authority and receives it without fail.

My grandfather's personal life is checkered with public successes and personal failures. He officially began his music career in 1955 and, when the schedule became too demanding, ironically resorted to the use of drugs to maintain a grip on his reality. This was both a personal and public failure—he was arrested in El Paso for attempting to "smuggle prescription drugs across the border," and the press knew it—and through the help of his family and his own spirituality, he rose from the ashes and went on to outsell the Beatles and land more pop hits on the charts than Michael Jackson.

In 1989, when he died on the operating table during open-heart surgery, he miraculously pulled through the operation and lived to tell his family that he spited the doctors for bringing him back from the white light. When he was recently diagnosed with Shy-Drager disease, a debilitating disorder affecting the nervous system, he didn't shrivel up and let his illness consume him. To quote him, "I refuse to give it some ground in my life."

However, this diagnosis turned out to be an error, and he is actually conflicted with a diabetic disorder—a disease which I also inherited from him. Now, did I mention that he's stubborn? He's 69 years old and, until recently, he ate as many candy bars a day as he wanted, he put five spoons of sugar in his coffee, and he ate mammoth bowls of Breyers ice cream.

But, he doesn't let his old age and his maladies immobilize him—he goes to Jamaica at least three times a year and he travels whenever necessary; if asked to visit an out-of-state friend, his reply will never be "I can't come, my arthritis is acting up."

But, while my grandfather is both great in soul and great in life experience, he is also shrouded in mystery to me. I didn't know my grandfather very well until recently. He was always touring and traveling until he officially retired in 1996. This lack of a relationship has cast him as a half-man, half-mythical figure.

I never knew he liked Roman history as I did until I told him I was in Latin class. After I told him about my taking Latin, he took me to the office in his bedroom and gave me a book written by Josephus. Since he has retired, I have grown to know Grandpa John more as a grandfather and less as an American icon, which is how I viewed him when I was 10 years old and younger. Rude, ignorant people ask me all the time, "What does your grandpa give you for Christmas? He's rich isn't he?"

Out of everything he's ever given me, the greatest gift is the newly established relationship which I will cherish long after he is gone; the American icon persona will fade—people will forget Johnny Cash—I will never forget my Grandpa John.

You Are Writing Your Own Story

No matter what you are doing
From cradle days through to the end
You're writing your life's secret story
Each night sees another page penned
Each month ends a thirty page chapter
Each year means the end of a part
And never an act is mistated
Nor ever one wish of the heart.

Each day when you wake the book opens
Revealing a page clean and white
What thoughts and what words and what doing
Will cover its surface by night
God leaves that to you, you're the writer
And never one word will grow dim
Till some day you write the word final
And give back your life's book to him.

Mrs. Ray Cash

Through all the ups and down my mother always says "God has his hand on you."

JIMMY TITTLE

Hendersonville, Tennessee

Shoe Size 12

*J*OHNNY CASH HAS BEEN written about, profiled, gossiped about, and it seems there's not much left to discuss, except appropriate stories that maybe only his close friends and family know. As public a figure as he was, he was extremely private and quiet. He was a voracious reader of wide ranges of books. He was a very learned man.

During the twenty-two years I was fortunate enough to be in his organization, both as an employee (I played bass in his band through the '80s) and in his later years (I was part of his production team as he worked with Rick Rubin and recorded some of his most moving work), he had a keen interest in ancient history and studied all religions and philosophies. He respected people of all faiths and was not judgmental toward anyone's beliefs. He felt that faith in whatever worship you chose was right for each individual.

John was a theologian and Bible scholar. As his daughter Rosanne has said, he was a "Southern Baptist with the soul of a mystic."

I had been a musician all of my life. I started touring professionally when I was sixteen years old and worked steadily with a few good bands. In 1974, I began to tour with Merle Haggard & The Strangers. That was my first real taste of big-time music. I spent several years with Merle and left in 1978.

I met John's daughter Kathy in 1981, and we fell in love almost immediately. When we met, I had no intentions of going back on the road with a touring band of any kind. Kathy and I dated for several months; during this time, she was working at her father's offices, the House of Cash, in the publishing business. I was a songwriter and had been for a long time. Kathy seemed to really like my songs and told John about me and my songwriting. He told her if she believed in me, that was good enough for him. I began recording my demos for his publishing company, Songs of Cash, and John liked them well enough to publish them. That was my first step into the door of professional songwriting.

Kathy also knew John was looking for a permanent bass player for his band. He had been using a few players out of Nashville, but John wanted his own guy who worked only for him and was available at all times. Kathy mentioned that I was a bass player and ran my resume down to him. John agreed to meet me and check me out.

That first meeting with me as a consideration for the job happened at W. S. Holland's house in Jackson, Tennessee. I'll never forget that day. Kathy and I drove down for the lunch and the "once over" from J. R. We arrived before John and the rest of the band; his arrival was somewhat spectacular.

Here's how it went down: W. S. Holland has a long driveway, and after we'd been there awhile, four black rental cars came roaring up to the house. The cars threw up a cloud of dust, and when the dust cleared, John and Marty Stuart rolled out of the cars.

John was in his usual long, black gabardine duster made by Manuel; in fact, everything he had on was black—*very* black. John and Marty strolled up to greet Kathy and myself, and I thought, *What an impressive man.* He was also very unique and charismatic. I noticed right away that John and Marty were wearing old Colt .45s in black leather holsters. I believe they'd been out shopping for old firearms. As he came closer to us, he pulled out his .45 and popped a few rounds off into the air. What a sound! Loud and lots of smoke. He was in some character, perhaps, or just being John. It was an amazing introduction and "greeting" on his part.

John was definitely your alpha male. He always did what he wanted, and I loved that about him. After the initial rounds, the smoke cleared, he re-holstered his gun, strode up to me, and looked me right in the eye. He introduced himself with a good, strong handshake. There was never a lot of small talk with John, although he was a really funny man.

Jimmy swaps licks with Ted Rollins at the 2004 Johnny Cash Jamaica memorial show.

I'd been around enough to know that artists of his caliber were very serious about the people that essentially became part of their traveling family. He was getting a read on me. I later learned that John could assess people and their intentions very quickly.

We went into Fluke's (W. S. Holland's) house and got right down to the business of a fantastic lunch prepared by his wife, Joyce. Southern cooking for a bunch of Southern men and women.

John sat at the head of the table to my right, with Kathy between us. He asked me about my days with Haggard, which we discussed, and I reminded him that ten years before I had actually played bass on an album he'd done, entitled *The Junkie and the Juice Head Minus Me*. I played on two or three songs, thanks to Helen Carter (who was my "second mother," and her son David was my best friend.) My first session with a superstar. This was just before my work with Haggard.

John ate, told stories, and finally looked at me and said, "Let's give it a try and see how it works." I was excited, to say the least. Someone at the table said they would record a live performance of John's show, which I could study and learn. There would be no rehearsal. I would show up, and he expected me to know and perform the show. I lived with that tape for days, playing along. A couple of weeks later, I flew to the concert and hit the stage, cold and nervous.

I made a couple mistakes, but I guess John liked it well enough to hire me. I've stood behind incredibly charismatic performers before, but I'd never seen or seen since anyone as heavy as Johnny Cash. It changed my life; thank you, Kathy, and thank you, John.

We toured constantly, doing concerts, television, and recording. About a year into my tenure with John, Kathy and I knew we wanted to marry. I was twenty-eight years old and had an intense desire to settle down. I wanted a wife, children, and a home. John wanted us to marry, and he had a sense it would last forever.

The world knows Johnny Cash was an iconic and super superstar. They know his voice the instant they hear it. Most people know he was one of the greatest American songwriters. We knew he was a master entertainer and that he had done things most artists, especially country artists, could never get away with. John's greatness was evident to all.

What isn't common knowledge is that he was also an ordained minister. It was John's idea to marry us, and I thought, *What a sweet and unique thing for a father to marry me to his daughter.* Another special gift of the many gifts he gave us. We were the first wedding ceremony he had ever performed. John was very excited about performing the ceremony.

We got our date books out and started planning the day when everybody was available. We toured so much back then, but we found a day that was perfect. We chose November 24, 1982, the day before Thanksgiving. Everyone would be at home in Hendersonville, Tennessee, that day.

On November 23, we were in Memphis, taping one of John's CBS Christmas specials. It was a long day and night, as TV tapings are. Kathy's eight-year-old son, Thomas, and I left Memphis about 2 a.m. the morning of the twenty-fourth.

I suppose we could have gotten really fancy with the wedding, but Kathy and I decided to keep it very simple, with only our immediate families: moms, dads, brothers, and sisters.

Rosey Carter, June's daughter, made the hors d'oeuvres as her gift to us. That was a perfect gift. Rosey introduced me to Kathy, and a year later we were getting married. John wrote the words he wanted to say, and we had a magical wedding. We married at the little cabin in John's compound across

The Johnny Cash road show softball team prepares for a fund-raiser game organized by a Las Vegas hotel. Jimmy Tittle is at top left.

the street from his lake house in Hendersonville. (This would be the same recording cabin where I would work with John on his final recordings over twenty years later.) Twenty minutes and it was done, perfectly.

Now here's something that I found very hilarious: John had a wicked little sense of humor. After the ceremony, he presented us with our wedding gifts. He gave me my gift first. It was Fleetwood's *Life of Christ*, an old, thick, impressive book that was practically ancient. I opened it up and saw that he had written these words inside:

Hendersonville, Tenn. Nov 24, 1982

To Jimmy Tittle upon your wedding day. This is the book I used quite a lot in studying the life of Christ for the making of "Gospel Road" in 1971. It is rich and enriches the word itself, (the Bible) is the best guide to the life of Christ. Use it. Enjoy it.
(The binding could use a little glue).

John

Then he gave Kathy her gift. She tore through the paper and it was a Walther 9mm handgun with a clip that held nine shots. I laughed and told John, "Your message had been received."

I loved John; I'll always love him and all that he taught me by his fine example. He's the greatest man I've ever met. He's in my heart, where he belongs, and joining us together as man and wife stuck in our hearts. Kathy and I gave him a grandson and a granddaughter who both adored him. He was the coolest grandpa ever. He loved being a grandfather, a dad, and a father-in-law.

ALMA JEAN TODD

Winston-Salem, North Carolina

Shoe Size 7½ MEDIUM

THE FIRST TIME I saw Johnny Cash was on his ABC-TV shows. I joined his fan club in 1971. I finally met him when he attended his Fan Club Breakfast in 1977. On May 6, 1978, as the North Carolina representative of his fan club, I was allowed to go backstage at Carowinds Park to meet with him again. After this meeting, my husband, Curtis, and I were allowed many meetings with John and June backstage at concerts. In 1984, we were asked to become co-presidents of their fan club with Ray and Jeanne Witherell. The four of us served as co-presidents until the fan club disbanded in 2001.

John Cash was many things in addition to being a great entertainer. He was serious, funny, kind, and generous. He loved practical jokes, and most of all, he was a loving person.

One of the most touching moments was at Fan Fair in 1986. John had come to the booth to sign autographs. He had been there for a while when a group of handicapped children came by and stopped to see him. A blind child was rolled up close, and John lay across the table, picked up the child, and talked and sang softly to the child. The child responded back with a big smile. This is a memory I treasure.

223

John was doing a concert at Duke University, and I had taken some gifts for him from the fan club. As he opened them, he said, "You know you don't have to do this." To which I replied, "I'm not spending my money—members keep sending me money for gifts, and I love to shop!" John said, "I wish I could shop with someone else's money, but everyone always shops with mine!"

John was smiling when he greeted his guests that were invited to celebrate his twenty-fifth wedding anniversary. When asked how he had stayed married for twenty-five years, he simply said, "It's a piece of cake." He was a gracious host—greeting each guest upon their arrival and later on saying good-night to each one. Even though it was very late, after the party John and June very graciously posed together for photos for us to use for their fan club.

For John's fortieth anniversary in country music, in 1995, the fan club asked June what we could get him that he would really love. She thought for a moment and said, "Trees." A recent storm had damaged many of the trees at his farm. We were going to have a landscape company plant them, but John had his office contact us and said he would like to have a check instead, because he wanted to pick out the trees and plant them himself. I sent the check overnight, and was later told that he was at Wal-Mart early the next morning buying trees. He said he would send pictures of him planting the trees, but I guess he forgot. I never received them. He did mention, however, that he had let June have a "little" of the money for hanging baskets.

Happiness was the news backstage at a concert on February 29, 1996, at the Silver Star Resort in Philadelphia, Mississippi. John met us with a big smile and said, "I have a new grandson—Joseph John Cash, born yesterday to John Carter and Mary Ann. We will be heading home to see him in a few days."

The fan club sent a sizable check to John and June for their thirtieth wedding anniversary, in 1998. John had someone call and asked if it would be all right with us if they gave the money to someone they knew who had a lot of medical bills. He said, "We have so much, and she has so little." All of us were proud of their unselfishness.

John became sick on the stage at Council Bluffs, Iowa, and had to re-schedule the concert. We spent the rescheduled date with John on his rounds. There was a book signing, a visit to the train station, and a visit to the hospital where he had gone when he became ill. There was a concert planned for that evening. We were to meet with him and June after the concert. We were asked instead to meet with them on the bus at the motel.

What no one (the fans) was aware of was that June had been in bed all day with a sinus infection, and John had a temperature of 103 degrees. They had performed a great concert with no one suspecting that they were both sick. There had been a bomb threat at the school where they were performing, so after our meeting, they left to go home.

Another time, at the Fox Theatre in St. Louis, Missouri, John was scheduled for a week of concerts. The second day, John's sister-in-law died in Nashville, and John wanted to go home to be with his brother. It was too late to cancel that day's concerts. John performed two concerts that night and no one knew until the last show, when John told the audience what had happened and how badly he was hurting. A group of us sat in the audience and were so proud of him. The remainder of the concerts were rescheduled.

Branson, Missouri, was a wonderful place to see John. One could attend ten to twelve concerts a week. John told me that Branson was good for him. He could perform and not be on the road traveling between concerts. He leased a house for a year on the lake near Branson and said he and June had spent ten days there without seeing anyone, and it was completely wonderful.

John's generosity is very well known. He was also generous to his fan club members. He always met with members when time permitted. While he was in Branson, each fan club member was invited to a concert and given a ticket. John and June met with all of us after the evening concert for a picture and autograph session. They also provided a buffet dinner. On another occasion, fan club members were invited to a brunch at the

House of Cash. John stayed until he had to spoken to each person, signed an autograph, and posed for photos.

Another time, members were invited to a radio show recording at the House of Cash. John, June, Helen, and Anita were there. Waylon Jennings and Jessi Colter were also there. Another buffet was served to all the guests. On yet another occasion, the fifteen top winners of a membership contest were invited to a party at John's home. There was a dinner, entertainment, and a gift of June's cookbook that she had signed for each winner. John also arranged for each winner to have a photo taken together with him before they left for the evening.

John Cash would do a benefit concert each year for Carter Fold in Hiltons, Virginia. He would do an afternoon concert and an evening one. It is a wonderful place for a concert, and when Johnny Cash was going to perform there, the 1,000 seats sold out quickly. People were allowed to bring chairs and blankets and sit on the mountainside. His concerts always had an overflow crowd. After the first concert, we were invited to have dinner with John and June between concerts. John, June, Helen, Waylon, Jessi, Joyce and her husband, Curtis, and I were seated at the table. I don't remember much about the food, but the conversation was fascinating. After dinner, John took us on a tour of the Carter Family Museum.

There were many other meetings with John at concerts and special events, and each one was special to me—even the one when I was telling him what I was doing, and he looked me straight in the eye and said, "I know everything you do." My

THE JOHNNY CASH AND JUNE CARTER CASH INTERNATIONAL FAN CLUB

Artists address;   Johnny Cash & June Carter Cash
                    700 Johnny Cash Parkway
                    Hendersonville, TN 37075

The club was established in July of 1971 by Virginia and Charles Stohler and the Todds and Witherells assumed co presidency in January of 1984. We are the only official Johnny Cash and June Carter Cash Fan Club and are members of the International Fan Club Organization (IFCO)

● IFCO
INTERNATIONAL FAN CLUB ORGANIZATION

                    CO PRESIDENTS

Curtis & Alam Todd   Ray & Jeanne Witherell
Rt. 12, Box 350   117 Duever Lane
Winston-Salem, NC 27107   East Peoria, IL 61611
(919) 769-2816   (309) 699-0240
Correspondence, orders, dues and inquiries should be directed to the Todds. Please send ANYTHING for the publications to the Witherells.

                  MEMBERSHIP DUES

$11.00 - USA (1st Class Mail)
 12.00 - Canada (letter rate/equivalent of First Class)
 17.00 - Europe, S. America (Air Mail-Printed Matter)
 18.00 - Australia, New Zealand, Asia, South Africa,
         Pacific Ocean Islands (Air Mail-Printed Matter)
PAYMENT MUST BE IN US DOLLARS; We cannot accept foreign currency (including Canadian) or foreign personal checks.

                MEMBERSHIP PRIVILEGES

February - Newsletter   Included with all new
April - Journal   and renewal memberships
June - Newsletter   is a membership card, bio,
August - Journal   and an 8 X 10 photo of
October - Newsletter   John and June.
December - Yearbook

Cups, calendars, photos and other souvenir items are available plus we publish any sources we know of for record collectors.

WE RESERVE THE RIGHT TO REFUSE OR WITHDRAW MEMBERSHIPS

Cover Photo by Ray Witherell - Champaign, IL. 2/88

Curtis, Alma, Ray and I would like to dedicate this Journal to the loyal club members who are consistently on hand to help with the booth. Thank you, we couldn't do it without you! From left to right, George & Kay Harney, Susan Nagle, Bill & Barbara Sather, Alma, Myrna Deasy, Louise Cline, Bernie Gaudreau, Judy Peterson, sort of hiding behind Theresa Becwar, Francois Baot, Paul Miner, Jeanne, Karen & Leon Morse. Missing are Curtis and Virginia Stohler, Jo Miner, I think, is hiding behind me and Ray is out front taking the photo.

Well, I did it again....no matter how I plan, something always seems to happen to interfere. When I picked my vacation times at the beginning of summer, I chose Fan Fair week and the first week of August. My plans were to use that week to do the Journal and get it out of the way early as late August and September always mean extra long hours for work. My plans did not work out - I got some kind of "bug" and was in bed the whole week that I was off work. Every day I told myself that I would feel better tomorrow and could at least get a start on the Journal but it just didn't happen. I went back to work almost straight from bed and am just now really beginning to feel well again. Now, I am torn between needing to put in extra hours at work and wanting to get the Journal done. I am really sorry that

If a red check appears here, your membership expires with this Journal. We hope that you plan to renew....please note the new dues on the inside of the front cover. If you are late renewing, PLEASE let us know if you want missed publications.

- 1 -

dinner with John and June between concerts. John, June, Helen, Waylon, Jessi, Joyce and her husband, Curtis, and I were seated at the table. I don't remember much about the food, but the conversation was fascinating. After dinner, John took us on a tour of the Carter Family Museum.

There were many other meetings with John at concerts and special events, and each one was special to me—even the one when I was telling him what I was doing, and he looked me straight in the eye and said, "I know everything you do." My reply was, "I hope not!" The way he said it, though, left me unsure if he really knew or not!

Johnny Cash was honored at the nineteenth annual Kennedy Center Honors held at the Kennedy Center Opera House on December 9, 1996. John and his family spent the weekend in Washington, D.C., and were entertained by President Bill Clinton. On the following Monday, we met John at his hotel in Anderson, Indiana, where we were to attend his concert on December 10.

John and June with fan club co-Presidents Curtis and Alma Jean Todd and Ray and Jeanne Witherell.

While talking with John about his weekend, he told us he had done the dumbest thing when he was introduced to President Clinton. John said he didn't know what to say to Clinton, so he looked down at the president's feet and asked, "Mr. President, what size shoe do you wear?" Mr. Clinton replied, "Size thirteen." John said he then told the president, "I have you beat, 'cause I wear size thirteen and a half."

John, June, Ray, Jeanne, Curtis, and I had our last business meeting together on the front porch of their mountain home in Hiltons, Virginia. We gave them birthday presents and had a wonderful visit with them. John told us that he and June had retired and he didn't need a fan club any longer. He told us we had done an excellent job with very little help from him, and he appreciated us caring enough to do a good job. He also told us that it was just June and him, and they were going to do what they wanted to for the rest of their lives. This was in early June of 2000. That night, John did a full Johnny Cash concert. It was wonderful to be there and see that magic once again. He made it a perfect evening by dedicating a song to us.

The saddest moment I ever witnessed in John's life was at June's funeral in May 2003. After many tributes from family, friends, and fans, John stood by her casket and kissed her goodbye. As he was taken up the church aisle, he was holding up his hand and saying, "Folks, thank you for coming." He looked so sad, and when I looked into his eyes, I could see the hurt.

The proudest I ever felt for John Cash was on June 21, 2003, at Carter Fold. It was June's birthday week, and for years John and June had cele-

brated her birthday at their home in Hiltons with lots of family and friends. I believe this was John's first public appearance since June's death in May. John was to do a tribute for June that night, and the overflow crowd spilled out onto the mountainside in anticipation of his appearance. When his limo arrived, the crowd came to their feet and started cheering. John was brought to the door in a wheelchair, but then he stood up and insisted on walking to the stage.

He did walk to the stage, with the help of family and friends—and all the way everyone cheered, clapped, and cried. He sang six songs in an emotional and strong voice. Among them was "Angel Band," for June, and "Far Side Banks of Jordan," with his daughter-in-law, Laura Cash.

John tried to express how he was feeling. He said, "The pain of losing June, after forty years, was so severe. It hurts so bad. It really hurts." He said, "Folks, this is the big hurt." Most of us had tears in our eyes as he proudly walked out to his limo and went home. This was the last time I saw John until his visitation and funeral in September.

John Cash will not easily be forgotten. His funeral was not open to the public, but the public lined the streets from the church to the cemetery to pay their respects. Some stood quietly with their heads bowed, and others held signs telling John how much they loved him. I was told there were a lot of people that visited his grave that night.

My husband, Curtis, and I will not forget the joy that was brought into our lives by John Cash. We still have his music, but we miss our friend. It is hard to realize that we will never again see that smile and hear John say to us backstage, "Hello, folks, how are you?" I will always still miss someone . . . Johnny Cash.

HUGH WADDELL

Joelton, Tennessee
Shoe Size 10

*A*S A BOY ANXIOUS to play my shiny new, twenty-eight-dollar tin drum set, the relevance of a particular Saturday night in February 1971 would not occur until decades later. My father, the late Herman Waddell, owned a hunting and fishing sports store in our hometown of Hendersonville, Tennessee. As my father was an accomplished local singer and Hawaiian steel guitarist, each Saturday evening at closing time, after cleaning the sports shop, I anxiously awaited the arrival of amateur musicians who would convene in the back office for impromptu jam sessions. These devoted weekend musical warriors made up in desire and volume whatever they lacked in talent.

Wanting so to be a part of these gatherings, I would keep time to their music with my hands by beating on my dad's desk or the arms of a nearby chair while I listened. This was very annoying to them, I later learned, and prompted my dad to consider getting me a beginner drum set for my birthday. That is, if I promised to never again pound on his furniture keeping time to music.

My thirteenth birthday finally arrived, and so did the drum set. On this night, the Big Daddy brand drum set, complete with its paper drumheads, tin cymbals, and plastic foot pedal, was presented to me.

One of the regular Saturday night attendees, William Hughes, who worked at the Ford Glass Plant in Nashville, often would talk about a singer named Johnny Cash, and William loved to sing Cash tunes. Of course, I had seen Johnny Cash on TV and now recall thinking back then that on the TV screen, he sure looked really, really tall.

The fellows got their instruments out and asked if was I ready to finally join them making some music. Having never played drums before, I remember holding those cheap rubber-handled brushes that were included with that drum kit and getting sweaty palms as I waited for the first song. Musically, I didn't know what to do or how to do, but I was going to do. William asked me to make a train rhythm sound on that toy snare drum with those brushes. I did the best I could, and in a moment, "Folsom Prison Blues" was being played, complete with the song's signature guitar licks. William attempted to sing that song like Johnny Cash; although I also do remember thinking he sounded more like Mr. Ed.

TONY JOE WHITE/WAYLON JENNINGS
PRESENT
A BENEFIT CONCERT FOR SARAGOSA TORNADO VICTIMS
SUNDAY AUGUST 16, 1987
MANOR DOWNS

WAYLON

That special night, in the small office of my father's sport shop stocked with fishing lures, boat paddles, minnows, fly rods, and spinning reels, I got hooked on drums and the sound of Johnny Cash music.

Little did I know that destiny, some twenty-odd years later, would have me sitting behind a set of drums, and once again playing on a snare drum with brushes, making that train rhythm sound for "Folsom Prison Blues." This time, however, it was Johnny Cash doing the singing.

In August of 1987, Waylon Jennings was hosting an outdoor benefit concert for tornado-ravaged victims in the tiny town of Saragosa, Texas. John, who was playing a concert at Billy Bob's in Fort Worth that weekend, had agreed to come down and perform a few songs and do a few duets with Waylon. Although having known John for years, I had worked for him as his publicist and personal aide for only five months.

There was no drummer on stage when Waylon called John to sing, so Cash motioned for me to go sit at the drum kit. John's longtime guitarist Bob Wootton had also made the trip down to Saragosa. The rest of John's band was on their way to Fort Worth. As Bob readied to kick off "Folsom," he told me I'd do fine. I had been master of ceremonies for large concert crowds, hosted TV shows, worked in radio, and in addition, had played drums profession-ally for many years. But nothing, I mean nothing, could have prepared me for the anxiety rush of sitting in with Johnny Cash.

John and June with Rosey Carter and Hugh in Las Vegas, 1986.

It was odd, for while sitting behind the drums on that hot August Texas afternoon, my quivering hands were once again nervously sweating while holding wire brushes. It was déjà vu. I remembered at that instant me as the kid in my father's sports shop on Saturday night and that first song I ever played on drums: "Folsom Prison Blues." My heart calmed down, and away we played. It was a great afternoon.

Our immediate families have known each other for almost thirty years. John's mother, the late Carrie Cash (or Mama Cash, as she was lovingly called), was a dear friend to my late grandmother, Marie Comer. My mom was friends with June and would attend June's private fur sales in the early

John stares down
Hugh's camera lens.

1970s, where they served afternoon tea. Some of my seven sisters were school friends with some of John and June's combined six daughters. Mama Cash included my grandmother's cheese sausage-ball appetizers and sweet Southern fruit tea recipes in Mama Cash's cookbook.

I loved Mama Cash as if she were my own flesh and blood. Mama Cash was also my good friend. She would make banana puddings for me almost every week when I was in town working at the House of Cash office. I loved how she would greet hundreds of visitors and tourists daily at the Johnny Cash Museum with a toot on her wooden train whistle and her greeting of "Come in and feel welcome!" She gave me that lipstick-stained train whistle of hers, and I cherish it still today. Mama Cash could and would talk John into hiring me back after I'd been fired, let go, downsized, laid off, or basically cut from the Cash payroll.

When my mother, Jackie Comer Waddell, passed away in February 1987, John and June called me to express their pain and condolences. Their words were gently prolific and comforting. They insisted I join them immediately on the road to soften my grief at home.

Two weeks later, John called again and insisted that I go on the road with them, advancing tour dates. My job was to help sell more tickets through promotion, newspaper interviews, and radio/television live feeds. I had been out on the road for years previously as a road manager, drummer, and publicist; however, during the next nine years I received quite a worldly education, John and June style. I learned fast. Traveling across the country and abroad with the Johnny Cash entourage and circus, there were so many special memories, such brilliant and incomparable scenery, hundreds of noteworthy characters, and those magical Johnny Cash live music moments.

Early on when I went to work for John, he wanted me to advance his concert dates, and he knew that a business card that proclaimed "Johnny Cash Sent Me" would at least get attention. He hastily designed my first business card on a legal pad and then signed his name ten times on a blank sheet of paper to get the right signature for my card. He also signed his name in German, Spanish, and Japanese, in case, as he said, "I decide to send you some other places."

All fresh and new to Johnny Cash touring protocol, I set up at least four or five live interviews for John on March 11, 1987, in Madison, Wisconsin, my first official day with John. I left Madison then and had gone on to the next town on the tour. I had a great and easy system to promote these shows using live mediums to promote day-of-show, walk-up ticket sales. How wonderful it all looked on paper. I left instructions for John's road manager/drummer, W. S. Holland, on who to call, when to call, and where they would set up.

Every little detail was prepared and set for John to arrive, do some live press in the Edgewater Hotel lobby, and then retire to his hotel room until leaving for the show. Well, W. S. called me late that night from Madison to inform me that my system was great, but the afternoon hotel press junket was a disaster.

W. S. called the media as I had instructed, and they showed up exactly as planned, setting up in the hotel lobby. The "problem" turned out to be that when John arrived at the hotel, he looked at the press assemblage, warmly waved, and just continued walking to the hotel elevator. He never came back down. It was his naptime. Nobody, living or dead, bothered Johnny Cash during his afternoon ritual naps. Especially not W. S., who knew better. Me, myself, and I knew nothing about John's road routine of everyday naps!

Hugh and John's long-time cook, Miss Leatha.

Several producers in Madison, Wisconsin, were ready to tar and feather me, or worse. These weren't typical interviews that could be post-poned and done later at the concert venue. They were live, afternoon and early evening radio and television pro-grams, running heavily promoted "Johnny Cash will be joining us here live in just a few minutes from the famous Edgewater Hotel" kinds of interviews.

And no Johnny, because Johnny was upstairs snoozing. Lucky for me, I was in another town setting up more live interviews there. At least from this I learned to be quiet and cordial while being deservedly chastised. I also learned that electronic media producers can and do harbor poor feel-ings and really like to vent. I also quickly learned how to cancel live after-noon interviews.

I joke with W. S. Holland, who drummed for Johnny Cash for almost forty years, that although as an employee he may have worked for John the longest; I probably worked for John the most. I was fired or laid off numerous times. I forget how many. Four, five, or six. Sometimes because I didn't keep my mouth shut when I should have, and sometimes because John and June were taking time off from road touring, or just laying off staff for health or vacation reasons.

Like some corporate human resources director, John had the ability to get out of you exactly what you were capable of. He seemed to know your limitations—or potential—at times better than you did. He knew how to

give you creative freedom to do your job. On a flight back
from Los Angeles, Waylon showed me his Franklin
Electronic Bible. I showed it to John. Later, when I
approached John about his possibly sponsoring Franklin
Electronic Publishers' Electronic Bible, he told me to "Do
it," and to "Just work it out." So, only weeks after running the idea by John, and after agent Lou Robin had
worked out percentages and financial details with
Franklin, Johnny Cash became the Franklin Electronic
Bible official spokesperson.

I did some literal "heavy lifting" for Johnny the
Cash, like helping June move large antique pieces of
furniture from place to place. Any male employee of
John or June's who has ever worked in Hendersonville
at their home or office has "moving June's antiques"
tales to share.

John would have me work on things or ponder
things that he knew would challenge me. He was like
that with everybody he was close to. Tasks such as finding a sponsor for the 1988 Country Music Hall of Fame
Johnny Cash exhibit, or having me put together piles of
home films and photos for use as new overhead-projection footage at his
concerts, or helping promote June's *Carter Family Cookbook,* or taking raw
video footage and producing it into the *Return to the Promised Land*
audio/video project, or helping his daughter Cindy organize the House of
Cash tape vault, or being the concert promoter for February 1988's
Affordable Art Tour.

On that particular short tour, John, Waylon, Jessi Colter, and June would
perform individually, paired up, and as a group, with a minimal backup
band. This was a pre-Highwayman tour and prior to the "unplugged" craze.
The concerts were booked at the main state university campuses of Illinois,
Missouri, and Oklahoma, and featured a reduced ticket price. John had
asked me to promote this tour, and I was thrilled at the opportunity. He had
me type and issue this press release he had written and dictated to me:

The prices for most country music shows have gone out of the ceiling and I believe that the average country music fan can't afford to take their family to a show.

June, Waylon, Jessi, and I are trying something different. With the Affordable Art Tour we are dropping show prices to a level that we believe the fans can afford. Tickets are $9.50 for everyone for a two-and-a-half-hour show.

In going back to basics, we are bringing a more intimate, simple show with little flash and flair. Less lighting, less sophisticated sound and instrumentation. We will do the songs the fans want to hear, but we'll do them without the high-tech schmaltz that has been the trend lately.

We want to reach people and allow anyone to see and experience a "homey" spontaneous production that has long been missing in our business.

The four of us have never toured together, and in our family and friends kind of band, we hope to share a look at ourselves that the gang has rarely seen.

We are excited about it and anxious to perform in a "loose" and "free" atmosphere. At $9.50, it's "affordable art."

After *Entertainment Tonight*'s Nashville producer, Dick Heard, told me that his bosses were not too interested in covering this special tour, I called Brooke Shields's office. Brooke and her mother, Teri, had become friends with John and June and had attended a few Cash concerts. After I yakked with Mrs. Shields, Brooke was added at the last moment as the tour's "special guest." With the lineup and the added celebrity appeal of Brooke, *Entertainment Tonight* was soon taping at the Affordable Art Tour concerts and did a nice feature. Of course, the exquisite Brooke Shields, with her tight denim laundry, didn't hurt the tour's ticket sales, either.

Johnny Cash knew how to evoke your thought process, and he let you figure things out on your own. Once after being laid off, John insisted that I read Og Mandino's *The Greatest Salesman in the World* before I could come back to work for him. He actually bought me a copy of the thin

JOHNNY CASH
hugh waddell
HOUSE OF CASH
P.O. Box 508 • 700 Johnny Cash Parkway • Hendersonville, TN 37077
Phone (615) 824-5110 • Fax (615) 822-7332

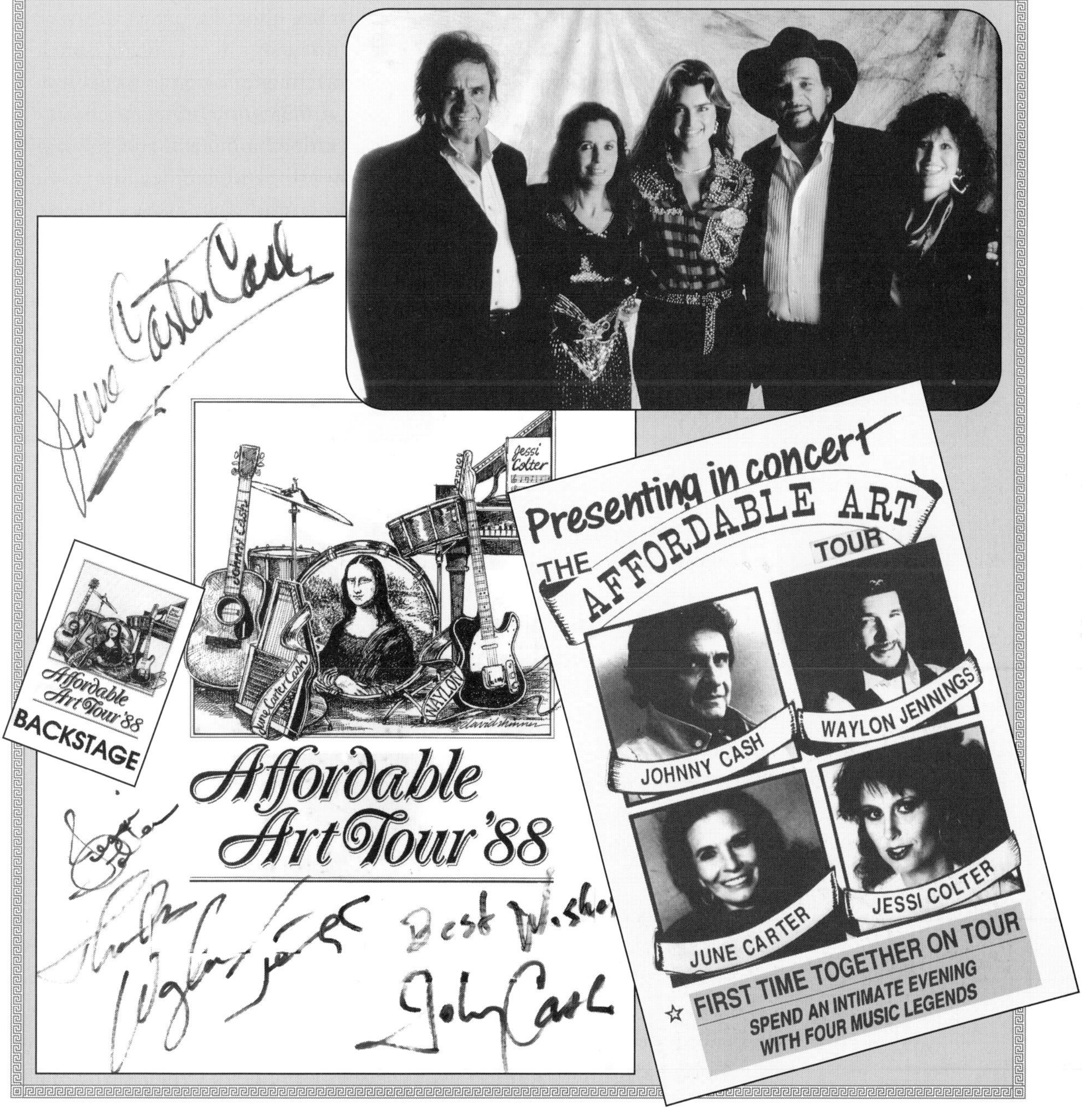

June Carter Cash

Affordable
Art Tour '88

Affordable
Art Tour '88
BACKSTAGE

Best Wishes
John Cash

Presenting in concert
THE AFFORDABLE ART
TOUR

JOHNNY CASH   WAYLON JENNINGS

JUNE CARTER   JESSI COLTER

★ FIRST TIME TOGETHER ON TOUR
SPEND AN INTIMATE EVENING
WITH FOUR MUSIC LEGENDS

paperback and quizzed me on the book to make sure I had read it. Shortly after, he hired me back at a higher wage.

We talked American history and suggested history books to each other. I'd give him *A People's History of the United States: 1492-Present* by Howard Zinn and tell him about Zinn's other works, and he'd suggest to me *Undaunted Courage: Meriwether Lewis, Thomas Jefferson, and the Opening of the American West*. John loved to tell you stuff you didn't know, and he loved to expose you to new things—whether describing his understanding of Mexican General Santa Anna, or telling the story of how the woodwork in his tour bus came from a home that Union General Ulysses S. Grant occupied in Chattanooga during the Civil War, or discussing his Roman coin collection.

He appreciated good singers and songwriters. John turned me on to great music from recording artists such as Johnny Horton, Tim Hardin, Leonard Cohen, Steve Goodman, Mahalia Jackson, Sister Rosetta Tharpe, Mississippi Mass Choir, Norman Blake, Roger Miller, and Alan Lomax's *Blues in the Mississippi Night*. Once, he had me go out and buy every Tim Hardin CD I could find in an afternoon and bring them, along with a portable CD player, to him in his room at Baptist Hospital in Nashville. Even if you had heard of the singer, John would invite you to explore their unheard song catalogs.

I went to California with June's daughter Rosey in the mid-1980s, and there I met Larry Murray, who had been one of the principal writers for many of John's television shows on the ABC and CBS networks. Larry was working on material for a possible upcoming Cash Christmas special. John had done many seasonal specials for CBS; however, this proposed special was only in the consideration stage. Larry mentioned that skits and songs for the program were written by freelance writers like himself, and I asked if I could "come up with some stuff" to send him. He didn't care.

Back home in Tennessee, I wrote this medium-tempo song, "You're My Holiday," for John and June to duet. I was not a songwriter, and this was my very first lyrical offering. It really wasn't a Christmas song per se, but I had visions of creative greatness, as I also came up with numerous Yuletide skits and segments for the special. I never sent anything to Larry, because just a month after our California visit, CBS decided not to do the Cash Christmas special that year. I produced tracks on my song anyway with corn-country crooner Vern Gosden singing the demo.

Years later I shared with John my "Larry Murray/California trip/illusions of scriptwriting grandeur" story, relative to his old CBS-TV Christmas specials. He asked me to play him the song, so I found and played the Vern Gosden version. John told me he liked it; I thanked him and then thought nothing more of it.

Johnny Cash was always about the song. He could record with anybody and feel at ease because, with him, it wasn't about the person or the personality; it was always about the song. I had suggested to John in 1988 that he record the Harry Chapin song "Cat's in the Cradle" and he did, putting it on his Mercury release *Boom Chicka Boom*. I had suggested to John in 1993 that he record an old song by Loudon Wainwright III called "The Man Who Couldn't Cry." I was out in California a lot that year with John, going with him for every recording session, while working with Rick Rubin. I was proud when a live version of "The Man Who Couldn't Cry" made John's 1994 Rick Rubin/American Recordings label debut.

However, I couldn't, and wouldn't, pitch a song I had written to John. He got enough of that from every direction. In 1997, Kelly Hancock called me from the House of Cash and asked if I had a tape and song lyrics to "my Christmas song." She said John wanted them. It took me a bit to find them, as I'm not a songwriter and had the tape stuffed in a box and the lyrics in a pile of papers.

As it turned out, Kenny Rogers had called John looking for material for Rogers's upcoming Christmas album recording sessions. John had asked Kelly for my tune, as it was the Christmas song he'd decided to send to Kenny Rogers. John also included a handwritten letter to Kenny asking for consideration of my song.

Rogers never did record "You're My Holiday," but that never bothered or disappointed me in the least. I was so impressed by the fact that John had remembered my song in the first place, after only hearing it just once three years earlier. I was also flattered that John actually liked my very first songwriting effort enough to offer it to Kenny Rogers. To me, that was weighty stuff.

John encouraged you when you failed. Promoting John's book *Man In White* in 1988, every public signing event had been very fruitful. That is until I booked a posh bookstore at the Beverly Center Mall, an exclusive shopping complex in the heart of Beverly Hills, California. Despite the newspaper and radio promotion, in less than fifteen minutes John had finished signing copies for the twenty or so folks who had shown up. He wryly smiled as I busily stacked more books for him to sign at the solitary table set up in front of the store. I knew at least that if John signed them all, maybe the bookstore wouldn't return them unsold to the publisher.

As John finished signing every single copy of *Man In White* the store had in stock, we sat there for several moments in silence. Ostentatious mall shoppers walked by, slowing to stare at this well-dressed and familiar man in black seated in front of the bookstore all by himself with his large stacks of books on the table. Quite surreal.

John waved and they moved on. So did we. His only words as he stood up were, "Hugh, you win some, you lose some." Nothing else was said. Coming from John Cash, those were some potent, yet succinct words to inspire me, despite this deplorable Beverly Hills turnout.

He had ways of expressing his displeasure when I messed up and, conversely, would support me when I came through for him. Such was the case in 1992, when John canceled a July photo shoot for *Family Circle* magazine. It happened that the photo session was for their sixtieth-anniversary October issue, which would feature three American families of note. Along with John and June and their children, only Walter Cronkite and his grandchildren and Eunice Kennedy Shriver with her children and grandchildren, were being photographed and profiled for this women's magazine and its 26 million-plus readers.

John and June decided an hour before the photo shoot that not enough family members were going to be present. I tried reasoning with John that the magazine would be happy with just him and June, because for what-

ever reason, we had canceled or postponed the session several times before and the magazine was now under deadline. John's retort was, "Who do you work for, them or me?" As he was communicating this to me through my cell phone in one ear, I was getting more unpleasantries in the other ear from some of the magazine's editorial hierarchy who had flown to Nashville from New York for this important and costly shoot.

The next moment was a defining personal reckoning for me, as I quietly replied to John, "I work for you, but you don't have to be an #*&@%$ about it." I then hung up on him. I truly expected to be fired, again.

Instead, two days later, while we were driving to Nashville, John apologized for putting me in that spot and told me he appreciated the fact that I told him what I thought, rather than what I thought he had wanted to hear. He mentioned that most everyone, when he asked for an opinion, out of courtesy, respect, or fear, would tell him whatever they figured would please Johnny Cash—not what they were actually thinking.

Subsequently, *Family Circle* magazine was very angry with John for this last-minute cancellation, and the Cash family was never featured in the publication.

John R. Cash was very nomadic. In my opinion, he loved being a restless Johnny. With so many diverse habitats he and June enjoyed, it truly seemed that they were always going, always outbound from someplace on the way to another. John did get "itchy feet" often.

Their arsenal of domiciles included, at one time or another, homes or apartments in Port Richey, Florida;

Hugh and June on Table Rock Lake near Branson, Missouri. Note John's black shoes on the deck; he's driving the boat.

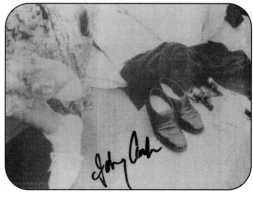

Supermodel Kate Moss with John and Hugh in 1994 during filming of the video for Cash's "Delia's Gone" single.

Hiltons, Virginia; Asbury Park, New Jersey; Central Park in New York City; acreage and a farmhouse in Bon Aqua, Tennessee; his noted Old Hickory Lake residence with its Cedar Hill Refuge Recording Cabin compound in Hendersonville; the numerous capacious log cabins on Cash Mountain, south of Cap's Gap, Tennessee; and even for a short while an unassuming duplex in Branson, Missouri.

When he felt like it, John Cash could hang and be "just one of the guys." And, as with a majority of red-blooded males, he appreciated beautiful and attractive women. He was a huge fan of Emmylou Harris, not only for her character, musical intelligence, and vocal talents, but also for her loveliness.

John would see a photo of a striking woman, such as actress Mary Steenburgen, and refer to her as "one of God's precious little creatures." Females were also attracted to John's aura and bravado. He counted many renowned and diverse handsome women as friends, from Kate Moss and Elizabeth Taylor to Jane Seymour and Brooke Shields.

Johnny Cash loved to give. One Christmas I received from him a California brown bear claw and a short Christmas note telling me the legal ramifications of his gift. I called it Santa Claw.

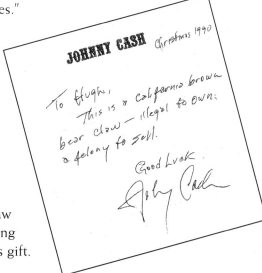

JOHNNY CASH   Christmas 1990

To Hugh,
This is a California brown bear claw — illegal to own; a felony to sell.

Good Luck.
Johny Cash

On another occasion, he presented me with an attaché case that I had vastly underestimated. On the outside of the worn Italian briefcase were a Braniff Airlines stick-on travel tag that said, in John's own handwriting, "Johnny Cash, Caudill Drive, Hendersonville Tennessee," and a late-seventies Emmylou Harris backstage pass.

I thought it was a nice hand-me-down gesture, and John explained a few days later that this well-thumbed briefcase was indeed his "stash" for a major portion of his traveling career. He had taken black shoe polish and inconsiderately changed the original light-tan shade to black.

The hidden inner case showed considerable evidence of the times he'd lost his key and ripped it open, then used extra-large amounts of Elmer's glue to make sloppy repairs. The inside lining had numerous ink pen stains and spill marks. John told me he gave me his old stash briefcase because he thought I'd appreciate it more than anyone else.

Johnny Cash was a real giver. He really did love giving people things sometimes, whether he knew them or not. Distinctive items given to me by John included the 500 C/M Hasselblad camera that the Victor Hasselblad Company of Sweden had presented to him, a leather Rolling Stones tour jacket, and many handwritten lyrics. When I traveled with John, I'd insist that he keep his original-first-draft song lyrics. He'd write and change the lyrics, then re-write the song out and want to throw his first draft away. So that I'd shut up and stop nagging him, he just gave many of them to me.

He loved to wear handmade silk shirts from Hollywood's Nat Wise, whom John referred to as "Shirt Maker to the Stars." Sometimes, however, June would buy him silk shirts off the department store rack. When we were out on the road, as he was packing for the next town, John would sometimes kindly sneak one of "June's gift shirts" to me and tell me not to mistakenly wear it while with them. I still have four or five of those shirts.

Once, while in the dressing room area just prior to going on stage, John lost a small ruby out of a nice handmade silver belt buckle he had on. I spent an hour or so with the lights off, crawling around the room with a flashlight, hoping to make it sparkle in the dark in order to find it. John walked in during the intermission, turned on the lights, and there I was, foolishly searching on my hands and knees with a flashlight.

He told me to forget about trying to find the lost, minuscule stone. That evening, on the way to the hotel, he gave me that silver belt buckle as a reward for having looked so hard and long for the missing stone.

On the road in New York or L.A., John would often call my hotel room in the evening around ten-ish and want to know why I wasn't out on the town. He'd tell me he didn't need me that evening and for me to come to his room. When I'd knock on his door, he would open it and hand me a hundred-dollar bill, sometimes two hundred dollars, and tell me I'd better not have any money left in the morning. John wanted me to go out and experience the city and not save the money to pay bills back home. His was a heart of benevolence and a mind for discovery.

Johnny Cash liked smoking cigarettes, and although he had often in the eighties and nineties publicly attempted to quit, he would sneak away from June for an occasional puff. Many times on the road, John would come down to my room for a quick smoke. He'd say, "You know, these things are bad for you. You got a light?" He was so quick-witted. When interviewers would ask him the main secret to his and June's many years of marriage, he'd simply reply, "Separate bathrooms."

One of the best places I enjoyed observing the visually amusing "Johnny the Cash" character was in New York City. I often called John "Johnny the Cash" when he'd go out in public knowing he would be asked for photos and autographs. He humorously referred to this as "getting swarmed." When cornered, John was most sincere and accommodating. Always. He was never rude to fans, working blue-collar folks, doormen, cooks, airline personnel, stagehands, waitresses, the elderly, and children. He could effortlessly handle politicians, from local councilmen to presidents.

Although he did politick a little by stumping in 1988 in Richmond, Virginia, during Albert Gore Jr.'s first run at the White House, the John I knew kept his personal political views to himself, as opposed to his Vietnam-era stands. He had his convictions, as we all do, but he avoided public political debate. John knew how not to sweat the small stuff. John didn't argue. He might disagree with you, state his own opinion, and let his view stand on its own merit.

Going to New York City with John was where I experienced the man in his most cerebral element. He and June had an apartment for years overlooking Central Park. John loved the streets of New York. He enjoyed walking endless blocks, going into stores and shops like Brentano's Book Store, Tower Records, and Banana Republic. He loved matzo ball soup from the Carnegie Deli.

One particular New York trip of note was a week in January 1992, when John was inducted into the Rock and Roll Hall of Fame in ceremonies at the Waldorf-Astoria Hotel on the evening of the fifteenth, then sang with Big Bird at a taping for a *Sesame Street* segment on the sixteenth, and then did an appearance on the *Late Show with David Letterman*.

Nick Lowe (left), Elvis Costello (top center), and a bevy of friends pay a visit to John and June backstage at London's Royal Albert Hall.

I'll never forget how, during the Rock Hall of Fame induction dinner, John returned from the restroom and shared with me that Keith Richards had patted him on the back while they were both standing at the urinals. John said Keith exclaimed at this moment, "I can't believe I'm taking a piss with Johnny Cash!" That week was so typical of John's diverse allure.

John was always open to meeting people I'd parade up to him, as long as I didn't embarrass him while doing so. At award shows, television tapings, and music events, John would ask me who certain up-and-comers were, as he liked their music but didn't quite know the names. One year, he was impressed with the all-woman band Wild Rose and songwriter Matraca Berg, and wrote to both simply as a music fan.

One particular Hugh-induced introduction occurred in Germany in 1989. I don't recall whether it was at our hotel in Munich, Berlin, or Hamburg, but I do know it was Germany. While checking in, I noticed Frank Zappa standing in the lobby. Being a Zappa fan, I approached him, introduced myself and tactfully asked if would he like to meet Johnny

Cash. I then went over to John and June, who were still standing in the lobby, and told them that Frank Zappa would like to meet them

John had definitely heard of Zappa, but June didn't quite know who he was until I hummed, "Watch out where the huskies go, and don't you eat that yellow snow."

John and former Beatle George Harrison.

As John, June, and Frank exchanged pleasantries, Zappa invited them to his concert that night some thirty miles from the hotel. John told him that if they felt like it, they would definitely try to make Frank's concert. Ultimately, they were too tired to attend the show; however, it so happened that Frank's concert was being recorded.

Frank's elation at meeting Johnny Cash that day in Germany can be heard on Zappa's live album *The Best Band You Never Heard in Your Life*, released in 1991, as he introduces his group doing "Ring of Fire." They had rehearsed the song during sound check that afternoon in Germany in anticipation of John showing up for the show. It is now a piece of Frank Zappa recording history.

I wish John had gone to the Zappa concert. John's career was full of cool pairings. John & Waylon, John & Sammy Davis Jr., John & Kirk Douglas, John & Billy Graham, John & Tom Petty, John & June, John & Ray Charles, John & Gene Autry, John & fill-in-your-own-blank. In the short period that I worked for him, John R. Cash recorded or performed with as veritable a plethora as could be fathomed.

These talents included Irish rockers U2, conductor John Williams and the Boston Pops, *Sesame Street*'s Big Bird, John Schneider (Bo Duke from TV's *Dukes of Hazzard*), Hank Jr., Paul McCartney, the Two Cookie Kid, Red Hot Chili Peppers, the Carter Family, Stevie Wonder, Mark O'Connor, the National Symphony Orchestra, Wayne Newton, horror-

fiction guru Stephen King, Bob Dylan, Gillian
Welch, Ray Stevens, Christian rockers One
Bad Pig, Bill Monroe, legendary deejay
Wolfman Jack, Tom T. Hall, Tammye Faye
Bakker (yes, *that* Tammye Faye), and, as John
wrote in his song "Backstage Pass," many
other "stars of flickering magnitude." His
recording career from early on was speckled
like that, with variety from Doc Watson to
Andre Kostelanetz.

John would, on occasion, do just whatever
you asked of him without reservation. He
played Starwood Amphitheater in Nashville for a charity event called One
for the Sun and played a Humane Society fund-raiser called Rock for the
Animals at my family farm. He met with NFL heavy-hitter Tex Schramm in
1989 in order to help Nashville get a possible National Football League
spring league team, prior to the Tennessee Titans.

John would always ask me why or how I had talked him
into stuff, usually after it had happened. I did totally
catch him off guard in February 1990 with
Billboard magazine's Johnny Cash 35th
Anniversary issue. I served as executive
editor of the section, and among
the features and good wishes
included were congrat-
ulatory letters from
all five living U.S.
presidents. Richard
Nixon referred to John as
"truly the voice of America,
as rich and strong as our
nation itself." Ronald Reagan
wrote that he knew John as "a
charitable and kindhearted man

John makes notes on the lyric sheet for *Return to the Promised Land* at the Bob Cummings studio.

who, by sharing your most personal experiences, inspired millions to regain faith and keep heart."

In 1988, John held a press conference in support of the Nashville Symphony and played its Italian Street Fair fund-raising concert. He supported AIDS awareness campaigns, the American Cancer Society's Jail-a-thon, Campus Crusade for Christ, and children's causes such as Feed the Children and Jamaica's S.O.S. Village. And nobody could ever know the exact amount of time or the exact number of shirts, boots, guitars, and other personal items Johnny Cash donated to charitable causes, just because they asked.

In March 1991, John let me throw a huge surprise party for John Carter. An overflow crowd—including Minnesota Fats, the Oak Ridge Boys, Waylon, Tom T. Hall, Larry Gatlin, Bill Monroe, and a "cast of hundreds"—packed the tiny Bell Cove Club in Hendersonville for John Carter's twenty-first birthday musical marathon, which I dubbed "John Carter Cash's Birthday Bash and Musical Bar Mitzvah." John let you run with your ideas and would pull you in only if you got too rambunctious.

I got pulled in quite often; however, it was the challenge to "do and do well" that drove me. John wrote in early 1990, "Hugh, you do a good job. You have improved in effectiveness about 90 percent in two years. Keep working on that 10 percent. It's sad, but that is the part that most people notice." John knew that 10 percent is where June got upset at me, and where I was most often misunderstood.

At the Billy Graham Crusade in Fargo, North Dakota, June felt that it was too hot on the podium for everyone. She had me go back to the hotel and fill up one of her suitcases full of ice, bring it back to the Crusade site, and then fill small bags of ice to put on people's feet, cooling them as they sat. This was so odd and so very practical at the same time.

John acted oh-so-serious while June was setting this up, yet behind her back, he and sister Reba Hancock and Jack Hale laughed endlessly at me, calling me "Iceman" as I walked behind them and Billy Graham on the way to the podium, struggling with June's bulky suitcase packed with melting ice. I would enjoy more creative moments.

Originally slated to be a 1992 Easter cable-television special, the entire *Return to the Promised Land* project was very unique, both in how it came to be and the final released results. It literally fell in my lap. John called me one morning in the spring of 1992 and asked me to go pick up the numerous raw videotape masters and see if I could do anything with them.

The Nashville Network cable channel had passed on the Easter Cash show. At this time, I was driving back and forth twice weekly from Nashville to Branson, working on the never-to-be completed Johnny Cash Theatre that some wide-eyed investor was attempting to build. John and June were staying at the Big Cedar Lodge just south of Branson.

An interesting fact is that, although the Johnny Cash Theatre never opened and the building was only half-finished at the time, Jim Bohannon guest-hosted the Mutual Radio Network's Larry King radio show live from the under-construction lobby to over a million listeners. John and June sang two songs and were on the air several hours with Jim. This was the same weekend as the Rodney King verdict in L.A. and the subsequent riots.

Return to the Promised Land took months to sort out. I spent every available moment looking at and logging the various content on those videotapes

JOHNNY
CASH
THEATRE

3701 West Highway 76 • Branson, MO 65616
417-335-CASH • 1-800-TRY-CASH

The Johnny Cash Theatre at Branson, Missouri, was never completed, but John and June still did a live segment of Larry King's radio show from the venue with host Jim Bohannon (top right).

shot in location around the Holy Land. The tapes traveled everywhere I did. The major portion of the hours of raw video footage was unusable due to technical glitches, failure to white-balance the camera, or just bad shots and angles. It was noteworthy that John had used Israeli cameramen and Arab production grips.

Most of the musical performances and sincere introductory words from the shoot were visually clean and possessed a notable rawness and deep spiritual connection. I couldn't lose that. We were able to piece the video together with cuts and edits and re-recorded the guitar tracks. Having only four audio tracks to record to in the digital D2 editor format, engineer Pete Cummings helped me build the music tracks.

As there was no theme song or melody tying the entire work together, I called my friend David Ray Skinner, who lives in Atlanta. David responded by calling back just two hours later, politely waited for the tone, and then played a wonderful melody on my answering machine. With the music theme now on tape to work with, Dave and I wrote the chorus and first verse. A few weeks later, after playing what we had for him at Bob

Cummings Productions' editing studio, John wrote the last verse just moments before he and June sang their vocals on it. Dave and I had now officially written a song with Johnny the Cash. Too cool!

We recorded that song, "Return to the Promised Land," in just over twenty minutes. Billy Graham's World Wide Pictures released the forty-five-minute *Return to the Promised Land* video in the fall of 1993. John told me he was very proud of *Return to the Promised Land*. Subsequently, the *Return to the Promised Land* audio CD was released in 2000, with several bonus Cash demo tracks and a ten-minute interview with Mama Cash, including her giving her recipe for banana pudding. Only 1,700 copies were ever manufactured, as the Renaissance Records label folded just before the CD was to be sent to reviewers and distributors.

John Cash used humor to break the ice and create mischievous tension in the ranks. When John asked me to play drums on his 1989 European tour, several members of his band wanted a rehearsal, because aside from John, no one had heard me play. This would be my first tour as Cash's drummer. During sound check in Cork, Ireland, the entire band waited for John to come out and rehearse with me. John made us wait an extra-long time. He finally strolled out. When someone asked what song we'd be going over first, he walked over to my drum riser, looked right at me, and proclaimed in a medium-loud Cash voice, "He doesn't deserve any rehearsal!" Then he just walked off the stage.

John Cash on a personal level was about as real a human being as I could know. He was all about admitting one's shortcomings, and he regarded atonement as an empowering strength. Sin and redemption. Since my days working for him, John had always told me that I could use him as a reference should the need arise. He wrote letters of recommendation for me. Up to the date of his passing, I proudly listed Johnny Cash as one of my references on my resume.

I have told many about the somber elation I felt at John's immense gesture of respect for my late father, Herman Waddell. When my father passed away in 1996, John called and asked if there was anything he could do. When I told John how my father loved his music, John offered to sing at my father's service. I told John the day of my father's funeral of my very

THE DORCHESTER
Park Lane London W1A 2HJ
Telephone 071-629 8888 Telex 887704
Facsimile 071-409 0114

April 8 1992

Dear Hugh,
Concerning the videos, stills,
etc for the Branson stage,
I thought it best to say
it out to you, then you
can get the information.
Jay Quaro in Branson
to Jay Quaro in Branson.
I think Jay went
home yesterday, I'm not sure.
Branson, I'm not sure.
reason, I am doing
this way is because of
you to get it done.
Following is Branson
as related to video

THE DORCHESTER
Park Lane London W1A 2HJ
Telephone 071-629 8888 Telex 887704
Facsimile 071-409 0114

Hugh, I cannot stand to
hear the sentence "It can't
be done." Please remember this
in your conversations with Jay.
I'll back you up if I need to.
I won't get to Branson
until about the 28th maybe
27th — so we'll only have
a day or two to rehearse.
I'll feel a lot better
till then knowing you are
handling this very important
thing for me.

Your Friend,
John

JRC

Hugh,
You'll never fly
like an eagle as
long as you run
with turkeys.

John

---

these 3
tapes are for
Rick Rubin. Please
make copies and
leave the originals
here so I can
take them with
me tomorrow

Thanks John

Call Heidi —
Ask her to please
choose some new
publicity photos.
I'm not too happy
with the scary
image.
Thanks.

Hugh, I wanted the
"America" tape alright, but
remember I told you that
I have it all typed out.
What I really need,
Audio and print is the
thing I did with
John Williams in Boston.

But I'm in no hurry
for it. Any time in
the next month is O.K.

"UNDAUNTED
COURAGE"

Thomas Jefferson
Merriwether
Lewis and the
great Western
Movement.

I need a tape on these
songs I have recorded:
1. Allegheny — w/Lyrics
2. The devil to pay w/lyrics
3. Pack up your Sorrows /..
I need lyrics on these:
1. Ballad of Barbara.
2. Big Foot
3. Bury me not on Lone Prairie
4. I Wish I was Crazy Again
5. No Earthly Good

JOHNNY CASH

Hi Bob,

Welcome to Hendersonville. Sorry I missed you. Gone on tour with the Highwaymen.

I know you'll enjoy the privacy at Monthaven. Hugh Waddell will take good care of you.

Should you want to get away to my house, you're welcome. There'll be security for you, and June said tell you that your room is ready.

Your friend,

John C.

Hugh Give this to Dylan if I dont get to see him

GERALD R. FORD

January 4, 1990

Dear Mr. Waddell:

Enclosed the letter to Johnny that you requested.

Best regards,

G.R. Ford

Mr. Hugh Waddell
House of Cash
700 Johnny Ca___
Henderson___ ___

SE OF CASH, INC.   P. O. BOX 508 • HENDERSONVILLE, TENNESSEE 37075

Inter-Office Memo

SUBJECT ROY ORBISON TRIBUTE

J.R.C.

HUGH   DATE

BARBARA ORBISON'S OFFICE CALLED AND SAID THE "RESCHEDULED" ROY TRIBUTE IS SET FOR FEB. 24th, NEXT YEAR. YOU HAVE A TWO SHOW CONCERT THAT NIGHT AT EL CAMINO COLLEGE IN NORTH L.A. AND I TOLD THEM THIS. THEY NOW WOULD LIKE TO KNOW IF YOU COULD TAPE A SONG, SAY A FEW WORDS AND THAT WOULD BE SHOWN THE NIGHT OF THE TRIBUTE, ALSO TO BE USED IN A SHOWTIME CABLE SPECIAL. DO YOU WISH TO DO THIS, OR WOULD YOU RATHER JUST PASS ON THIS. PLEASE LET ME KNOW.

I'd like to tape a song and say a few words for the tribute

JOHNNY CASH

THE WASHINGTON COURT
ON CAPITOL HILL

July

Bono, I'm trying to be and statesman-like when I see the great reviews on Zooropa, and when I read all the nice things that you and Edge and the others say about me, I say, "Yeah, that's nice." But inside I'm exploding with Joy.

I'm richly blessed to have been "the chosen one"

I heard about a video. I'll make myself available if and when the time comes.

Your room is ready at my house when you come to America. June sends love. Thanks to you all.

John Cash

P.S. ___

JOHNNY CASH

Dear Mr. President,

Thank you.

As of today with Baker in Geneva, there seems to be a faint hope for peace.

May God bless you, and give you great wisdom and discernment in dealing with the middle East situation.

For Peace

June and Johnny Cash

This September 28, 1993, concert in the Country Music Hall of Fame parking lot, celebrating the release of the Carter Family stamp by the U.S. Postal Service, was one of the last times that June and her only two sisters, Helen and Anita, and her only two daughters, Rosey and Carlene, performed together.

first drumming experience as a thirteen-year-old, playing "Folsom Prison Blues" with my dad at the little sports shop. Words cannot do adequate justice to the appreciation I felt as John sang "These Hands" and "Peace in the Valley" during my father's tribute.

Whether one liked John's music or not, to me, there was a comfortable feeling knowing that new Johnny Cash albums were coming out, and with each release a new Cash revival. To me, John's albums were where good songs had a chance to be heard. He always seemed to get out of a song what the songwriters put in. It will always be trendy to play Johnny Cash music. It has been since 1955.

I reflect on my personal friendship with John and offer my own Johnny Cash memory-evoking tour. I think John would approve.

• Stop at the Johnny Cash rest area on Interstate I-40 West, at mile marker 170, near Dickson, Tennessee. Sit on the bench by the Johnny Cash sign and write a poem.

• Go to Bon Aqua, Tennessee, and smell the honeysuckle, while listening to the Cash songs "Any Old Wind that Blows," "Saturday Night in Hickman County," and "I'm Gonna Sit on the Porch and Pick on My Old Guitar."

• Read a story in the Holy Bible about Jesus and listen to the tune "Redemption" from Johnny Cash's first Rubin-produced 1994 American Recordings album, *Cash*.

• Buy a cassette or CD from any struggling singer or songwriter and offer them words of encouragement.

• Drive to the east side of Hendersonville, Tennessee, and sit on the westbound side of U.S. Highway 31 East by the Johnny Cash Parkway sign. Wait until the next eastbound train rumbles through on the tracks nearby. Meditate on it.

• Drive by the local jail, workhouse, or prison in your area while listening to John's songs "Folsom Prison Blues," "San Quentin," and "Dark as a Dungeon" at high volume.

• Order a soft-serve ice cream cone from the drive-thru at McDonald's. (On numerous occasions when returning home from Nashville, John, June, and I would stop at McDonald's for these treats. After ordering through the tiny speaker, John would jokingly mimic their standard reply of "Thank yeeew. Pleeez drive round.") Just under your breath, replicate Johnny's mimic.

• Go to Kingsland, Arkansas, and have your picture made next to the brick and brass "Birthplace of Johnny Cash" memorial.

• Attend the Carter Fold in Hiltons, Virginia, and ask them about Johnny Cash.

• Read a book about the Civil War. Or just read a book.

• Go to Center Point Barbecue in Hendersonville and order a Johnny Cash-sized portion of fried pork rings. Call first, as they only make them on certain days.

• Drive through a small town around 7 a.m. on a Sunday while listening to Johnny's single "Sunday Morning Coming Down." (Obvious, but still a rush when the last verse plays as you drive.)

• Go to Dyess, Arkansas, in Mississippi County, and look at Johnny Cash's childhood home on County Road West 924. Play any of the following Cash recordings of "Big River," "Pickin' Time," "String Cheese Incident," "Understand Your Man," "Flesh and Blood," "Dirty Old Egg-Sucking Dog," "Beans for Breakfast," "Man In Black," "Chicken In Black," or "Without Love." Or play Johnny's album *Precious Memories* that he dedicated to his late brother Jack.

• While in Dyess, look at the front façade of the old Dyess Theater. (The roof and walls have collapsed, but you can imagine the Cash children on Saturday afternoons joining all the other area kids for those weekly westerns.) For an added attraction, look at photos of your own family while in Dyess.

• Visit a National Park while listening to Cash albums *Come Along and Ride This Train*, *Lure of the Grand Canyon*, *Bitter Tears*, *America*, *Sea to Shining Sea*, and particularly John's song "Sold Out of Flag Poles."

• Spend at least an hour talking to a Vietnam veteran, but first listen to Johnny's songs "What Is Truth" and "Singin' in Vietnam Talkin' Blues."

• Go to the House of Cash (formerly the Cash museum and gift shop) in east Hendersonville and sit in your car out front for a short moment (it's private and now closed to the public). Listen to "Ragged Old Flag," which was recorded live at the House of Cash for a CBS Records luncheon on January 28, 1974. Imagine Johnny's late brother Roy running the Stars and Stripes up the flagpole. Imagine Johnny's sister Reba planting Arkansas cottonseeds in the brick driveway walls, where the shrubs are now. Imagine Mama Cash beckoning you to "come on in and feel welcome!" Circle around the back as you leave, and wonder how many countless times Johnny Cash used that rear metal staircase.

Optional: Imagine how many cigarettes Johnny smoked on that rear landing.

• Put lots of pomade or styling gel in your hair and watch Johnny's 1961 feature film *Five Minutes to Live*, later released under the title *Door to Door Maniac*.

• Cough very loudly and then start any sentence with "Well, son . . ." as you walk, taking big strides while swinging your arms. Try not to sound like Mr. Ed.

• Last, find someone—anyone—who needs financial assistance and anonymously make a donation to them, while wearing all black.

As related by each individual in this tribute book, Johnny Cash had the ability to make you feel that your relationship with him was uniquely special. And it was. He made almost everyone in his inner circle feel they were exclusive. And they were.

I was at life's personal worst in 1994, when my first love went away. I had lost thirty pounds and was mostly keeping to myself. John appeared in my office, shut the door, put his arm around my shoulder, and told me I was bringing everyone in the office down because I was not my usual "up self." He said, "I can't take the pain away, Hugh, but no matter what, tomorrow the sun will come up. What you do under that sun tomorrow is up to you."

He walked out of my office, shutting the door behind him, allowing me to soak up the meaning of what he had just said. And he was right. The sun did come up, time eased my pains, and with each new sun, my life moves on. I hope that I've tried to live up to my own potential each day and will continue to do so each tomorrow. That's all my friend John R. Cash ever asked or wanted out of me.

Stills from John's video for his 1989 Mercury Records single "Let Him Roll." Waylon appears with John in the top photo.

BILL WALKER

Brentwood, Tennessee

Shoe Size 9

GOOD NIGHT, BILL WALKER." This simple phrase was first spoken by Johnny Cash at the end of the first show of his three-year-long ABC television series, which began in 1969. From then on, and for the next thirty years, he would repeat this phrase at the end of every one of his television specials, as well as for any other performance on which I served as his music director.

This simple phrase also marked the beginning of, and paved the way for, a very long and satisfying career for me in network television. Thank you, Johnny Cash! However, 1969 was not my first time to be on a show with Johnny Cash. Because of my love and respect for the Johnny I got to know so well, the following story was never recounted to him.

In 1964, I was brought to Nashville to serve as music director for Jim Reeves on his upcoming television series. Unfortunately, Jim was killed in an airplane crash the very week I arrived in the United States. I moved to Nashville anyway, and through a series of fortunate events, I became Eddy Arnold's music director, arranger, and pianist. At a high point in Eddy's long and successful career, we were in New York to be featured on a Steve

Lawrence television special called *Nashville Comes to Broadway*.

Johnny Cash and the Tennessee Three were to begin the closing segment of that show and were to perform "I Walk the Line." This would lead into a medley of popular country songs by various country and Broadway artists. In the rehearsal, it went well. When we started the dress rehearsal, Johnny had gotten very, very high (this was during the time of his most severe substance abuse). Because I had never met him before, I had no idea what to expect from him.

Bill and John with rock music pioneer Jimmie ("Honeycomb") Rodgers.

The show director counted down to the start of the segment. The Tennessee Three started the well-known vamp intro to "I Walk the Line." I was poised in front of the orchestra waiting for the segue into my orchestral arrangement. Johnny hummed the start of the song. Johnny hummed again. He hummed again, and then again, but he never did start the actual song. The director yelled into the headset system for me to get Johnny started, but my part of this segment did not begin until the end of Johnny's song, and I, of course, had no control over his humming performance. He was too "out of it" to make it through his song and, unfortunately, had to be taken out of the segment completely.

That was my first introduction to my dear friend Johnny Cash. To my knowledge, he never remembered that situation, and I certainly never mentioned it to him. I was so gratified to watch his battle with and victory over his addictions, with the help and support of God and the love of his life, June Carter.

Three years later, I was called by the Bill Caruthers Company in Los Angeles who offered me the job of music director on the upcoming *Johnny Cash Show* variety series to be taped at the Ryman Auditorium for the ABC television network. I, of course, accepted their offer. After meetings in Los Angeles with the production company, I then had my next encounter with

Bill with John, June,
Barry Gibb, and Lulu.

Johnny Cash himself. I went out to his house to discuss his ideas for melodies to be used as themes for each segment of the show, i.e., comedy segments, guest artist segments, *Ride This Train* segments, etc.

His ideas for background music were excellent, and I was impressed with his understanding of composition and orchestral background music. As we discussed all the music for the show, he suggested, and I readily agreed, that it should appeal to both the country audience and the urban audience, and that a full orchestra would be needed to successfully accomplish this. Of course, for Johnny, June, and the Carter Family songs, the Tennessee Three were incorporated into the orchestra's rhythm section as a featured part of the show, in order to maintain Johnny's signature sound with its universal appeal.

The Johnny Cash Show was a true variety show with all manner of world-famous musical artists, actors, comedians, and groups as guests. One particular guest appearance that stands out in my memory as having special meaning to John was when Louis Armstrong wanted to "reproduce" one of his earliest recording sessions that had consisted of Louis on trumpet, his wife on piano, and a guitarist, whose name I cannot remember. Our re-creation consisted of Louis on trumpet, Johnny on guitar, and me on piano. I don't even remember the song, but as big a thrill as it was for me, Johnny talked about that spot for weeks.

Johnny was equally "at home" with all the guests on his show, no matter what area of entertainment they represented, whether they be country, rock, pop, Broadway, or jazz. Appearances on his show helped promote the blossoming careers of artists such as Linda Ronstadt, Anne Murray, and the Carpenters; and celebrated the popularity of such names as Ray Charles, Peggy Lee, Neil Diamond, and many others.

After the third season's show tapings had been completed, John and

June were called to New York to renegotiate for the upcoming season. Coincidentally, that was the day of my wedding to Jeanine, and John called me to express regrets that they would not be able to attend because of this. That same morning, Harold Cohen of ABC had already met with me to sign my contract for the upcoming season. Everything was looking really rosy, and Jeanine and I went merrily on our way to Hawaii and Australia for our honeymoon. At the same time, Johnny and June, the Tennessee Three, the Carter Family, and the Statler Brothers (also my very special friends) were beginning a tour, which included Honolulu, Hawaii, and Sydney, Australia—right where we were going to be.

While we were in Honolulu, Johnny asked me to conduct his show in Sydney (my hometown), as he was doing that show with an orchestra. The afternoon rehearsal with the Sydney musicians was very good, and all was set for the evening performance. When we arrived at the Randwick Race Course for the show, Johnny was met by a barrage of newspaper reporters asking him how he felt about his hit show being canceled.

Backstage with John, Ray Charles, Waylon, and Bill.

Unbeknownst to us, the American FCC had ruled that all three major television networks had to give an hour of prime-time programming back to the local stations. This resulted in the cancellation of almost all musical variety shows, which included *The Ed Sullivan Show*, *The Andy Williams Show*, our show, and about fifteen others. Needless to say, Johnny was very angry about this! Not only had the network gone back on their agreement with him, they had left it to the news media to inform him of the situation.

I don't even know how he was able to go on with his show that night, but he did, and he did a terrific show to a standing-room-only crowd who absolutely adored him. His tour of Australia was fabulously successful, and he had to promise to do another one very soon.

A representative of another network approached Johnny with an offer to take over his show, but Johnny declared a moratorium on television and refused to appear on any television show for quite a while. I just watched in despair as all my potential income flew out the window. But I didn't die, and I didn't starve. By God's grace, many other shows and recording sessions did come along for me, and all went well.

One special experience with John and June stands out in my mind. On Johnny's next tour of Australia, which also included Hawaii and New Zealand, his road band piano player was unable to make the trip. Since I knew all his material, he asked if I could possibly go and play piano for him. He also invited Jeanine to go along with us, and she filled in with the Carter Family, along with Jan Howard and Carl Perkins. It was a wonderful opportunity to see New Zealand and Australia in the very best of circumstances, and Johnny looked after all of us very well.

After our performance in Hobart, Tasmania, Johnny and June decided that it would be a special treat to take a bus ride instead of an airplane across the island of Tasmania to our next venue in Devonport. It was great! We all felt sort of like teenagers going to camp. We stopped at a little village called Ross halfway across Tasmania, where several of our group took horse and buggy rides, and where June fell in love with all the antiques she saw there.

Not long after this very successful tour, Johnny agreed to again host several television specials each year. This time they were for the CBS network and included Christmas specials, Easter specials, autumn and spring specials, and general variety specials. This was great news for all concerned, as it kept the Man In Black, and all he had to offer, in front of the television public for many years to come.

Through the years, Johnny and I became very close on many levels. He would often call me out of the blue to discuss a new spiritual book he had just read, or a new idea he had. We spent many wonderful evenings at his house for the many dinner parties that he and June hosted. At these dinner parties, the main entertainment would be his famous "guitar pullings." Many well-known songwriters and performers got their first audiences in Johnny's living room. And he treated each one as if they were his very favorite.

Johnny Cash was one of God's special gifts to this world, and although he experienced a lot of torment within himself, he also experienced a lot of triumph over his adversities. And until I get to see him again on the "Far Side Banks of Jordan," I would like to use this simple phrase and say, "GOOD NIGHT, JOHNNY CASH!"

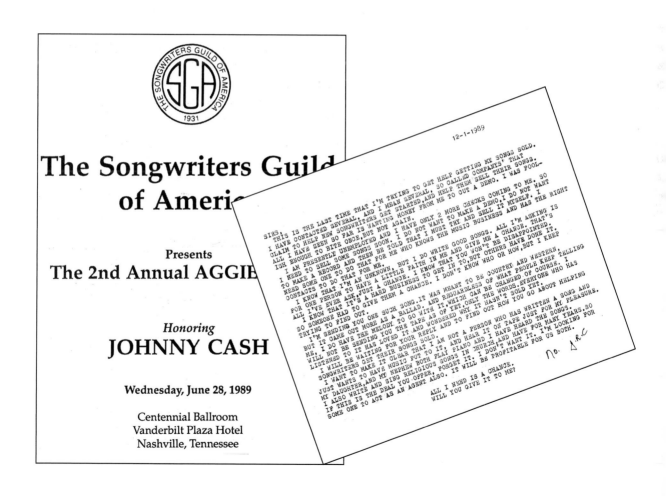

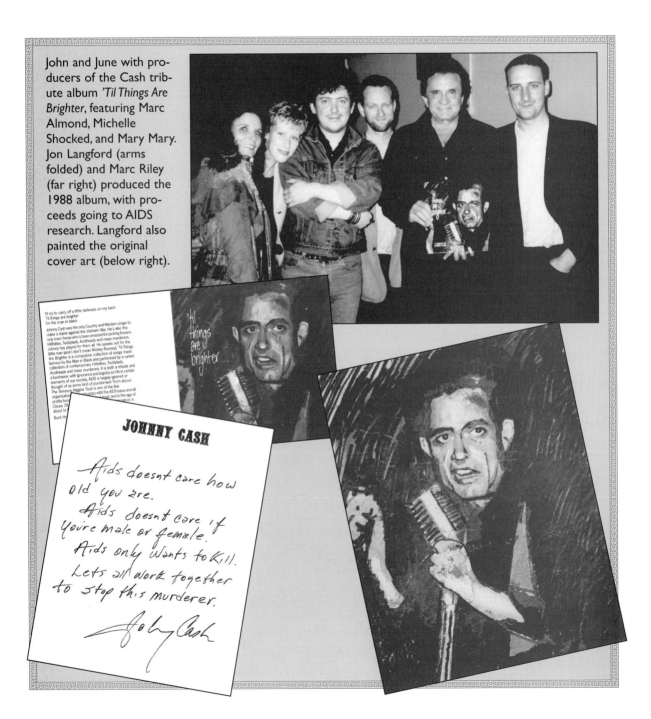

John and June with producers of the Cash tribute album *'Til Things Are Brighter*, featuring Marc Almond, Michelle Shocked, and Mary Mary. Jon Langford (arms folded) and Marc Riley (far right) produced the 1988 album, with proceeds going to AIDS research. Langford also painted the original cover art (below right).

'Til Things Are brighter...

JOHNNY CASH

Aids doesnt care how old you are.
Aids doesnt care if you're male or female!
Aids only wants to kill.
Lets all work together to stop this murderer.

Johnny Cash

JOHNNY WESTERN

Wichita, Kansas

Shoe Size 9 1/2

*J*OHNNY CASH WAS A giver. In July of 1956, in Toronto, Canada, Johnny Cash gave me his hand in friendship. I was working for Gene Autry as featured singer on his show. We were playing at the Canadian National Exhibition, and Johnny was playing the Casino Theater in downtown Toronto doing six shows a day, with the Louvin Brothers opening for him. I would go see John every night and catch his show. When we met backstage, he stuck his hand out, and we shook hands to a friendship that would last our lifetime. In November of 1958, he gave me a featured spot on his stage show for three dates in California. He said, "It will just be you, me, Luther, and Marshall, and you can ride with me." I could have never guessed that ride would go on for thirty-nine years.

In August of 1959, he gave me the chance to play guitar on his Columbia Records sessions. We recorded over seventy sides (songs) together over the years. In January of 1964, when "Ballad of Ira Hayes" reached the national Top Ten charts, Johnny Cash gave me an Apache Teardrop stone on a gold neck chain that he had gotten from Ira Hayes's mother on the Pima Reservation in Arizona. Ira was one of the Marines to raise the flag at Iwo Jima. I've been wearing it every day of my life for forty years now.

In May of 1964, Johnny gave me his new D-28 Martin guitar in Boston. In the summer of 1978, he gave me a silver belt buckle that says "Johnny Cash is a friend of mine." I have worn it on shows all over the world. In February of 1988, backstage in Norman Oklahoma, during John's Affordable Art Tour, he gave me his very expensive Alvarez-Yiari stage guitar that he'd been using for years, scratches and all. He signed it on the front with "Johnny Western is a friend of mine." Through the years, until his passing on September 12, 2003, he continued to give me clothes, books, mementos, and things of his that he thought I'd like to have for my western memorabilia collection. He was so right, for I have treasured them all these years.

The one thing he offered to give me, that it turned out I didn't need after all, was truly a gift of true friendship. Labor Day weekend of 1976, the Bicentennial year, I was traveling from Reno, Nevada, to Cheyenne, Wyoming. My band and I had been appearing at the Ponderosa Hotel in Reno for a two week engagement there and

OLD CHUNK OF COAL
DECIA
LET THE TRAIN BLOW
THE BEAST IN ME   DRIVE ON
WHY ME LORD
THIRTEEN
COWBOYS PRAYER
BIRD ON A WIRE
TENNESSEE STUD
REDEMPTION
DOWN THERE BY THE TRAIN
LIKE A SOLDIER
MAN WHO COULDNT CRY
TO BEAT THE DEVIL

FOLSOM   JACKSON
GET RHYTHM   IT AINT ME BABE
I WALK THE LINE   CARPENTER
SUNDAY MORNING
I STILL MISS SOMEONE
BIG RIVER
GHOST RIDERS
ORANGE BLOSSOM
GUESS THINGS HAPPEN
DONT TAKE YOUR GUNS

were headed east for a sold-out Labor Day show at the Little America Hotel in Cheyenne.

The annual Jerry Lewis Telethon for Muscular Dystrophy was going on, and earlier I had done a live-televised cut-in from Reno for the charity broadcast. We started driving for Cheyenne in two vehicles. I rode with my drummer, Tom McCoy, in a new pickup truck with a camper. Tom had his drum kit and dirt bike back there. My longtime band leader, Gene Hoover, was still gathering up the rest of the band and would follow in the group's van with all of our instruments and our sound equipment.

We drove all across Nevada and Utah, and when we crossed the Wyoming line we decided to stop at the Little America, Wyoming, truck stop for a meal and bathroom break. To our great surprise, when we went into the coffee shop we ran into several members of the Kimberlys, a great Nevada show group that I had worked with for years. They bought our breakfast, we visited for a while, and then headed out again for the final leg of the trip to Cheyenne.

A backstage gathering of musical luminaries, including John, June, George Jones (second from right), and Johnny Western (right).

It was around 4 a.m. on September 5, 1976, when we started out again. I had been driving for many hours previous to our meal break, so Tom took over. About thirty miles west of Rawlins, Wyoming, on Interstate 80, Tom fell asleep at the wheel going about seventy miles per hour. I was asleep on the passenger side and awoke to find Tom over-correcting as we veered into the gravel on the right side of the road. Then we shot across the freeway and raced down into the median at about a 45-degree angle.

When we hit the bottom of the median, the truck started flipping and rolling to the right. The Wyoming Highway Patrol estimated that we were ejected on about the third rollover. They found fifteen different

John with Johnny
Western's wife, Jo.

impact marks total from the truck's continuous flipping. We were not wearing seatbelts, and this one time that saved our lives.

The truck was totaled, and the roof had caved in until it was mashed down against the seats. The engine had come up through the firewall, and even "Little" Jimmy Dickens could not have survived in that tight squeeze, much less two guys our size. We were laying out on the grass near the interstate when truckers started stopping to help us, and they used their CB radios to call the Highway Patrol and an ambulance.

A trucker, Nick Nichols, from Flora, Illinois, saved my life by holding the severed arteries in my neck and head together with his fingers till the EMT people got there forty-five minutes later from Carbon County Memorial Hospital in Rawlins. Tom was badly cut and bruised, and he must have crashed into me when we rolled, as I had broken ribs and lots of arterial bleeding, in addition to a concussion and a broken front tooth.

They put me in the intensive-care unit right away and then called my wife, Jo, in Scottsdale, Arizona. She made plans to fly up to be with me after a series of calls to family and friends. The media got hold of news of my accident in Nashville, thanks to the international fan club organization. While in the ICU, they found that I had two ribs that had gone through and collapsed my left lung. The emergency room doctor, Timothy Hobson, saved my life when he finally got my lung re-inflated.

During my third day in the ICU, Dr. Hobson came into my room with a phone (which they never do) and said Johnny Cash was on the line. When I answered, "Hello," he said, "Johnny, it's Johnny Cash. I don't want you to be worried about the medical bills. I just want you to get well. I've already told the doctors there to send all the bills to me at the House of Cash."

I was stunned, and I guess I cried a bit with his kind and generous offer. Soon after the call, a telegram came from him. I had it framed on my office wall for years. As it turned out, Jo had contacted a State Farm Insurance agent in Rawlins, and he told her that I was completely covered through my policy. Though I was not the driver, Wyoming was one of the first no-fault states in the country for these type accidents.

A week later, I was transported to Denver Presbyterian Hospital for more treatments on my broken ribs. A week later, I finally got to fly home to Scottsdale for several weeks of rehab. The total of all my medical expenses was over $17,000. Johnny had offered to pay all my bills, no matter how much the amount turned out to be. This was 1976, when that was one heck of a chunk of money.

Johnny and John onstage in Wichita, Kansas.

That was the Johnny Cash I knew and loved for forty-seven years of my life! He gave me many things during our years together, but the thing that was most valuable was the gift he gave of himself. Johnny Cash gave of himself to me time and time again through the years. As time went by in the past few years, we didn't see as much of each other as we had in the 1950s and 1960s, but I always knew he was there.

And he will be with me always! We went from those first three Johnny Cash shows in 1958 to the last one on which we appeared together, October 14, 1997, outdoors on a Monday night, here in Wichita in front of 15,000 people. From 1958 to 1997, Johnny Cash and me played many concerts together, from Carnegie Hall in New York City to L.A.'s Hollywood Bowl and every place you can play, big and small, prisons included. On the way to those shows in 1958, he said, "Johnny Western, you can ride with me." Well, thank you, John. It was one hell of a ride!

Rev. COURTNEY WILSON

Hendersonville, Tennessee

Shoe Size 11 1/2 C

ANY TRIBUTE TO JOHN Cash must include words about his wife, June, who was a gift from God when John was sinking deeper and deeper into the life of a druggie. June probably saved his life many times. It also must include something about his father, his mother, and his family.

John had a wonderful mother and father. His mother, Carrie, was a woman of deep Christian faith and commitment. She loved the Lord. John and his mother were very close. She was a woman of substantial strength. She was more of an influence on Johnny as he grew older and became used to the fame.

John realized the heart of happiness was in serving God and doing His bidding in real life, and that's what he tried honestly to do. He had a very strong faith. His books and his music became a testimony to his faith in Jesus Christ. He struggled with addiction to the pills, but Johnny was a person who never quit struggling. He continued his fight and, to me, he won a victory over it. To know a little about Johnny and what made him the person he was, in addition to his faith in God, you need to know something about his father, Ray, and his mother, Carrie Cash.

Mr. Ray Cash told me this story: He had a small garden out on the road leading to son John's home. One day he was working in his garden, digging potatoes, and a lady who was a tourist stopped to chat. She asked, "Do you know where Johnny Cash lives?" Mr. Ray answered, "Yes," as he pointed to John and June's home across the street, "that's where he lives." And then she asked, "Do you know him?" Mr. Ray replied proudly, "Oh yes, he is my son."

John with mother Carrie and father Ray Cash.

She asked, surprised, "You are Johnny Cash's father, and you are out here digging potatoes and working in the dirt?" Mr. Ray humbly said, "Lady, I am just an Arkansas dirt farmer, and some of that Arkansas dirt farmer background became very much a part of who and what Johnny Cash is." When I told this story to Johnny, he laughed and said, "That's Dad, all right." John's background was from a poor dirt farm, and his father taught him not to give in. Yes, Johnny Cash had struggles, but he never gave in. He fought all his life.

I think there are two lessons that we might learn from Johnny Cash's life. One thing I hope people will learn is that drugs are no substitute for good living. It doesn't really lead you to the good life. But God is a helper to those who turn to Him, even those who make mistakes in life. John found his sustaining strength in his battles for life, in his faith in Jesus Christ.

I think we might learn from the fact that Johnny loved his family and he was good to his family. His wife, June, his father, his mother, his children, and any other members of his family. His love for June and for the family, all his family, was his strength. That speaks well for a man, especially a man who has become quite famous. His mother and father were strong, dedicated Christians, and that and his faith in God helped John through his personal trials and struggles.

Sometimes there is a tendency to forget those you love and those who have been with you along the way when you are successful. But John didn't forget. It is my prayer that these words might encourage all those who struggle and those who seek a faith to live by, and help us see the gift that is in us and the blessed value of each of our lives. God bless. Go and be the touching hand of God in a needy world.

NAT WINSTON, M.D.

Nashville, Tennessee
Shoe Size 10¹/₂

I HAD HEARD THE NAME Johnny Cash, but it really meant nothing to me that year of 1967 when June Carter came by my house one night in Madison, Tennessee, and said, "Nat, you've got to go out and help Johnny Cash, he is about to die." I had known the Carter family for many years. Mother Maybelle lived for a short while in my hometown of Johnson City, Tennessee, working with Bonnie Lou and Buster Moore, who later had an ongoing show in Pigeon Forge, Tennessee. We used to get together at night when I was in practice there in psychiatry and had great times jamming. June knew that I understood the country musician's life and style and problems.

Johnny was living in Hendersonville all by himself in a unique house built on a bluff overlooking Old Hickory Lake. When we arrived and went up to the bedroom where Johnny lay in obvious distress, I immediately saw the need for help. He was a large man, I knew, and he looked like he didn't weigh more than 150 pounds. He was anxious and nervous and lying on the round bed in the master bedroom. June had told me that he had been taking massive amounts of amphetamines. Indeed, Johnny said he had been taking twenty and thirty at a clip, three and four times a day, and then taking a tranquilizer, Equanil, twenty or so at night, to try to get some rest. He was indeed quite ill.

As so often happens, Johnny became inadvertently hooked on the amphetamines. He was many years later to tell *Larry King Live* in an interview that when he took the first Ritalin tablet he said to himself, "The good Lord made this just for me." In those years, Johnny would get on his bus and ride several hundred miles, say, to Kansas City, and have to give a concert in an hour. He would take an amphetamine and be rejuvenated and get onstage and give a tremendous concert. Then he might get back on the bus and drive to New Orleans. There again, he would have to be up and ready to go in an hour, dead tired but restored by taking the Ritalin tablet. Then, as is the case, it took two, then three, then four, then five, and so forth to get the same effect. He was hooked, and he really didn't realize it.

John and June's lakeside home in Hendersonville, Tennessee.

At the time, I was Tennessee State Commissioner of Mental Health and was not in private practice. Most reluctantly, I agreed to help John, but he refused to go to the hospital. I had common sense enough to know that if I forced him to go, he would sign out in two or three days and all efforts to get him back into psychiatric care would be lost. We, therefore, organized babysitters to sit with him around the clock to make sure he didn't take more of the amphetamines. We knew he had caches all over the house, and indeed we found several as we searched it.

At the time, I was speaking almost nightly at some city across the state and would not get back to my house until ten or eleven at night. Every night, however, I went out to talk to Johnny and see what progress we were making. I carefully withdrew him, instead of abruptly, which would conceivably lead to severe seizures and possibly death. John was a great soldier. He cooperated all the way, although on one occasion I felt that he had "snuck" a

couple of pills from the caches that we did not find. In about three weeks'
time, he was totally withdrawn and doing great. He was real tough.

During that time, his mother called from California. She was, I could tell,
a very dead-serious, dedicated, Christian woman who said, "Please take care
of my boy; he's worth it, he's the best talent in the world. Please help him."

I got to know Ray Cash, Johnny's father, later on. He was full of fun
and jokes and just the opposite of his wife. I had the pleasure of riding to
Houston, Texas, once with Ray Cash and his oldest son, Roy. Ray, who
had fought Pancho Villa on the border of Texas and Mexico many years
ago, just before World War I, was going back to be the grand master of a
parade honoring the downfall of Villa. We enjoyed our ride together.

Johnny was not the easiest patient I had ever treated. He could not com-
fortably sit still and talk one-to-one as the average patient in my practice
did. Instead, we would take long walks in the dark at night or get in his
Jeep and ride great distances when we talked about his past. Later on, after
he built a log house in the wooded acreage adjacent to the main house, we
would sit in the log house by a fire and talk about his past. I recall vividly
two episodes in his life that probably had the greatest impact on him.

When he was a boy of twelve, he looked up to his older brother Jack,
who was fourteen and was killed in a log mill accident. This had a profound impact on John at that early age in learning about death and the
realities of life. Many years later, one of his guitar players, Luther Perkins,
died in a tragic fire at his house. John told me that Luther had called him
the night before he died and begged John to come over, that he needed
help. John realized that he was drunk and told Luther, "I will be there in
the morning." In the morning, he was dead. Again, this had a devastating
impact on Johnny's life.

The relationship between John and June was beautiful and at the same
time had the ups and downs of any marriage. As a psychiatrist, I, of course,
was privy to many of the intimate and personal experiences between them
that no one else knows nor should know. I remember June telling John that
if he stayed clean for a year, she would marry him, but they married after
eight months because they were going to Israel to film a movie on Christ.

On his return I continued to see John on a regular basis. There was one major relapse, which is usual in a case of withdrawing from addictive drugs. This was weathered, but there were other ups and downs over the years. Without any question, however, the devotion they had for each other was unshakable.

As time went by over the next few years, I made the error that a psychiatrist should never make. That is, a psychiatrist should always maintain his professional distance. But Johnny and I became close personal friends, and I really lost my ability to help him, although at that time he needed no further help. We were almost always at their house for banquets with all of the celebrities in country music and other fields, and he usually seated me on his right-hand side. This flattered me very much.

The fun side of Johnny Cash is what I enjoyed the most. I lived in Madison, Tennessee, halfway from downtown Nashville to his home in Hendersonville. Often, coming back from visits to the doctor or other errands, they would stop by our house and chat. We had a fenced-in three acres, and back there we had what is known as nervous goats. These were goats bred by Vanderbilt University in Nashville to study epilepsy. If you would make a loud noise, the goats would go into an epileptic seizure, fall on the ground, and then in the tonic stage you could pick them up by their heels and move them all over anywhere.

I would take my bugle and go out in the back (by that time we had eight goats), and I would blow a loud blast on the bugle and all eight would go into a seizure, fall on the ground, and we could move them around. Neighbors used to say, "Here comes the crazy psychiatrist to blow the bugle at his nervous goats." The billy goat of the eight was a massive animal with massive horns. John loved to try to wrestle him down. Every time he came by the house, he would go out and grab that billy by the horns, but he never succeeded in putting him down. I think this frustrated John very much.

I will never forget the day on the way back from the gynecologist that John and June stopped by and exclaimed, "We're pregnant!" I pointed out that June had two daughters by two husbands, and no boys, and that John had four daughters by one wife, and no boys, and that there was no way they could have a son. They laughed and said, "We know it is going to be a boy!" This, of course, was before the days of ultrasound, and the gender of the child was not known until birth. They would stop by on their frequent visits to the gynecologists, and one Friday afternoon about 12:10, I was the first person Johnny called, and he said, "Nat . . . John Carter Cash is here!" They could not have been happier or more proud.

As is true with all the famous personalities, particularly in the country music field, they loved the adulation and attention they received from their fans, but every now and then they got fed up. I had a houseboat on Old Hickory Lake about ten miles from John's house, and he called me up one Friday afternoon and said, "Nat, let's go out tomorrow and just ride around on the boat, fish, cook, talk, and swim." I spent the night, Friday night, and got the houseboat down a little after breakfast time.

We went out into the lake and anchored and had a great time cooking, picking, talking about the old days, talking about his experiences and our goals in life, fishing, swimming, and waiting until about six o'clock before heading back. When we got back to his dock, there were, just outside the house and behind the fence, about twelve tourist buses, with hundreds of tourists hanging over the fence taking pictures of the Cash house. Johnny almost broke his legs to get off the boat and run up to start signing autographs. He couldn't resist the temptation!

On another occasion, Johnny was giving a concert in my hometown area of upper East Tennessee. I was there in the morning and said, "John, let's drive up to my cabin and my waterfall just across the line in North Carolina." We drove up, and on the way I pulled off on a side road on Whitehead Creek and stopped the car. Without telling him why, we walked across the creek on a foot log and up a little knoll to a family graveyard. There were two stones that stood out. The stone of Tiger Whitehead stated: "James T. Whitehead, the noted hunter, killed 99 bears. Died 1905. We hope he has gone to rest." On his wife's tombstone it said, "Sally Garland, wife of James Whitehead, age 97 years. She was not only a friend to mankind but to animal-kind as well, as she gave nurse to two cubs and a fawn. She is now resting from her labors."

We stood there and read those poignant stones, and then we continued our drive up to my waterfall in North Carolina. Johnny pulled out an envelope from the glove compartment, and by the time we reached the cabin he had penned "The Ballad of Tiger Whitehead." It wasn't his most famous song, but it's my favorite. Incidentally, we sat there on the porch looking up at the 145-foot churning waterfall and Johnny mentioned, "Do you have any snakes around here?" and I replied, "Yeah, we had lots of copperheads." That ended our visit, and John gingerly walked back to the car, and we drove back to give his concert.

I got a call from the Reverend Billy Graham inquiring about John Cash one day. We were both mountain Presbyterians, Billy and I, growing up sixty-five miles apart from each other in the mountains. His father-in-law, who was a Presbyterian minister to China, as I recall, had dinner in our home one Sunday after having preached at our church. Billy had heard of my treatment of John and he asked, "Is he a born-again Christian, and is he clean of drugs?"

I told him that indeed he was and gave him John's home phone number. He called and we met together out at Johnny's house. They became instant friends, and from that time on, John and June were part of many of Billy Graham's crusades. We frequently had dinner at his house together.

I could go on and on telling other anecdotal material, but I hope some of these stories give insight into this great man.

As a psychiatrist, I tell all my patients, "Know your roots." The more you know about your past—although your ancestors may have been horrible people, or excellent people, or both, or a combination thereof—the more you can set your goals for the future. I feel Johnny Cash knew as much about the value of this as anyone. He was an avid historian, in particular about the American Indian.

He was proud of his small percentage of Indian blood. He had an empathy for the underdog. Contrary to popular belief, he was never in prison, but he felt for the prisoners and the hopelessness they felt. He befriended many of them, and as all know, he performed many times in various prisons around the country. He had a phenomenal feel for the past, for the everyday miseries of the common man, the triumphs of the wealthy, the dedication of the persistent, the good and the bad of life, its pitfalls and dangers, and its triumph. These are the makings of a great man, and I can truly say that, to me, Johnny Cash was a Gentle Giant of a great man!

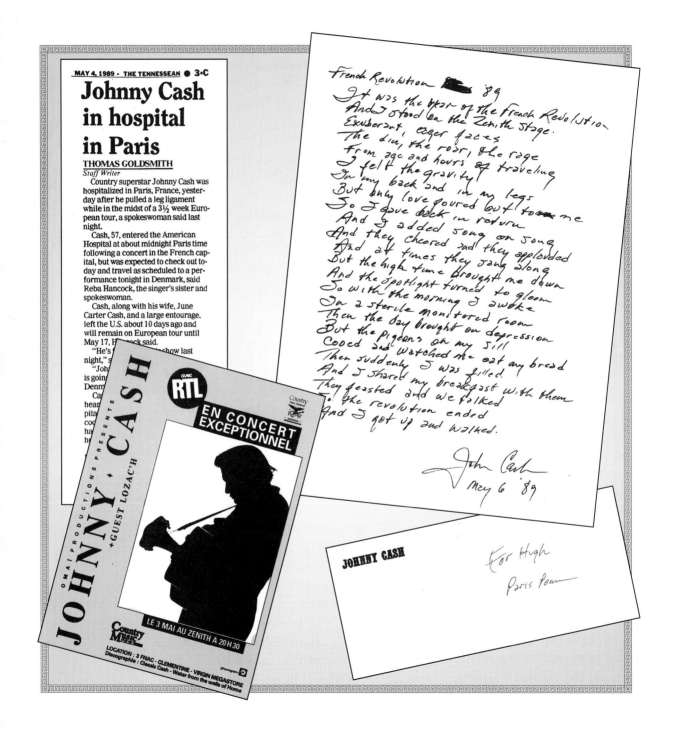

MAY 4, 1989 · THE TENNESSEAN ● 3·C

Johnny Cash in hospital in Paris

THOMAS GOLDSMITH
Staff Writer

Country superstar Johnny Cash was hospitalized in Paris, France, yesterday after he pulled a leg ligament while in the midst of a 3½ week European tour, a spokeswoman said last night.

Cash, 57, entered the American Hospital at about midnight Paris time following a concert in the French capital, but was expected to check out today and travel as scheduled to a performance tonight in Denmark, said Reba Hancock, the singer's sister and spokeswoman.

Cash, along with his wife, June Carter Cash, and a large entourage, left the U.S. about 10 days ago and will remain on European tour until May 17, Hancock said.

"He's _____ show last night," _____

"Joh_____ is going _____ Denm_____

Ca_____ hear_____ pita_____ coo_____ ha_____ h_____

OMAI PRODUCTIONS PRESENTE

avec **RTL**

JOHNNY · CASH
+ GUEST LOZAC'H

EN CONCERT EXCEPTIONNEL

Country Music

Country Music

LE 3 MAI AU ZENITH A 20 H 30

LOCATION : 3 FNAC - CLEMENTINE - VIRGIN MEGASTORE
Discographie : Classic Cash - Water from the wells of Home

phonogram

French Revolution '89

It was the year of the French Revolution
And I stood on the Zenith Stage.
Exuberant, eager faces
The din, the roar, the rage
From age and hours of traveling
I felt the gravity
In my back and in my legs
But only love poured out to me
So I gave back in return
And I added song on song
And they cheered and they applauded
And at times they sang along
But the high time brought me down
And the spotlight turned to gloom
So with the morning I awoke
In a sterile monitored room
Then the day brought on depression
But the pigeons on my sill
Cooed and watched me eat my bread
Then suddenly I was filled!
And I shared my breakfast with them
They feasted and we talked
So the revolution ended
And I got up and walked.

John Cash
May 6 '89

JOHNNY CASH

For Hugh
Paris Pour

JEANNE WITHERELL

East Peoria, Illinois
Shoe Size 8½ *NARROW*

*M*Y HUSBAND, RAY, AND I, along with Curtis and Alma Todd of North Carolina, became co-presidents of the official Johnny Cash and June Carter Cash International Fan Club at the beginning of 1984. It may have seemed a bit odd for two couples that lived so far apart to attempt such a collaboration, but in all the seventeen years that we worked together, I can honestly say that we never had a disagreement about anything. Sometimes we thought so much alike that it was scary. I believe that our mutual love for John and June, and wanting to do the very best that we could for them, made the fan club a labor of love for us.

I had been a member of the club for many years and had designed Fan Fair booths, handled photo orders, and sent out newsletters as a club representative for the previous club presidents, Charles and Virginia Stohler, so I had a little experience in fan clubbing, but it did not fully prepare me for the time and effort that the club work would entail. We divided duties, with the Todds handling the correspondence and most of the orders, while I was responsible for gathering the material for all of the club publications, having them printed, assembling and binding them, and mailing them to

Jeanne and John, 1970.

members. I also handled orders for any special publications, such as the calendars.

I met John before we became co-presidents of the club. I'm very sure that everyone remembers their first meeting with John, and I am no exception. I had been corresponding with Marie Wolf, a friend of John and June's, and we were both attending a concert in Indiana. Although I don't remember doing it, I must have told her our seat location, as we had never met and she would not have recognized me. As a surprise, she brought us from the audience and took us backstage to meet John.

I was so totally in awe that I do not remember one word of our conversation, but Ray took a picture of us together. I remember going back to our seats, and when I sat down my knees were shaking so badly that you could actually see them moving. I have never seen my knees bounce around like that under any other circumstances. When the film was developed, John had his eyes closed and I had that look of a deer in the headlights, but, oh, how I treasured that photo, especially later when I got it autographed.

Through the years, there were many backstage visits with John, but none seemed as earth-shattering as that first one, although many were more fun. By their very nature, backstage visits were usually hurried and hectic, as there was fan club business to discuss and always the quest for photos. I sometimes felt guilty, as we always seemed to be seeking photos, but they were really a big requirement for the club publications, plus taking that "extra good one" for the annual yearbook. When I overheard John tell someone that Ray took some really good photos, I felt better. Even better when one was used for a publicity photo. I was deeply touched that one of our photos of John and June appears in John's "Hurt" video. It was included in the part that was filmed in the old Cash museum. It seemed that everyone always wanted photos, and I am grateful that John was so patient about posing for pictures for us.

We were always welcome backstage to eat meals with the band and crew. Sometimes John and June would join us if they were not eating on their bus. We would look at photos, or they would tell us about upcoming recordings, television shows, etc., and they were always proud to talk about their children and their many accomplishments.

We tried very hard never to be in the way backstage and to give John his space, as I'm sure many times his mind was on the upcoming concert. One night I must have overdone this, as I was talking to band members and John walked up behind me, tapped me on the shoulder, and said, "Hey, remember me?" There is no doubt that I will always remember him!

Although birthday, Christmas, and anniversary gifts from the fan club were most often delivered backstage, sometimes we were asked to take them to John and June's hotel room. Those were among my favorite times, much more private and more relaxed moments as the concert was behind them. It was nice to just sit and visit with them. At one of these visits we had purchased books for John's birthday, and after he had opened the package and looked at the books, he asked me to write on the flyleaf of each book that they were from the club, and the occasion and the date. I had not thought to do that, and it really impressed on me John's appreciation of the gift and that at any later date he wanted to be able to remember how these books were acquired. I believe that books were his favorite gift, with maybe one exception.

We left a Franklin Mint Civil War chess and checker set at House of Cash for John, and although it was several weeks before we saw him at a concert, his first words were to express his thanks for the sets and to let us know how much he liked them. The chess set had been highly advertised, and John said that he had seen the advertisements and had wanted the set, but it had to be ordered as a series and he did not want to

Rosanne Cash sings to her dad at the June 10, 1989, debut party for Mother Maybelle Carter's cookbook.

get involved in that process. I didn't tell him that I had called the Franklin Mint and ordered the complete sets. We found that the mention of Johnny Cash opened many doors.

John was not above surprising you by opening doors. One night when we took gifts to his hotel room after a concert, he opened the door wearing a nightshirt. It was nice that he felt that comfortable with us.

I witnessed many acts of kindness through the years of things that probably did not seem like much to John but that meant the world to others. Some examples of his kindness to us included being invited into his hotel suite with other friends to view a tape of his recently filmed Christmas show before it was shown on television, going to the private opening of the Johnny Cash exhibit at the Country Music Hall of Fame, being invited to attend John and June's twenty-fifth wedding anniversary celebration, attending John Carter's wedding, book-launching parties, and so much more.

It was especially heartwarming to see John with special-needs children. One young girl from our area was at a local concert, and John's love and compassion were very much in evidence. Her parents must have been impressed with his attention to their daughter, because when that young lady died several years later, her devotion to Johnny Cash was mentioned in her obituary.

Anyone who knew John was aware that he was not fond of Fan Fair. Although we always built the best booth that we could each year and hoped that he would be there, his visits were few and far between. He was usually out of town on a concert tour, but maybe absence does make the heart grow fonder, because when he did attend, the fans were very enthusiastic and appreciative.

If John was in town and did not want to come to Fan Fair, he would sometimes greet fans and sign autographs at House of Cash. He attended the club get-togethers when he was in town, and the club members were always thrilled to be in the same room with him. They also appreciated the fact that he wanted it to be open to club members only. He would sometimes sing a new song or tell us about some new venture, but he always took time for photographs and to sign autographs.

He was very generous when we asked for personal items that we could use for prizes and gave us some unbelievable things to give away, including one of his gold albums. One year, he invited all the fan club representatives to his house for lunch and spent time with us, and June gave us a tour of their home.

When John was scheduled to appear in Branson in 1994, we thought it would be great to have a club party there. Other events had always been held in Nashville during Fan Fair, so we thought it would be great to see a Johnny Cash concert and have a party. We asked John if he would attend. That was all we asked: Would he attend? We got so much more! Not only did John provide a free ticket for every club member who could attend, he had a lovely buffet served on the balcony of the theater after the show. He and June generously shared the remainder of the evening with very happy club members.

We had a birthday gift to give to June at this party. It was a limited-edition porcelain doll. When John saw it, he had a good laugh and said that it looked just like June—not only did it have auburn hair and freckles but its mouth was open!

John also hosted a brunch at House of Cash in honor of his fortieth anniversary in country music, and invited club members. An invitation to a book-launching party at their Hendersonville home was offered as a prize for the winners of a fan club membership drive. It worked better than any other incentive we had ever offered!

One of the best laughs I shared with John was over a story that I told him. Our teenage daughter was the babysitter for a neighbor's child, and she thought that it would be fun to teach the little girl a Johnny Cash song as a surprise for me. The child was three or four at the time, and when the day came for her performance, all was going very well until she sang out,

"I'm stuck in some fool prison and time keeps dragging on," instead of "Folsom Prison." We all dissolved in laughter, as John did when I told him of the incident. He wondered if he should be changing the lyrics.

John had a very active sense of humor, sometimes a little offbeat. He once met with a line of women fans backstage by going down the line greeting each one with a hug or kiss. Ray was standing in the line, and John tried to keep, a bit unsuccessfully, an unsmiling face as he looked at him and said very seriously, "Well, Ray, I'm not kissing you," as he held out his hand.

Although we attended many shows, I was never lucky enough to catch the tossed harmonicas, and at later shows John stopped throwing them out into the audience. One night we had front-row-center seats, and as John finished "Orange Blossom Special," he paused, looked me right in the eye, smiled that mischievous smile, and said, "Well, come and get them," as he held out the harmonicas to me. I could have sold them several times on the way out of the theater, but I'm sure you know that I still have them.

When Curtis, Alma, Ray, and I met with John and June in the summer of 2000 to discuss the future—or more precisely, the end—of the fan club, it was very difficult. We knew in our hearts that it was time to end the club, and John and June agreed. John was no longer able to tour, and his personal assessment of the situation was that it would be difficult to maintain the quality of the club on his release of an album a year.

My personal assessment was that it was six older folks sitting on a porch in Virginia letting go of something that had been an important part of their lives. It was a sad time as we drove away from that house. I knew in my heart that I would probably never see John and June again, and I was very nearly correct.

I really believed that this was my saddest experience with John, but I was wrong. Seeing him face the loss of June could truly break one's heart. She looked so beautiful and peaceful, and he looked so utterly lost. There was no way that you could not be deeply affected. He had lost a piece of himself, and, for me, June's funeral was sadder than John's. It hurt that he was forever gone from our lives, but I felt that he and June were reunited.

John is no longer with us, but he will always be a presence in my life. Because of him, our lives were enriched by travel that would never have taken place, and I treasure the wonderful friends that our association with him brought into our lives. Due to Ray's health problems, my world has become much smaller, and I find myself turning more and more to the music John left us. Videos, photos, and mementos all help to fill empty days with happy memories.

This trip down my Johnny Cash memory lane was harder than I thought it would be, and it has brought tears along with the smiles. I feel that it was an honor to be invited to be part of this book, just as I always felt that it was an honor to be co-president of John and June's fan club. John brought an exciting dimension to my life, and I will forever be grateful to him for allowing me into one small corner of his life.

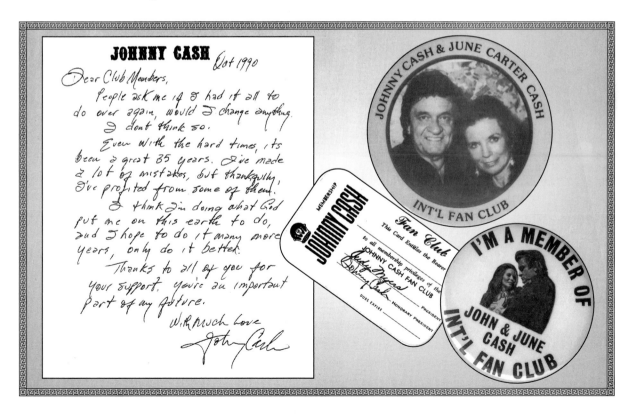

You are special to us

Please come to our house

for our

Silver Wedding Anniversary

March 2, 1993

Open House   6 p.m.

Johnny Cash and June Carter

200 Caudill Drive

Hendersonville, Tennessee

R.S.V.P. 615-824-5110

Performance Guide   **1994**
Vol 7, No. 1 $35.00

COUNTRY TALENT

Johnny Cash and June Carter Cash

America's Favorite Country Couple
For Over 25 Years

VARIETY/CORPORATE ENTERTAINMENT ON OPPOSITE SIDE

THE VICE PRESIDENT
WASHINGTON

March 3, 1993

Johnny Cash and June Carter Cash
200 Caudill Drive
Hendersonville, Tennessee   37077

Dear Johnny and June:

Thank you for asking Tipper and me to join you in celebrating your Silver Wedding Anniversary last night. We are sorry that we could not be with you and your friends and family on this special occasion.

Please accept our belated but warm congratulations on your twenty-fifth anniversary. We wish you many more years of happiness together.

Again, thank you for the invitation. Your friendship has always meant so much to Tipper and me and we hope to see both of you again soon.

Sincerely,

Al Gore

THE WHITE HOUSE
WASHINGTON

March 2, 1993

John and June Carter Cash
700 Johnny Cash Parkway
Hendersonville, Tennessee   37075

Dear Johnny and June:

Hillary and I are delighted to send our best wishes as your friends and family gather to celebrate your 25th wedding anniversary. We hope that the coming year will bring you good health and much happiness.

Happy Anniversary!

Sincerely,

Bill Clinton

BOB WOOTTON

Philadelphia, Mississippi
Shoe Size 9

*H*ELLO, I'M JOHNNY CASH." Probably four of the most memorable words ever said together in entertainment. Personally, to me, they rank with other timeless phrases, like "President Kennedy has been shot," or "Elvis has left the building," or even perhaps "God created man."

I met Johnny Cash in 1966 in Tulsa, Oklahoma, at Cain's Ballroom. It was an exciting moment in my life. I played guitar and sang in church and also sang some of John's songs, like "I Was There When It Happened" and "Suppertime." I was a big Johnny Cash fan! I met him after his show and even got an autographed picture. In a day or so, my life was back to normal.

In 1967, I put together a band called Bob Wootton & The Commancheros. We played the music of Haggard, Jones, Tubb, Elvis, and Cash. I tried to do the songs exactly like those artists that made the hits. My problem was that no one in our band could play Cash's distinct boom-chicka-boom sound on guitar, so I finally decided to learn to play it myself.

Sadly, in August of 1968, Tennessee Three guitarist Luther Perkins, the patriarch of John's original sound, died in a house fire in Hendersonville, Tennessee. Shortly after Luther's passing, I tried several times to contact

Tennessee Three
guitarist Luther Perkins.

John to possibly audition for a job playing guitar with him. For whatever reason, I couldn't get through to John. I also didn't know that fate was about to step in and play an important part in my life.

In September of 1968, my band was doing real good. We were playing seven nights a week. One Saturday night a Greyhound bus driver came in and listened. After the show he approached me and said, "You really like Cash, don't you?"

My reply to him was, "He's the best!" During our conversation, he said he was going to Fayetteville with a load of supporters for Arkansas Governor Winthrop Rockefeller's re-election rally and asked if I would like to go. I wasn't into politics, but he told me Johnny Cash was having two shows there for the rally, and so, hearing that, I decided to go. I would have walked every step of the way to get there after hearing that Cash was playing there!

When it came time to go, I decided to drive with some friends. As we approached Fayetteville, we were listening to the radio and the announcer said, "Johnny Cash's plane is landing at the city airport right now." I looked up and actually saw a small plane, so we turned and headed for the airport, following that plane.

When we got there, a man in a suit asked,

"Are you with Johnny Cash's group?" Before I could think I said yes. He led me to a limousine, and after getting in, he drove us to a city park where there were about eight thousand people around the flatbed trailer that was set up for the rally.

Johnny was on that flatbed-truck stage, with W. S. Holland playing drums. It was the afternoon matinee, and Johnny and W. S. were doing the show with only Johnny's acoustic guitar and W. S.'s drums. June Carter was behind the trailer. I walked directly to the front of that flatbed-trailer stage and rested my chin almost on Johnny's shoes, looking straight up in awe and admiration!

Marshall Grant and Carl Perkins had been delayed in Memphis due to weather, and so, onstage, waiting, it was only John, W. S,. and June. There was a second show coming up, and the other band had still not arrived. While I was watching, my friend went behind the stage and asked June if John would like to have a guitar player. June then asked him, "Do you know someone that can play Johnny's songs?" He replied to June, "Do you see that guy with his chin on John's shoes? He can play!"

I started hearing someone. *"Psst, psst, psssst."* I looked around and saw June motion for me to come to her. I actually crawled under the truck bed to get around back, and then June asked, "Can you play guitar?"

I said "Yes ma'am!" June called John off stage and said, "I have a guitar player for you." And the first words John said to me was, "Tune my guitar." I tuned it, we went onstage, and I knew every song, every key they were

played in, and John could not believe it. After the show, he told me Carl Perkins was playing guitar for him at the time, but for me to give him my phone number and he would stay in touch. John also offered to pay me, and I told him no, that it was my pleasure to be onstage with him. And I got to play with Johnny Cash using Carl Perkins's guitar plugged into Luther Perkins's amplifier.

I went home and told everyone that I was going to work for Johnny Cash. I had quit my job playing music, quit my job driving a truck, and had packed my clothes. I knew in my heart that my dream was coming true. Two days later, the phone rang. I answered and heard, "Bob, this is Johnny Cash. Would you like to meet me in Arkansas and discuss a job?" I went to Memphis and then to Knoxville with them, and the rest is history.

Thirty of the best years of my life I got to spend onstage with my hero, idol, friend, and brother. There are no words to describe how I feel about Johnny Cash. We had our ups and our downs, but the best of relationships have those. I got to know Johnny Cash as a man, not just

an entertainer, and believe me when I say the man was much greater than the image of the entertainer.

On September 12, 2003, for me, the music truly died. I often watch the shows we did over the years, I look at all the things Johnny had given to me, and it amazes me to know that I was part of that. I remember every moment spent playing live onstage, in recording studios, on TV sound stages and huge movie sets, at parties, and mostly, the private moments in each other's homes and on the bus. I relive them daily.

To some, Elvis was the "King," but not to me. It was then, and always will be, Johnny Cash. I have been asked several times to play with other people onstage, but my reply is always no. After being with the best entertainer in the world, everything else would pale in comparison.

Johnny Cash allowed you to be on your own unique terms with him. He expected you to do your best, and other than his solid friendship, he never told you how to do your job, or acted like a boss. He trusted you and let you be yourself around him. So many people around Johnny's life had that kind of individual one-on-one relationship with him. I am blessed to have been one of those people.

I know that Heaven's choir was rejoicing that September day those pearly gates swung open wide and they saw that tall, dark-haired man stick out his hand and say, "HELLO, I'M JOHNNY CASH."

DR. HARRY YATES

Gallatin, Tennessee

Shoe Size 10

I AM PASTOR OF NASHVILLE Cowboy Church and one of only two surviving brothers-in-law of Johnny Cash. But I didn't start out for it to be that way, nor was it a life's quest to be known as Johnny Cash's sister's husband.

I ran away from home when I was twenty-six years old to come to Nashville to see my sister and meet some country music stars. The first night I was here, my sister Mary took me to a church and I met Connie Smith. Six months later, Joanne Cash came to that same church and I met her. A year later, we went on a tour to the Holy Lands with a group of people from church, and we "fell in love" in Tel Aviv, Israel, came back home, and were married three months later. That was 1971.

I, of course, knew who Johnny Cash was. I grew up listening to his music and loving every bit of it. Little did I know that I would be in the family later. We had talked generically many times, but it was what he said at our wedding that endeared me to the man Johnny Cash. Actually, it was in a letter that he gave to me, and it said:

Dear Harry,

Some things are only necessary to say once in a
whole lifetime. That one thing I have to say to you is
this: you are now my brother. I love you as a brother.
I stand beside you before God. Your problems are my
problems. Your joys are my joys. Your people are my
people. I am always the same in these things. Be
understanding with Joanne as she needs you. I love
her, too. Always take care of her. God bless you both.
                                                    John

John with sister Joanne
and brother-in-law Harry
Yates.

That was the way John was. If you were in the
family, you were family. He accepted you for who
you were and allowed you to be yourself. He encouraged you to excel in
your talents, even if they were not what he thought you ought to be
doing. Joanne and I were on the road for fifteen years as well, and many
times our paths crossed with John's. At each one of these times we were
accepted at his show as if we were part of the show. Most of the time he
even asked Joanne to sing with him. There was one time that we were able
to return the favor.

We were in Alberta, Canada, at the same time as John, and we told him
about this wonderful place where he could rest, a place called Circle
Square Ranch. So he brought the entire Johnny Cash Show to the ranch
and slept in the bunkhouses and enjoyed a few days of real rest in the middle of a long tour. Incidentally, both buses full of the show stopped at a
department store in a small town to get boots because it was cold. Within
a few minutes, the entire town went running for their little Brownie
Hawkeyes to take pictures of Johnny Cash. By the way, they bought all
the boots in the whole town.

Another one of my favorite memories was to go to the farm that John
owned in Bon Aqua, Tennessee. It is one of the most peaceful places
around, and Joanne and I would be privileged to go there once in a while
to rest and meditate. The first time we went there, John left us a letter

Gospel / Spiritual

1. How Great Thou Art
2. His Eye is on the Sparrow
3. He Touched Me
4. He'll Understand and Say Well Done?
5. ~~...~~?
6. Peace in the Valley
7. You'll Never Walk Alone?
8. Precious Lord Take my Hand
9. I'd Rather Have Jesus
10. When He Reached Down His Hand
11. My God is Real
12. Why Me Lord
13. In the Garden
14. Sweet Hour of Pray
15. The Ninety and Nine
16. Whispering Hope
17. There's No Secret
18. The Old House
19. ... the Riverside
20. ... the wheel
21.

Spirituals

1. This Train is Bound For Glory
2. Strange Things Are Happening Every day
3. I'll Have a new Life
4. Gospel Boogie
5. The Fourth Man
6. On the Jericho Road
7. Satisfied
8. On the ...
9. Where We'll Never Grow Old
10. God Put a Rainbow in the Cloud
11. Look Down Look Down That Lonesome Road
12. Do Lord Remember Me
13. Got Shoes (Shout all over Gods Heaven)
14. Go Tell it On the Mountain
15. Workin on a Building
16. Lonesome Valley
17. O Mary Don't You Weep Don't you Mourn
18. Down By the Riverside
19. Ezekiel Saw the wheel

Believer Sings the Truth

20. Jo 3.
21. I'll be ridin back
22. Gunslinger
23. Walk of Life?
24. Mama's Recipe for love
25. Tecumseh
26. Hello Out There
27. Drive On
28. Doodle Blues

that really showed what the man was. This is what the letter said:

Harry and Joanne:

Welcome here. Be at your ease. Go to bed when you're ready. Get up when you please. The light of His love shines upon you. This is your house. Use it as you would your own. This house was built in 1837 by Captain Joseph Weems. He is buried in the cemetery across the field behind the house. There is plenty of firewood in the garage. Go through the back porch to get to the door of the garage. If you blow a fuse, there are extra fuses in the top dresser drawer just off the kitchen. The kitchen is well-stocked with food. Keep your weight up Harry. By the way, the key is in the jeep. You'll enjoy driving over the gravel roads all over Hickman County. That's the only way to see America.

John

My personal favorite recollections of Johnny Cash have nothing to do with music. They are the memories of the enormous spiritual quality of the man. Whether talking about the Apostle Paul, Peter, or Jesus, John was one of the most knowledgeable Bible scholars that I knew personally. He would always have a book or tape that he was reading or listening to. He would ask me what I thought about some of the things he was studying. I have personally three doctorate degrees in Bible education and still felt dwarfed by his overwhelming knowledge of the Bible, and not only his knowledge but his wisdom and discernment in using his knowledge. Johnny Cash has been what he said he would be in the letter he wrote to me when I married his sister. He has been a true brother and, even more than that, a "friend who sticketh closer than a brother." Even at the time of his own immense physical problems, he was always thinking about others. It is not an accident that his initials are J. C.

I miss my spiritual friend and brother.

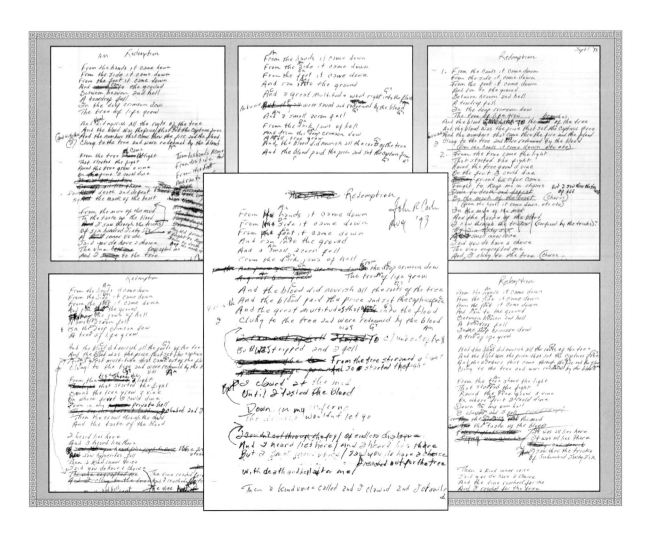

JOANNE CASH YATES

Gallatin, Tennessee

Shoe Size 6¹/₂

*M*Y MIND AND HEART are so full of precious memories of my beloved brother Johnny Cash. I am the youngest sister of John. Tommy is the youngest of the seven of us—Roy, Louise, Jack, John (J. R.), Reba, Joanne, Tommy. I have tremendous mixed emotions of loving him so much, and the hurt and loneliness of him not being here with me now.

When was the first time I ever remember John? We grew up together on a cotton farm in northeast Arkansas, although John was born in Kingsland. The family moved to Dyess in 1937. I was born the next year. The cotton fields were our livelihood. Daddy's philosophy was, "It's a gift from God to be strong and be able to work and earn a living!" (He put that "gift" into practice every day!)

It was hot in the cotton fields in the summer and "shaking" cold in the winter. Our house was a two-bedroom (with Mama and Daddy and seven of us, that was interesting). We had a living room, dining room, and Mama's small kitchen. There was a black iron woodstove in the kitchen where Mama cooked three times a day for all of us. I remember especially Mama's biscuits! They were big and a lot of them for all of us.

Not too long ago, I was in the kitchen in John's house in Hendersonville, having breakfast with him. He said, "Joanne, do you remember what we had for dessert when we were kids and wanted something sweet?" I said, "What do you mean?" He told June to pass him and me a biscuit. He put butter on the steaming biscuit and added a little sprinkle of sugar on it. I said, "Yes! I do remember!" We both just sat there eating "sugar biscuits" and reminiscing. Try it. If Merle Kilgore or Hank Williams Jr. are reading this, I know that they will go immediately and get some "Johnny Cash" sugar biscuits! Enjoy!

Our school was a simple, spread-out, white-washed building called Dyess School. I remember walking one-half a mile each morning and afternoon to Road 3 to catch the bus to and from school. Rain or shine, that was a daily thing. Once, when I was about seven, the weather was very stormy when the rain-soaked bus stopped at Road 3 to let us off. It was pouring rain! John got off the bus and had one umbrella. He said, "Come on, I'll keep you from getting wet!" He held the umbrella over Reba, Tommy, and me, and he took the rain. We walked the half-mile to the house—John was soaked and we were dry. That was Johnny Cash. Even to this day, I do not know where he got that umbrella. Very few people then even owned one.

The time in our lives that had probably the most profound effect was the events surrounding the death of our beloved brother Jack. Jack was fourteen, Johnny was twelve, and I was six. Johnny and Jack had to stay out of school sometimes during the week to help Daddy in the fields, so at times they would make up school work on Saturdays. This was the case that day with Jack. He and Johnny were planning to go fishing, but Jack said, "I have to finish cutting some fenceposts." A terrible accident happened, and Jack basically fell into the saw. For eight anguishing days he lingered between life and death. On the last day, we were gathered at the little Dyess hospital to say "goodbye." We were all so devastated! Jack was saying things like, "I see a river." "They are coming to get me." "That's

where I am going." "Can you see the angels?" "Can you hear the music?" "The angels, they are beautiful!" Then—he was gone.

All of our lives changed from that day. John told me many times that was the turning point in his life. Not very long ago he told me that he could not wait to see Jack.

There were many touching moments we all shared in growing up. In all of these moments, John was always just who he was. He did not have a selfish bone in his body. I was working at the House of Cash in the early 1970s as a receptionist and would greet people when they would come in. This one particular day a man about twenty-five to thirty years old came in looking for Johnny. He said that his name was Bobby Cash, and he wanted to see his brother Johnny who had been looking for him for many years. I said, "Tell me about it." He went into this long, unbelievable story. Then he was upset and said, "I want to see Johnny now. Who are you to not let me see him? I'm his brother!"

John was upstairs, heard the commotion, walked down the stairs, and said, "Are you bothering my sister?" The look on Bobby's face was one of shock, and he almost fainted! Johnny then told him that if he needed money, to be nice, do not lie, and do not raise your voice. To make a long story short, John gave him a check for $300, he thanked him, and he left. We laughed and thought that would be the last we would hear of Bobby. Not so. He took that check, used it for identification for hotels and meals with a promise to pay when he got the check cashed, and even bought a sewing machine in my name! Oh, well. People used or abused John that way many times, but he always said, "It's all right. I know they are using me. What really hurts is when I do not know!"

In 1971, John and June had just finished doing the movie *The Gospel Road*, a film about the life of Jesus. I was still working at the House of Cash. I had told John about my conversion before and how I was living for the Lord. I now told him that I thought that I was in love with Harry Yates. He told me that if I loved him, really loved him, to marry him, and I had his blessing. He smiled and gave me a big hug and kiss and said, "It's going to be all right." He also asked me then if I wanted to go to the land of Israel. If so, I could take a copy of the film and show it to the people over there who had been in it. (Almost all of the film had been shot in Israel.) I had always wanted to go to that special land. Going there to me was one step from Heaven.

Harry Yates was on that same trip. We fell in love in Tel Aviv, came home, and got married December 27, 1971. My whole family was there. What a day!

John has given me "little things" over the years—his understanding, his humor, as well as tangible things. A week before he went to Heaven, I was visiting him in his bedroom, and he wanted me to sit down with him. I never knew what he would want, either to give me something—from a word of encouragement to something tangible—or just to talk with him. This particular day he said, "What has the Lord said in His word today— what's the word for today, Baby?" He needed that (and so did I). He opened his desk drawer and took out five of the biggest, ugliest watches (he was always buying different kinds of watches) that I had ever seen. He wanted me to give one to Harry, and I could wear the rest at different times. Then he gave me one personally. He told me it was a good watch, if you just wanted to know what time it was. I now really cherish those watches. He also gave me one of his treasured black silk shirts, as well as many other things over the years.

One of the most spiritual gifts that John gave me was when we talked the very last time just before he passed away. He asked me this question: "If you were walking on the shore of Galilee and you saw Jesus walking toward you, you knew He was going to say one thing to you, what do you think you would want Him to say?" John was very serious, so I replied, "What I believe I would want Him to say to me is, 'You are doing what I called you to do,'" John looked at me and said, "He would say to you, 'Feed my sheep.'" (Harry and I pastor a

John took this photo of his dad, Ray, raising the Stars and Stripes.

church.) I told him that I thought that Jesus would say something like that and that we are doing just that.

Then I turned it around on him and asked him the same question. "Oh, that's easy," said John with tears in his eyes, "'Come unto me all ye that labor and are heavy laden, and I will give you rest. Take my yoke upon you and learn of me, for I am meek and lowly in heart, and you will find rest unto your souls, for my yoke is easy and my burden is light.' That is what He would say to me." I felt the presence of the Lord in that room that day in a very wonderful way. I really did not realize until a few days later that John may have been saying goodbye to me for now. Now I look back on it and think that maybe he was telling me to do what God has called me to do and that he (John) was going home, and he pointed upward when he finished speaking. He had told me once that living without June was like being a half a pair of scissors—he just could not cut it! He was tired.

John was, and still is, a part of me and I of him. Family is family is family! I am thankful to be a Cash. My brother J. R. still daily inspires me with who he was—funny, strong, tender in heart, and most of all, his incredible love for truth, God, me, and other family—unconditional love!

Now he is in Heaven with June, Jack, Roy, and other family and friends. I still wonder what Jack really looks like. I can sometimes feel John laughing and saying, "Wait till you see, Baby, wait till you see!"

ACKNOWLEDGMENTS

MUCH ADMIRATION AND RESPECT is expressed to the friends and family of Johnny Cash who graciously contributed their time and emotion-filled memories to *I Still Miss Someone*. A little bit more lore is now added to John R. Cash's rich legacy by their willingness to share those experiences and thoughts.

Great appreciation is almost not enough to convey my gratitude to Susie Q. Gustke and John Mitchell. They have been in the trenches with me since the production start of this book, putting in countless hours with all the words, images, and photos that are included herein. This volume would not have come to fruition without your continued dedication to my vision. You both learned to tolerate me and the methods of my madness. Thank you so very much.

And an extra special heartfelt note of thanks to Brother Joe McKinney, one of the ministers of the Church of Christ at Joelton, who, as my best friend, has supported me from the very inception of this tribute project.

Memorabilia and photographs courtesy of: Jay Abend, Russ Busby, Cindy Cash, Mark Cash, Tommy Cash, Jack Clement, Garland Craft,

Morelia Cuevas, Dennis Devine, Luther Fleaner, Wanda Fleaner, W. S. Holland, Tim Hudson, Dmitri Kasterine, Pat Katz, Merle Kilgore, Alan Messer, Bill Miller, Lisa Meideffer, Al Qualls, Lou Robin, Michele Rollins, Ted Rollins, Fern Salyer, Maury Scobee, Mark Seliger, Rev. Jack Shaw, John L. Smith, Dustin Tittle, Jimmy Tittle, Alma Jean Todd, Hugh Waddell, Bill Walker, Johnny Western, Jeanne Witherell, Dr. Harry Yates, and Joanne Cash Yates.

INDEX

A

ABC Television, 87, 109, 114, 116, 141, 209, 223, 238, 258-259, 261
Abend, Jay, xv, 3-5
Abraham Lincoln High School, 49-50
Adams, Nick, 114
Adelaide, Australia, 199
Affordable Art Tour, 3-4, 4, 212, 235-236, 237, 266
AIDS awareness, 248, 264
Air Jamaica Jazz & Blues Festival, 164
"All Hail the Power of Jesus' Name," 135
Allen, Duane, 37
Allen, Joe, 89
Almond, Marc, 264
America, 208, 256
American Bandmasters Hall of Fame, 69
American Cancer Society

Jail-a-thon, 65, 248
American Recordings, 129, 149, 153, 239, 254
Ames, Iowa, 100, 209
Anderson, Ind., 212, 227
Andy Williams Show, The, 261
"Angel Band," 228
"Annie Palmer, The White Witch of Rose Hall," 164
Anto Distinguished Shirtmakers, 189
"Any Old Wind that Blows," 254
Apostle, The, 67, 132, 186, 294
Armando, 26
Armstrong, Louis, 87, 260
Arnold, Eddy, 105, 258
Art Direction Magazine, 138
Artist Consultants Productions, 151
"As Long as the Grass Shall Grow," 206, 208
Asamba, Minister, 165

Asbury Park, N.J., 242
Asheville, N.C., 182, 184, 186-187
Atkins, Chet, 111
Atlanta, Ga., 41-42, 113, 250
Atlantic City, N.J., 78-79
Autry, Gene, 19, 140, 246, 265

B

Baggett, Reverend, 132
Baker, Julian, 71
Bakker, Tammye Faye, 247
Ball Busters, 172
"Ballad of Ira Hayes, The," 265
"Ballad of Tiger Whitehead, The," 277
Bannon, Jim, 19
Baptist Hospital, 139, 173, 197, 238
Barnard, Helen, 48
Barnard, Russell, 48

Barnhill, Mike, 61
Baron, Arthur, 206-207
"Beans for Breakfast," 255
Beatles, 69, 130, 216
Belcourt Theater, 139
Belgium, 152
Bell Cove Club, 136, 248

Berg, Matraca, 245
Berlin, Germany, 127, 245
Best Band You Never Heard In
    Your Life, The, 246
Beverly Center Mall, 240
Beverly Hills, Calif., 189, 240
Bicentennial Tour, 25-26, 122
Big Bird, 245-246
Big Cedar Lodge, 249
"Big Foot," 126, 207-208
"Big River," 212, 255
Billboard magazine, 24, 105, 247
Billy Bob's, 231

Billy Graham Crusade, 131,
    136, 138, 182, 184-185,
    188-189, 248-249, 277
Bitter Tears, 256
Black Hills, 206
Blake, Norman, 238
Bloomington, Ill., 212
"Blue Suede Shoes," 76-77
Blues in the Mississippi Night, 238
Bob Cummings Productions,
    248, 250-251
Bob Wootton & The
    Commancheros, 287
Bohannon, Jim, 249-250, 250
Bon Jovi, 3
Bond, James, 12
Bono, 253
Bonsall, Joe, 35
Boom Chicka Boom, 239
Boone, Pat, 209
Bossier City, La., 103
Boston, Mass., 266
Boston Pops, 246
"Boy Named Sue, A," 85-86,
    106-107, 209
Bramlett, Dave, 149
Brentano's Book Store, 245
Brentwood, Tenn., 258
British Isles, 152
Browning, Elizabeth Barrett,
    161
Buck Lake Ranch, 20
Buffalo, N.Y., 197
Burgess, Sonny, 75
Bush, George H. W., 146
Butler, Larry, 64

C
Cain's Ballroom, 287
Camp Rudder, Fla., 149
Canadian National
    Exhibition, 265
Cap's Gap, Tenn., 242

Carbon County Memorial
    Hospital, 268
Carnegie Hall, 195, 269
Caroline, 93-94
Carowinds Park, 223
Carpenters, 260
Carson, Johnny, 80
Carter, A. P., 176
Carter, Anita, 42, 47, 49, 84,
    104, 107, 226, 254
Carter, Carlene, 135, 164,
    166, 172, 178, 254
Carter, Helen, 42, 47, 49, 51,
    107, 220, 226, 254
Carter, Janette, 176
Carter, Joe, 130, 176
Carter, Mother Maybelle, xv,
    36-37, 47, 49, 65, 107, 272,
    281
Carter, Ora, 177
Carter, Rosey, 49, 130, 221,
    231, 238, 254
Carter, Sarah, 176
Carter Family, 45, 177
Carter Family Cookbook, 235
Carter Family Museum, 226
Carter Fold, 176, 178, 208,
    226, 228, 255
Cash, Bobby, 298
Cash, Carrie Rivers "Mama"
    (mother), v, 16, 20, 23,
    149-150, 217, 231-232,
    251, 270-271, 271
Cash, Cindy (daughter), 6-
    10, 8-10, 15, 17, 35, 136,
    172, 210, 235
Cash, Jack (brother), 28, 255,
    274, 296-298, 300
Cash, Jessica (granddaugh-
    ter), 9
Cash, John Carter (son), 11-
    15, 12, 14-15, 136, 148, 165,
    172, 178, 248, 276

Cash, Joseph John (grandson), 224
Cash, June Carter (wife), xi, xiii, xv, 4, *12*, 25, 38, 42-43, 45, 47, 49, 51, *52*, 54, *66*, 68, 97, 101, 104, 110, *111*, 118, 129, 130, *130*, 131, 136, *136*, *138*, 139, 142-143, 146, 154, 158, 160, 164, *165*, 166, 175, *175*, *177*, 181-182, 184, *187*, *191*, *198*, 203, 207-208, *209-210*, 221, 226, 228, 231, *231*, 235, 237, 241, *241*, 245, *248*, *250*, 259-260, *260*, 263, *267*, 272, 279, *283*, 289, *290*
Cash, Laura (daughter-in-law), 228
Cash, Mark (nephew), 16-17, *17*
Cash, Mary Ann (daughter-in-law), 224
Cash, Ray (father), 20, *23*, 49, 270-271, 274, *271*, *299*
Cash, Rosanne (daughter), 35, 163, 172, 185, 218, *281*
Cash, Roy (brother), *23*, 199, 256, 274, 296, 300
Cash, Tommy (brother), xv, 19-29, *23-24*, *27-28*, 51, 296
Cash Box magazine, 24
Cash Mountain, 242
Casino Theater, 265
CBS Records, 256
CBS Television, 34, 64, 109, 221, 238-239, 256, 262
Cedar Hill Refuge Recording Cabin, 159, 242
Center Point Barbecue, xvi, 255
Centerville, Tenn., 54
Champaign, Ill., 3
Chapin, Harry, 239
Charles, Prince, 153

Charles, Ray, 246, 260-261, *261*
Charleston, S.C., 156
Chattanooga, Tenn., 238
Chesser, Eustace, 7
Cheyenne, Wyo., 266-267
"Children Go Where I Send Thee," 179
Cincinnati, Ohio, 193
Cinnamon Hill, 12, 125, 133-135, 139, 166, 169
Cinnamon Hill Golf Course, 161
Cinnamon Hill Great House, 161, 164-166
Circle Square Ranch, 293
Circle Star Theater, 34
Clapton, Eric, *203*
Clark, Guy, 130
Clarke, Terry, 136
Clement, "Cowboy" Jack, 30-32, *31*, 37, 118, 194
Clinton, Bill, 227
Cohen, Harold, 259
Cohen, Leonard, 238
Colter, Jessi, 12, 226, *232*, 235-236
Columbia, Mo., 211
Columbia, S.C., 131, 136, 188
Columbia Records, 77, 129, 153, 265
Comer, Marie, 231
Copperwood, 161-162
Cork, Ireland, 251
Cornwall Regional Hospital, 163
Corona, Calif., 140
Cosby, Bill, 151
Costello, Elvis, *245*
Country Music Association, 109, 111
Country Music Hall of Fame, 96, 105, 188, 235, 254, 282
Country Music magazine, 48

Craft, Garland, xv, 34-39, *35*
Crazy Horse, 206
Cream, 87
Cronkite, Walter, 240
Crosby, Bing, 141
Cummings, Bob, 248
Cummings, Pete, 250
Czechoslovakia, 91, 152

D
Dangler, Bob, 46
Darrah, Saundra, 50
Dauro, Jay, 41-45, *42-43*
Davis, Sammy Jr., 190, 246
De Pere, Wis., 98
Dean, Eddie, 19
Deckerman, Bud, 75
Delaware, University of, 164
"Delia's Gone," 242
Denver, Colo., 138, 142, 148, 269
Denver Presbyterian Hospital, 269
Deputy, The, 206
Des Moines, Iowa, 48, 168, 205, 208-209
Devine, Della, 46, 49, 52, *52*
Devine, Dennis, xv, 46-52, *47*, *50*, *52*
Devine, Dennis Jr., 48
Devine, Harold, 49
Devine, Jean, 48
Devine, Joe, 48
Devine, Norman, 48
Devine, Paul, 46, 49
Devonport, Tasmania, 262
Dewey, Bill, *53*
DeWille, Tom, 42
Diamond, Neil, 260
Dickens, "Little" Jimmy, 268
Dickson, Tenn., 54, 254
"Dirty Old Egg-Sucking Dog," 255

"Don't Take Your Guns to Town," 82, 176
Doobie Brothers, 68
Door to Door Maniac, 256
Doors, 140
Douglas, Kirk, 118, 246
Dublin, Ireland, 152
Duke University, 224
Dukes of Hazzard, 246
Duvall, Gayle, 132
Duvall, Robert, 131-132
Dyess, Ark., 19-21, 25, 102, 255, 296-297
Dyess School, 297
Dyess Theater, 19, 255
Dylan, Bob, 18, 86-87, 136, 247, 253

E
Earle, Steve, 139
East Germany, 152
East Peoria, Ill., 279
Eastwood, Clint, 144
Ed Sullivan Show, The, 261
Edgewater Hotel, 233-234
El Paso, Texas, 216
Elfstrum, Ron, 207
Elliott, Kent, 42, 44
Entertainment Tonight, 236
Epic Records, 24
Evangel Temple, 63-64
Everly Brothers, 37

F
Fabian, 79
Family Circle magazine, 240-241
Fan Fair, 100, 223, 279, 282-283
Far East, 106
"Far Side Banks of Jordan," 228, 263
Fargo, N.D., 249
Farm Aid, 209-210
Farmer, Brian, 45
Fayetteville, Ark., 288
Finish Line Motel, 50-51
Finland, 152
Five Minutes to Live, 256
Flatt, Lester, 82
Fleaner, Chad, 57
Fleaner, Jeff, 57
Fleaner, Luther, xv, 54-62, 57
Fleaner, Wanda, 56, 61
"Flesh and Blood," 255
Florida Ranger Camp, 149
Folsom Prison, 109, 175
"Folsom Prison Blues," 20, 22, 141, 212, 230-231, 253-254, 284
Fonda, Henry, 206-207

Ford, Gerald R., 253
Ford, Joy, 136, *136*
Fort Campbell, Ky., 148
Fort Walton Beach, Fla., 147
Fort Wayne, Ind., 204
Fort Worth, Texas, 231
Fox Theatre, 41, 225
France, 195
Franklin, Aretha, 68
Franklin Electronic Bible, 197-198, 235
Franklin Electronic Publishers, 235
Franklin Mint, 281-282
Frix, Bob, 148-149

G
Gallatin, Tenn., 16, 177, 292, 296
Gander, Newfoundland, 148
Madison Square Garden, 119
Garfield, James, 145
Garland, Sally, 276
Garrett, Louise Cash (sister), 23, 296
Garrett, Matt, 42, *42*, 45
Gatlin, Larry, 39, 164, 248
Geraldine, 134
"Ghost Riders in the Sky," 71-72
Gibb, Barry, 260
Gibbs, Irene, xv, 63-67
"Gift of the Magi, The," 149
Giltner, Neb., 46
Golden Boot Awards, 150
Goldie, 69
Goodman, Steve, 212, 238
Gore, Albert Jr., 244
Gosden, Vern, 239
Gospel Quartet Hour, 102
Gospel Road, The, 207, 222, 298
Graceland, 77

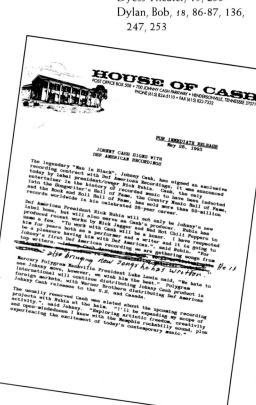

Graham, Billy, xi-xii, *xii*, 23-24, 65, *70*, 131, 133, 136, 138-139, 163, 181-189, *182*, *187*, 246, 249, 251, 277

Graham, Franklin, ix, 181-182

Graham, Ruth, xi-xii, *xii*, 12, 182, *182*, 184, 186-187, *187*

Grammy Awards, 105

Grand Island, Neb., 46

Grand Ole Opry, 4, 106-107, 130

Grant, Marshall, 20, 35, 41-42, 47, 76-83, *77*, *79*, 85, 88-89, 120, 205, 265, 289

Grant, Ulysses S., 238

Greatest Salesman in the World, The, 236

Green Bay, Wis., 98

Greenville, Del., 160

Greenville, S.C., 160, 187

Greenwood Great House, 161

Guantanamo Bay, Cuba, 152

Guccioni, Bob, 132

Guild Guitars, 5

Gunfight, A, 118

H

Haggard, Merle, 110, 218, 220, 287

Hale, Jack, xvi, *43*, 68-73, *69-70*, 136, 249

Hale, Jack Sr., 68

Hale, Ralph, 69

Hall, Tom T., 56, 247-248

Hamburg, Germany, 245

Hammond, Ind., 81

Hancock, Kelly, 145-146, 239

Hancock, Reba Cash (sister), 23, *23*, 51, 56, 60, 64-65, 149, 117, 119, 190, 249, 256, 296-297

Hardin, Tim, 238

Harris, Emmylou, 60, 242-243

Harrison, George, *246*

Hasselblad, Victor M. Co., 93-94, 243

Hastings, Neb., 46

Hastings, Harlan, 163

Hastings, Jennifer, 163

Hawaii, 152, 155, 261-262

Hayes, Ira, 265

Heard, Dick, 236

Helsinki, Finland, 152

Hendersonville, Tennessee, xvi, 11, 19, 34, 37, 68, 218, 221, 229, 243, 254, 270, 273, 287
Hendrix, Jimi, 140
Hershey, Pa., 120
"Hey Porter," 20, 42, 97, 174
Hidden Jesus, The, 133
Highwaymen, 44, 136, 209-210, 213
Hiltons, Va., 226-228, 242, 255
Himons, Aashid, 130
Hobart, Tasmania, 262
Hobson, Timothy, 268
Holiday Inn, 118, 193
Holiff, Saul, 47, 151
Holland, Joyce, 78, 90, 220
Holland, W. S. "Fluke," xv, 47, 75-92, 76, 80, 88-89, 91, 122, 130, 219-220, 233-234, 289
Holly, Buddy, xvi
Hollywood, Calif., 70, 80, 116, 243
Hollywood Bowl, 269
Holmes, Oliver Wendell, 201-202
"Holografik Danser, The," 203
Holt, Sterling, 61
Holy Land, 250, 292
"Honeycomb," 259
Hong Kong, 152
Honolulu, Hawaii, 261-262
Hoover, Gene, 267
Hope, Bob, 67
Horton, Johnny, 103-104, 103, 238
House of Cash, xvi, 35-36, 45, 64-65, 67-68, 93, 118-119, 138, 154-155, 190, 194, 203, 208, 219, 226, 232, 235, 239, 256, 268, 276, 281-283, 298

Houston, Texas, 72, 274
Houston Symphony, 72
Howard, Jan, 262
Hughes, William, 230
Hungary, 152
Hunt, Mark, 42
Huntsville, Ala., 41
"Hurt," 24-25, 92, 111, 280

I
"I Walk the Line," 22, 97, 144, 204, 212, 259
"I Was There When It Happened," 287
"If I Were a Carpenter," 38
"If You Could Read My Mind," 29
Illinois, University of, 3, 235
"I'm Gonna Live the Life I Sing About," 182
"I'm Gonna Sit on the Porch and Pick on My Old Guitar," 254
International Entertainment Buyers Association, 102, 105
Ireland, xv
Irwin, Sam, 51
Israel, 66, 274, 292, 299
Italian Street Fair, 248
I've Been Everywhere, 152
Iwo Jima, Japan, 266

J
Jackson, Mahalia, 182, 238
Jackson, Michael, 105, 216
Jamaica, xi, 9, 12, 93, 123-125, 132, 134-135, 160-164, 166, 168, 172, 203, 216, 248
Jamaican Safari Village, 12-13
Japan, 106, 108
Jean, Norman, 46
Jefferson, Thomas, 238

Jennings, Waylon, xv-xvi, 4, 12, 44, 60, 67, 130, 130, 132, 137, 209-212, 226, 231-232, 232, 235-236, 246, 248, 257, 261
Jerry Lewis Telethon for Muscular Dystrophy, 267
Jesus Christ, 171, 193, 202, 207, 254, 270-271, 294, 298-300
Jim "the Gorilla," 13, 15, 258
John, Barbara, 209
John, Elton, 105
Johnny Cash and June Carter Cash International Fan Club (John and June Cash International Fan Club), 97-110, 101, 223-225, 227, 268, 279-281, 283-285
Johnny Cash at Folsom Prison, 141
Johnny Cash Is Coming, 150
Johnny Cash road show softball team, 222
Johnny Cash Show, The, 107, 108, 108, 114-115, 117, 259-260
Johnny Cash—The Man, His World, His Music, 39, 106
Johnny Cash Theatre, 249-250
Johnny Cash: Unearthed, 154
"Johnny Yuma," 114
Johnson, Larry, 42, 44
Johnson City, Tenn., 272
Johnstown, Pa., 193
Jones, George, 46, 267
Jones, Tommy Lee, 190
Josephus, 216
Joyner, Dickie, 170-171
"Junkie and the Juice Head Minus Me, The," 220
Just As I Am, 211

K

Kananga, Ross, 12-15, *13*
Kansas City, Mo., 273
Kasterine, Dmitri, 93-95
Kasterine, Nicholas, 94
Katz, Pat, xv, 97-101, *99*, *101*
Keach, James, 51
Kennedy, John F., 287
Kennedy Center Honor, 105,
  145-146, 148, 227
Kennedy Center Opera
  House, 227
Khayyam, Omar, 73
Kilgore, Merle, xv, 61, 68,
  102-105, *105*, 297
Kimberlys, 267
King, Larry, 249-250, 273
King, Rodney, 249
King, Stephen, 247
Kingsland, Ark., 255, 296
Knott's Berry Farm, 109
Knoxville, Tenn., 290
Kostelanetz, Andre, 247
Kristofferson, Kris, 39, 44,
  137, 168
KRNT, 205

L

La Crosse, Wis., 212
Lakeland, Fla., 119
Lane, Penni, xv, 106-111
Langeneggar, Doris, 49-50
Langford, Jon, *264*
Larry King Live, 273
LaRue, Lash, 19, 147
Las Vegas, Nev., 35, 88, 98,
  120, 222, 231
Las Vegas Hilton, 35
Late Show with David Letterman,
  245
Laughlin, Nev., 98-99
Laughner, Jim, 131
Laughner, Vancie, 131

Lawrence Co.,
  S. M., 76
Leatha, Miss, *234*
Leave It to Beaver, 141
Lee, Buddy, 24
Lee, Peggy, 260
Leno, Jay, 190
"Lessons I Learned
  From My Father,
  The" 179-180
"Let Him Roll,"
  257.
LeTourneau
  College, 181
Lewes Beach,
  Del., 163, 166
Lewin, Bob, 68-69
Lewis, Curly, 80-
  81
Lewis, Jerry, 190
Lewis, Jerry Lee,
  75
Lewis,
  Meriwether, 238
Lewry, Peter, 152
Life Of Christ, The, 222
Lightfoot, Gordon, 29
Lincoln, Abraham, 49-50, 52,
  90, 168
Little America Hotel, 267
Lomax, Alan, 238
London, England, 71, 123,
  136, 245
London Palladium, 123
"Long-Legged Guitar Picking
  Man," 175
Longview, Fla., 181
Los Angeles, Calif., 69, 80,
  109, 151, 154, 157, 235,
  259
Los Angeles Forum, 69
Lost Highway Records, 154
Louisiana Hayride, 103, 174

Louvin Brothers, 265
Love Without Fear, 7, 255
Lowe, Nick, *245*
Lowe, Tiffany Anastasia, *164*,
  166
Lulu, *260*
Luna Tech, 41-42

M

Maces Springs, Va., 174, 176
Madison, Tenn., 272, 275
Madison, Wis., 97, 233-234
Madison Square Garden, 119
"Man Can't Live With a
  Broken Heart Too Long,
  A," 164
Man In Black, 66
"Man In Black," 27, 255
Man In White, xi, 50, 67, 186,
  240
"Man Who Couldn't Cry,
  The," 239
Mandino, Og, 236
Mann, Carl, 78
Manny's Music, 158
Manson, Charles, 109
Manuel, 25, *74*, 150, 219

Marshall, Jim, 130
Martin, Chance, xv, 13, 15,
  113-127, *114, 118, 124*
Martin, Dean, 59
Mary Mary, 264
Mayo Clinic, 183
McCarthy, Joseph, 215
McCartney, Paul, 246
McCoy, Tom, 267
McQueen, Steve, 124
Mead, Walter, 176
Memphis Horns, 68-70
Memphis Symphony, 69

Mercury Records, 137, 239
Mercy Hospital, 49-51
Merle Haggard & The
  Strangers, 110, 218
Messer, Alan, xv, 129-139, *136*
Messer, David, 133
Messer, Michael, 135-136
Michelle Shocked, 264
Michl, June, 166
Microsoft, 105
Miller, Bill, 140-146, *141*
Miller, Dick, 48-50
Miller, Jordan Cash, 145
Miller, Roger, 238
  Miller, Shannon, 141,
    141, 146
  Millersville
    Pentecostal
    Church, 132
  *Million Dollar
    Quartet, The*, 75
  Miniconju, 208
  Minneapolis,
    Minn., 99-100
  Minnesota Fats,
    248
  Mississippi Mass
    Choir, 238
  Missouri,
    University of, 211
  Mitchell, Joni, 87
  Molly Hatchett, 3
  Moman, Chips,
    132
  "Mona Lisa," 78
  Monroe, Bill, 247-
    248
  Montego Bay,
    Jamaica, 152, 161
  Monthaven, 130
  Montreat, N.C., xii,
    181-182, 187
  Moore, Bob, 131

Moore, Bonnie Lou, 272
Moore, Buster, 272
Moore, Roger, 124
Moses, 202
Moss, Kate, 242, *242*
Mount Vernon United
  Methodist Church, 177
Munich, Germany, 245
Murphy, Eddie, 190
Murray, Anne, 260
Murray, Larry, 24, 238-239
Music Row, 63, 114
Mutual Radio Network, 249
"My Friend, the Famous
  Person," 30-32
Mystery of Life, The, 138

N
Napoleon, 62
Nashville Cowboy Church,
  292
Nashville Now, 77, 150
Nashville Symphony, 248
Natchitoches Red River Bait
  Co., 103
National Football League, 247
National Medal of Arts, 146
National Symphony
  Orchestra, 246
Neil, Bob, 75
Nelson, Lanette, 141
Nelson, Willie, 44, 86, 137
Netherlands, 195
New Orleans, La., 273
New York, N.Y., 73, 94, 158,
  160, 201, 242, 244-245,
  269
Newport Beach, Calif., 143-
  144
Newton, Wayne, 141, 246
Nichols, Nick, 268
Nickelsville, Va., 176
Nirvana, 142-143

MAR 28 '98 15:54 MUSIC CITY NEWS

FROM: JOHNNY CASH

Music City News®

The World's Largest Monthly Country Music Magazine

MOTHER'S FULL NAME: CARRIE CLOVEREE RIVERS CASH

WHAT PHYSICAL OR PERSONALITY ATTRIBUTES DID YOU INHERIT
FROM YOUR MOTHER?

Height. Voice

WHAT IS THE BEST ADVICE YOUR MOTHER GAVE YOU?

Trust in God

DID YOUR MOTHER ENCOURAGE YOUR CAREER IN MUSIC?

yes

WHAT IS YOUR BEST MEMORY OF YOUR MOTHER?

When she welcomed me
home with love after I'd
been in jail.

Nitty Gritty Dirt Band, 148
Nixon, Richard, 110, 145, 247
Norman, Okla., 266
Northern Ireland, 152

O
Oak Ridge Boys, 34-37, *35*, 39, 248
O'Connor, Mark, 246
Ojai, Calif., 80, 83
Old Fireball lure, 103-104
Old Hickory Lake, 136, 167, 171, 242, 272, 276
Omaha, Neb., 46-48, 50, 53
One Bad Pig, 247
One-Eyed Jack, 13, 124-125
One Man Show cologne, 138, 188
"Orange Blossom Special," 48, 51, 142, 284
Orbison, Roy, 75
Orlando, Tony, 59
"Over the Next Hill," 37, 64

P
Pacino, Al, 190
Pale Rider, 144
Palmer, Annee, 162-164
Panama City, Fla., 150
Paramount Theatre, 46
Paris, France, 7, 102
Parton, Dolly, 193
Parton, Stella, 130
Paul, Saint (Saul), xv, 67, 186, 246, 294
Paxman Horn Shop, 71
Pee Hill, 135
Pella, Iowa, 212
People's History of the United States: 1492-Present, A, 238
Perkins, Carl, 47, 75-78, *76*, 85, 89, 142, *210-211*, 262, 289-290

Perkins, Clayton, 75-76
Perkins, J. B., 75-76
Perkins, Luther, 20, 47, 53, 76, *77*, 79, 205, 274, 287-288, *288*, 290
Perkins Band, 76
Perronet, Edward, 135
Perth, Australia, 196
Peter, Saint, 152, 294
Petty, Tom, 246
Philadelphia, Pa., 224, 287
Phillips, Dewey, 76
Phillips, Sam, 75-76
"Phoenix Rising," 214-216
"Pickin' Time," 255
Pigeon Forge, Tenn., 272
Pima Reservation, 265
Pine Ridge Reservation, 207
Pioneer Award, 102, 105
Pittsburgh, Pa., 195, 206
Plains Indians, 205
Polygram Records, 129, 153
Pompano Beach, Fla., 167
Ponderosa Hotel, 266
Pop, Iggy, 130
Port Richey, Fla., 241
Portland, Ore., 179, 185
Poughkeepsie, N.Y., 94
"Precious Memories," 178, 255, 296
Presley, Elvis, 35, 75, 77, *77*, 156, 174, 287, 291
Press On, 133, 162
Professional Club, 63
Public Television Network, 206
Pusser, Buford, xv, 65

Q
Qualls, Al, 147-150, *148*
Qualls, Donny, *148*, 150
Qualls, Polly, 150

R
"Ragged Old Flag," 256
Ramada Inn, 114
Randwick Race Course, 261
Rapid City, S.D., 206, 208
Rawlins, Wyo., 267-269
Reagan, Ronald, 190, 247
Rebel, The, 114
Record World magazine, 24
Red Hot Chili Peppers, 246
"Redemption," 254
Reeves, Jim, 69, 258
Reilly, Billy, 75
Renaissance Records, 251
Reno, Nev., 266-267
Return to the Promised Land, 235, 248-249, 251
Rhinelander, Wis., 20
Rhythm Oil—The Sessions with Terry Clarke and Jesse "Guitar" Taylor, 136
Richard Nixon Presidential Library, 145
Richards, Keith, 245
Richmond, Va., 244
Ride This Train, 42, 256, 260
Riley, Marc, *264*
"Road to Kaintuck," 174
Robin, Karen, 45
Robin, Lou, xv, 41-42, 45, 48-49, 88, 97-99, 143, 151-154, *152*, *154*, 185, 235, 272
Rochester, N.Y., 183
Rock and Roll Hall of Fame, 105, 245
Rock for the Animals, 130, 247
Rockefeller, Winthrop, 288
Rodgers, Jimmie, *259*
Roe, Dave, xv, 155-159, *156*
Rogers, Kenny, 166, 239-240
Rogers, Roy, 19, 140
Rolling Stones, 71, 130, 243

Rollins, John, 160-163, *161,*
163-164, 166
Rollins, Marc, 164-165, *164*
Rollins, Michael, 162-166,
164-165
Rollins, Michele, xv, 160-
166, *161, 164*
Rollins, Michele (daughter),
162, *164*
Rollins, Monique, 162 *164*
Rollins, Peggy, 163
Rollins, Randall, 163

Rollins, Ted W., xv, 167-173,
168, 170-172, 220
Ronstadt, Linda, 110, 115-
116, 260
Rose Hall, 133-135, 161-166
Rose Hall Great House, *134,*
162, 164-166
Rosebud Reservation, 206
Ross, Tasmania, 262
Round Hill, 160
Royal Albert Hall, 71, 245
Rubaiyat of Omar Khayyam,
The, 73
Rubin, Rick, 153, 212,
218, 239
Rustic Rhythm maga-
zine, 21
Ryman Auditorium,
107, 114-116, 208,
259

S
St. Croix Falls, Wis.,
97
St. Francis, S.D., 207
St. John, Al "Fuzzy," 19,
71
St. Louis, Mo., 25, 225
Salyer, Fern, 174-178, *175*
Salyer, Joey, 175
Salyer, Marcus, 176, *176*
Salyer, Phil, 175
Salyer, Shane, 175
Salyer, Walt, 175
Sambora, Ritchie, 3
San Antonio, Texas, 108
San Carlos, Calif., 34, 43
San Francisco, Calif., 106,
108
"San Quentin," 85, 255
San Quentin, 123
San Quentin Prison, 106,
130, 209

Santa Ana, Calif., 153
Santa Anna, Antonio Lopez
de, 238
Santa Barbara, Calif., 108
Saragosa, Texas, 231
"Saturday Night in Hickman
County," 254
Schneider, John, 246
Schramm, Tex, 247
Schwarzenegger, Arnold, 190
Schwoebel, Tara Cash
(daughter), 7, 173, 179-
180, *179*
Scobee, Maury, 181-188, *182*
Scottsdale, Ariz., 268-269
Sea to Shining Sea, 256
Seely, Jeannie, 106
Sepetjian, Anto, 189-191
Sepetjian, Jack, 189
Sepetjian, Ken, 189
"September When It Comes,"
163
Sesame Street, 245-246
Seymour, Jane, 242
Shaw, Grace, 199
Shaw, Jack, xv, 193-202, *194,*
196, *198*
Shaw, Sarah Grace, 199
"Shenandoah," 73
Sheraton Hotel, 102
Shields, Brooke, xv, 4, 212,
230, 236, 242
Shields, Teri, 4, 236
Shreveport, La., 103
Shriver, Eunice Kennedy, 240
Shy-Drager syndrome, 134,
216
Silver Star Resort, 224
Silverstein, Shel, 85
Simon and Garfunkel, 151
Simonitsch, Heinz, 163
Sinatra, Frank, 190
Singapore, 152

TITLE: J. CASH: DON'T TAKE YOUR ONES TO TOWN

PRODUCTION #: 23-0000   SHOW/ITEM #: WILD   2.

WRITER: CASH/CERF

AUDIO IN: _____ DIRECTOR: _____ TIME: _____

VIDEO IN: _____ AUDIO OUT: _____ AD _____ PA _____

PROD. DATES: _____ VIDEO OUT: _____
VT 1: _____
VT 1: _____ VT 2: _____ CASS: _____
VT 1: _____ VT 2: _____ CASS: _____
VT 2: _____ CASS: _____

GOAL(s): ENUMERATION

SCENIC: NEST AREA, SESAME STREET

CHARACTERS: JOHNNY CASH, BIG BIRD, BARKLEY, THE COUNT, THE COUNTESS, AMS; COW, HOESE, FROG

PROPS: LOTS OF NUMBER 1's, SADDLE BAG, CRATES
COSTUMES: COWBOY OUTFIT FOR BIG BIRD
MUSIC: SONG: "DON'T TAKE YOUR ONES TO TOWN",
WHICH REQUIRES TV TRACK OF "DON'T
TAKE YOUR GUNS TO TOWN"

BIG BIRD, DRESSED AS A COWBOY, IS IN THE NEST
AREA WITH JOHNNY CASH. BIG BIRD HAS A SADDLE
BAG TYPE SATCHEL ON HIS HIP. IT'S FILLED WITH
1'S AND HAS A "1" ON IT.

BB: (TO CAM) Hi! My friend Johnny Cash
and I are going to do a song for you about a
cowbird named Birdy Big! Ready Johnny?

JOHNNY: Ready Big!

JOHNNY CASH SINGS:

VERSE #1:

A young bird named Birdy Big
Had learned to count to one
He said it's time to leave the nest
And go and have some fun
So he (packed up) (gathered) all the number ones
That he could find aroun'

BIG BIRD PUTS 1'S IN THE SACK.

But his good friend cried as he walked out:
"Don't take your ones to town, son
Leave your ones at home, Bird
Don't take your ones to town"

3461/1

"Singin' in Vietnam Talkin' Blues," 256
"Six White Horses," 24
Skinner, David Ray, 250-251
Smith, Connie, 27, 292
Smith, Fred, 42
Smith, John L., xv, 204-212, 206
Smith, Smokey, 205
Smith, Warren, 75
Snow, Hank, 63
Snow, Jimmy, 63
"So Doggone Lonesome," 22
"Sold Out of Flag Poles," 256
Songs of Cash, 219
Sonny and Cher, 215
Sonny Burgess & The Pacers, 75
S.O.S. Village, 163-166, 248
Sousa, John Phillip, 69
Spain, 118-119
Spin magazine, 132-133, 169
Springfield, Mo., 199
Stars Incorporated, 75
Starwood Amphitheater, 247
Statler Brothers, 39, 47, 89, 142, 261
Steel Pier, 78
Steel Pier Club, 79
Steenburgen, Mary, 242
Stevens, Ray, 247
Stohler, Charles, 279
Stohler, Virginia, 279
Strawberry Cake, 123-124
Streisand, Barbara, 105
"String Cheese Incident," 255
Stuart, Marty, 60, 209-211, 219
Sugarman, Bonnie, 102
Sullivan, Ed, 69
Sun City, Nev., 98
Sun Records, xiii, 75-77, 156, 174, 211-212, 247

"Sunday Morning Coming Down," 255
"Suppertime," 287
Sutton, Glen, 24
Swan, Dottie, 63
Sydney, Australia, 261
Syracuse, N.Y., 78-79

T
Table Rock Lake, 241
Tasmania, 262
Tate, Sharon, 109
Taylor, Elizabeth, 186, 242
Taylor, James, 87
Tel Aviv, Israel, 292, 299
Tender Mercies, 132
"Tennessee Stud," 105
Tennessee Three, 79-80, 81, 88, 92, 205, 259-261, 287-288
Tennessee Titans, 247
Tennessee Two, 78-79
Tennessee, University of, 113
Terry, Gordon, 83
Tharpe, Sister Rosetta, 238
"That's Just Like Jesus," 36
The Nashville Network, 249
"These Hands," 254
"Thing Called Love, A" 64
Three Rivers Club, 78
Tijuana Brass, 151
"'Til Things Are Brighter," 264
Tinkley, Allen, 42, 151
Tittle, Dustin (grandson), 214-216, 214, 219-221
Tittle, Jimmy (son-in-law), xv, 38, 164, 172, 190, 218-222

Tittle, Kathy Cash (daughter), xv, 17, 35, 171, 217, 218-222
Todd, Alma Jean, 100, 223-228, 224-225, 227, 279, 284
Todd, Curtis, 223, 226-228, 227, 279, 284

Tokyo, Japan, 106
Toronto, Ont., 265
Tower Records, 245
Trask, Diana, 209
Triad Records, 132
Tubb, Ernest, 287
Tulsa, Okla., 287
Two Cookie Kid, 246

U
U2, 246
Ullman, Tracey, 188
Undaunted Courage: Meriwether Lewis, Thomas Jefferson, and the Opening of the American West, 238
"Understand Your Man," 255
USAir Club, 201-202

V

Van Zandt, Townes, 130
Vanderbilt University, 275
Varney, Jim, 60
Vassar College, 94
Veterans Hospital, 52
Vienna, Austria, 158
Villa, Pancho, 274

W

Waddell, Herman, 229, 251
Waddell, Hugh, xv, 8, *15*, 50,
    52, 129-130, 135-138, 155-
    156, 181, 183, 185, 188,
    217, 229-257, *231*, *235*, *237*,
    242, *248*
Waddell, Jackie Comer, v, 232
Wainwright, Loudon III, 239
Waldorf-Astoria Hotel, 245
Walken, Christopher, 190
Walker, Bill, xv, 72, 130, 258-
    263, *259-261*
Walker, Jeanine, 261-262
Walking Tall, xv
Washington, D.C., 227
Watertown, S.D., 212
Watson, Doc, 247
Wayne, John, 140, 149-150
Weems, Joseph, 294

"Weight, The," 136
Welch, Gillian, 247
Wendt, Maribeth, 64
Westlake Village, Calif., 151
Western, Jo, 268, *268*
Western, Johnny, xv, 265-
    269, *266-267*, *269*
"What Is Truth," 256
"When the Saints Go
    Marching In," 71
White, Tony Joe, 130
White House, 110, 173, 244
White Witch of Rose Hall, The, 133
Whitehead, James T., 276
Whitehead Creek, 276
Wichita, Kan., 265, 269
Wild Rose, 245
Wilderness Road, 174
"Wildwood Flower," 38, 70,
    131-132
"Wildwood Weed," 70
"Will the Circle Be
    Unbroken," 139, 148, 212
Williams, Hank Jr., 246, 297
Williams, John, 246
Wilson, Courtney, 270-271
Winston, Nat T., xv, 272-277
Winston-Salem, N.C., 223
Wise, Nat, 189-190, 243

Witherell, Jeanne, 100, 223,
    227, *227*, 279-285, *280*
Witherell, Ray, 223, 227, *227*,
    279-280, 282-283
WMAK, 113-114
Wolf, Marie, 280
Wolf Trap, Va., 160, 168
Wolfman Jack, 130, 247
Wonder, Stevie, 246
Wootton, Bob, 42, 89, 125-
    126, *156*, 231, 285-291,
    288, *291*
World Wide Pictures, 251
Wounded Knee, S.D., 205-
    208, *211*

Y

Yates, Harry (brother-in-law),
    292-295, *293*
Yates, Joanne Cash, (sister),
    23, 292, *293*, 295-300, *297*
Yates, Mary, 292
Young, Faron, 83-84
"You're My Holiday," 239-
    240

Z

Zappa, Frank, 245-246
Zinn, Howard, 238

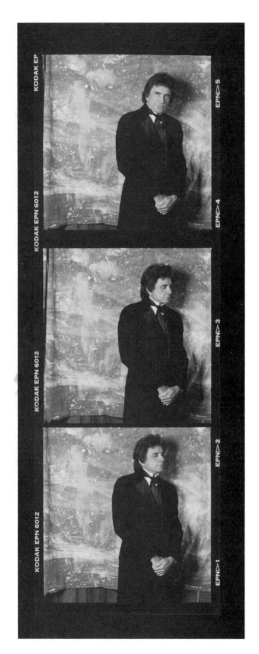

No man is an island.
Everyman is a piece of
the continent, a part of
the man.
    So your death dimmishes
me. therefore I never
ask for whom the Bell
tolls, It tolls for me.

        John Donne